# Media Access
## and Organization

# MEDIA ACCESS AND ORGANIZATION
## A Cataloging and Reference Sources Guide for Nonbook Materials

CAROLYN O. FROST

1989
LIBRARIES UNLIMITED, INC.
Englewood, Colorado

LIBRARIES UNLIMITED, INC.
P.O. Box 3988
Englewood, CO 80155-3988

---

**Library of Congress Cataloging-in-Publication Data**

Frost, Carolyn O., 1940-
  Media access and organization.

    Includes index.
    1. Cataloging of nonbook materials. 2. Libraries--
Special collections--Nonbook materials. 3. Reference
books--Nonbook materials--Bibliography. 4. Nonbook
materials--Bibliography. I. Title.
Z695.66.F78  1988      025.3'4      88-27302
ISBN 0-87287-583-0

*In Memoriam*

CHARLES SUMNER FROST
EMMA McKINNEY PLEASANTS
FRANCES BETHEA

*Lifelong Friends and Supporters*

# Contents

θθθθθθθθθθθθθθθθθθθθθθθθθθθθθθθθθθθθθθθθθθθθθθθθθθθθθθθθθθθθθθθθθθθθθθθθθθθθθθθθθθθθθθθθθθ

# *Preface*

θθθθθθθθθθθθθθθθθθθθθθθθθθθθθθθθθθθθθθθθθθθθθθθθθθθθθθθθθθθθθθθθθθθθθθθθθθθθθθθθθθθθθθθθθθ

## PURPOSE

The major purpose of this book is to offer a comprehensive approach to the organization and access of nonbook materials. While the focus is on descriptive cataloging, attention is also paid, where appropriate, to subject organization and access. A key feature of the book is its extensive listing of reference tools which complement the cataloging process, and which assist the reference librarian in finding information contained in nonbook formats.

The objectives of the book are twofold: (1) to assist librarians in dealing with the organization, description, and retrieval of nonbook materials through discussion and illustration of cataloging rules, and identification of reference sources that support the cataloging process and (2) to assist the reference librarian in retrieving nonprint and nonverbal information through identification of sources that provide access routes beyond the catalog.

## SCOPE

The scope of the book includes a wide variety of nonbook and nonprint formats. For cataloging purposes, there have as yet been no satisfactory definitions of the terms *media, nonbook, nonprint, nonverbal,* and *audiovisual.* The scope of materials included in this book will be those formats covered by the following chapters in *AACR 2*: cartographic materials, sound recordings, graphic materials, motion pictures and videorecordings, microcomputer software, three-dimensional artefacts and realia, and microforms.

## APPROACH

For each type of material, as appropriate, the chapter will begin with a commentary and analysis of problem areas in bibliographic control, organization, and descriptive cataloging. The discussion will include key rules from the 1988 revision of *AACR 2* (*AACR 2*, 1988 rev.), and important manuals developed especially for individual formats. Some chapters will include an overview of classification and other systems for subject organization and access. Alternative methods for organization and description also will be considered. The discussion will be followed by examples. Each example will:

1.  provide relevant information about the item to be cataloged, so that the reader will be able to ascertain the reason for decisions made

2.  provide a catalog record according to level 2 of *AACR 2*, 1988 rev.

3.  provide MARC coding and tagging in the OCLC format

4.  document and comment on *AACR 2*, 1988 rev. rules used to formulate the record

A major part of this book is intended for use with *AACR 2*. For a thorough understanding of the discussion on descriptive cataloging, the reader will need a basic familiarity with *AACR 2* and its principles.

Attention will be focused on decision areas — situations in which the cataloger is presented with choices or options, with ambiguities in the rules that are subject to varying interpretations, or with external difficulties that pose problems in implementation of the rules.

Second, each chapter provides annotated lists of reference sources, manuals, and professional literature. One use of these sources is to assist the cataloger by providing definitions of terms that may appear in *AACR 2*, the MARC format manuals, or on the item to be cataloged. For many types of special formats, the cataloger may require technical information given in sources that provide background on particular physical formats; for example, to assist in determining what is meant by terms used in *AACR 2* such as *anamorphic map*, or *sound cartridge*, or *filmloop*. At other times, the need may be for background information of a subject nature; for example, some knowledge of cartography may be necessary in the cataloging of maps, or a knowledge of musicology in the case of sound recordings. Some sources are particularly valuable in providing information about the publishing industry of a particular medium. Such sources may help the cataloger to understand the roles of different types of publishers, producers, and creators, or offer names and locations needed for the catalog description. The discussion of *AACR 2* rules for each medium will point out situations in which the cataloger may need to consult reference sources in order to understand and apply the appropriate rules.

For the reference or catalog assistance librarian, the primary value of the annotated list of sources is the provision of additional access routes for locating information contained in nonbook materials. Frequently, the catalog does not provide access points at the level of detail required or in the manner of the desired approach; for example, a user may be interested in determining if the library has films by a particular actor, or which films in the library's collection are Academy Award winners. While the catalog does not normally provide access points under the names of actors or awards, access routes for this type of information are provided in certain reference sources. In addition, the catalog record is necessarily selective in the information it provides about a given bibliographic title, while exhaustive information about the production, credits, and history of a film can be found in reference sources that supplement the catalog's description.

My previous book, *Cataloging of Nonbook Materials: Problems in Theory and Practice*, dealt with most of the types of materials covered in the present volume. However, while the emphasis of the previous book was on descriptive cataloging and the history of the development of cataloging standards, the present book devotes greater attention to decision areas encountered in the process of cataloging, and expands coverage to include subject organization and reference sources. Also, since the publication of the first book, substantial revisions in rules for computer files have resulted in more widely accepted bibliographic standards for this medium. Thus the present book includes computer files among the materials covered. In addition, the present book reflects the 1988 revision of the *AACR 2* rules.

# ACKNOWLEDGMENTS

Two colleagues and special friends are due humanitarian awards for their willingness to read through a large portion of the manuscript. Sheila Intner and her class at Simmons offered crucial suggestions in getting the book on track in its earlier stages. Dana Rooks, University of Houston, made the exceptional sacrifice of reading through the narrative chapters, *AACR 2* in hand, from the perspective of the cataloging layperson. Her careful textual analysis yielded invaluable suggestions for improving both substance and style.

At the University of Michigan, Karen Markey gave suggestions for the graphic materials chapter, and Bonnie Dede reviewed the cataloging examples. Additional assistance with individual examples was provided by University of Houston catalogers Keiko Cho, Marilyn Craig, and Jack Hall. Their efforts are all much appreciated.

Teaching is a pleasure when an educator can learn from and be enriched by the ideas of students. Several classes at Michigan's School of Information and Library Studies have provided helpful insights, criticisms, and background information. Special recognition is due to the contributions of Nancy Becker Johnson, Sue Weiland, Karen Sinkule, Ruth Pierce, Craig Summerhill, Judy Tsou, Barbara Murphy, Ann Owen, Paul Conway, Elizabeth Lane, Kathy Litka, and Barbara McMillan.

After completing the preparation of this manuscript for publication, I owe my survival to the unfailing energy, reliability, resourcefulness, and good humor of my research assistant, Patti Soderberg. Her future employers will be fortunate indeed.

# *Abbreviations*

| | |
|---|---|
| *AACR 2*, 1988 rev. | *Anglo-American Cataloguing Rules, Second Edition, 1988 Revision.* Edited by Michael Gorman and Paul W. Winkler for the Joint Steering Committee for Revision of the AACR. Chicago: American Library Association, 1988. |
| *AACR 2* | *Anglo-American Cataloguing Rules. Second Edition.* Edited by Michael Gorman and Paul W. Winkler. Chicago: American Library Association, 1978. |
| | Note: the term *AACR 2* has been used in this book to refer to the 1978 edition. However, in the discussion and citation of rules, all references to rules in *AACR 2* will apply as well to the 1988 revision, unless stated otherwise. When substantive differences occur between rules in the two editions, these differences will be specifically pointed out, and a distinction made between the original and the revised *AACR 2* rules. |
| *AACR 1* | *Anglo-American Cataloging Rules. North American Text.* Chicago: American Library Association, 1967. |
| ALA | American Library Association |
| CSB | Library of Congress. *Cataloging Service Bulletin* |
| GMD | General Material Designation |
| SMD | Specific Material Designation |
| LC | Library of Congress |
| *LCSH* | *Library of Congress Subject Headings* |
| MARC | Machine-Readable Cataloging |
| OCLC | OCLC Online Computer Library Center, Inc. |

# 1

# *Introduction*

This chapter will focus on the organization of *AACR 2*, and on sections of the rules that have special significance for nonbook materials. Since these standards have evolved over a period of decades, the chapter includes a look at predecessors of the present rules. Supplementing the discussion of descriptive cataloging is an overview of key considerations in subject access and organization, and a look at the impact of the MARC formats and bibliographic utilities on bibliographic control of nonbook materials. At the end of the chapter is an annotated list of general works dealing with the description, organization, and retrieval of nonbook materials. Reference sources for specific media are discussed in the individual chapters that follow.

## *AACR 2*: ORGANIZATION

### Part One: Description

Part One of *AACR 2* deals with descriptive cataloging and is divided into chapters which, for the most part, are arranged according to media groups. Chapter 1 is set aside for the description of media in general, and is applied to the several individual chapters covering specific media.

#### CONSISTENT DESCRIPTION FOR ALL MATERIALS

Within the structural framework of *AACR 2*, all media formats are treated alike. Chapter 1 contains general rules for description and serves to bring about an "integrated and standardized framework for the systematic description of all library materials" (p. viii). The individual chapters are to be used in conjunction with the general chapter. Thus, for example, in cataloging a map, the general rules in chapter 1 would be used in conjunction with the rules governing cartographic materials in chapter 3, for all points of the description. A basic premise of *AACR 2* is that general precepts can be identified which apply to the description of all materials. It is assumed, for example, that elements of description such as title, edition, publisher, and date are common to all materials, and that detailed rules can be specified in the general chapter which will apply to most materials. When specific rules are deemed necessary for individual types of media, these provisions are dealt with in the various chapters for specific media. *AACR 2* provides a consistent system of numbering to facilitate the identification of analogous rules among the different chapters. For example, rule 1.1B in the general chapter deals with the recording of the title proper for all materials. In chapter 3 (cartographic materials), the corresponding rule is 3.1B, in chapter 6 (sound recordings), the rule is 6.1B, and so on. If no specific rules for an element of description are needed in the chapter for a given type of material, the cataloger is referred back to the general chapter. Thus, in chapter 3's rule 3.1B1, the cataloger is told to "transcribe the title proper as instructed in 1.1B." Rule 3.1B2, however, provides specific instruction relating to scale information in the title proper. The chapters of the media groups are:

cartographic materials

manuscripts

music scores

sound recordings

motion pictures and videorecordings

graphic materials

computer files (formerly, "machine-readable data files")

three-dimensional artefacts and realia

microforms

## DEFINING CHARACTERISTICS OF
## MEDIA CATEGORIES

The media groups named above are comprised of diverse formats which have in common some basic characteristic underlying their physical form or intellectual content.

The various media making up the category of cartographic materials share the characteristic of "[representing] ... the earth or any celestial body." Another category of materials determined by intellectual content — or, more precisely, by the manner in which it communicates its message — is music.

Static two-dimensional visual representations form the category of "graphic materials." Dynamic visual materials include motion pictures and videorecordings. The category of three-dimensional artefacts and realia consists of a diverse assortment of materials ranging from natural objects to sculptures. The groups of materials included in the latter categories are related more by their physical format than by their intellectual content. The same can be said for the categories of microform and computer files.

In contrast to *AACR 1*, which allowed an item to be assigned to only one category, the categories in *AACR 2* are not regarded as mutually exclusive and can be used in combination. This may occur when there is an intersection of content, form, or — in the case of serials — mode of issuance. Thus, it is inevitable that some types of material that are independent of content, such as serials and microforms, will belong to more than one category. For example, a set of music scores reproduced in microform format and issued on a serial basis would be in three categories.

The code assists the cataloger by suggesting possible combinations and indicating the chapter most appropriate as the basis for description. For example, the introduction to the chapter on manuscripts points out that manuscript cartographic items belong in the chapter on cartographic materials. Likewise, direction is given for the treatment of manuscript music, recorded music, microform reproductions of music, sound track film (not accompanied by visual material), and microform reproductions of printed texts.

The code also provides guidance by recognizing other bases for determining the organization of categories. For example, the term *graphic materials* might logically be construed as including maps, microforms, motion pictures, and microscope slides. *Three-dimensional artefacts* could logically include relief models and globes. In each of these cases, the reader is referred to the appropriate chapter.

## MULTIMEDIA MATERIALS

Multimedia items are comprised of components from more than one media category; for example, a filmstrip with accompanying tape cassette. The general rules for description prescribe that multimedia items be described in terms of the predominant component, if there is one; subsidiary components are then described as accompanying material. Another alternative provided for treatment of multimedia items is cataloging each item as a separate record. (See the discussion of kits later in this chapter.)

## SERIAL PUBLICATIONS

By *AACR 2*'s glossary definition, serials can be "a publication in any medium." A serial is defined by its mode of issuance: It is issued in successive parts and is intended to be continued indefinitely. As such, a serial is independent of physical format or intellectual content. *AACR 2* permits the cataloger to describe serial publications in any type of medium by combining the appropriate chapter for the media format with the chapter for serials. The *AACR 2* rules are organized to allow an integrated description of all aspects—physical format, intellectual content, and mode of issuance.

## AREAS OF DESCRIPTION

The content, sequence, and punctuation of the bibliographic record prescribed by *AACR 2* have been derived from an international standard, the International Standard Bibliographic Description (ISBD). Rules are provided for the eight areas of description which may be included, as appropriate, in each record. These areas are:

Title and Statement of Responsibility

Edition

Material (or Type of Publication) Specific Details

Publication, Distribution, Etc.

Physical Description

Series

Note

Standard Number and Terms of Availability

## Part Two: Access

*AACR 2*'s Part Two covers the choice and form of access points to be used as headings in the catalog. These rules, for the most part, apply to materials in general and are not specific to individual media.

## *AACR 2* RULES OF SPECIAL SIGNIFICANCE FOR NONBOOK MATERIALS
### Problem Areas and Considerations in Bibliographic Description and Access

While *AACR 2* presents one set of rules for the consistent description of all materials, some concepts that are implicit when applied to book materials may require reexamination or refinement when applied to nonbook materials. These are:

- the concept of *title page* and its application to rules for sources of information

- the concept of *publisher*

- the concept of *author* and its application to rules for choice of access points, and for ascription in the statement of responsibility and notes area

Another key concept, that of *media designation*, has its origin in rules for nonbook materials, and thus has no precedent in book-based traditions. Rules for physical description deserve our attention because this aspect of the description is most likely to be shaped and determined by the nature of the material in hand. Since many nonbook materials could be considered as "kits," options for the treatment of this category will also be discussed.

## Sources of Information

With many types of nonbook materials, bibliographic information can appear on the item itself, as a label affixed to the item, or on the container of the item, among other possibilities. Cataloging codes determine which of these sources comes closest to serving as a title-page substitute. Principles reflected in the rules are based in part on those properties of the title page which make it so attractive as the chief source of information for books. *AACR 2*'s title-page approach is based on the assumption that for all media we can determine a chief source of information, or ideal place from which bibliographic information is to be transcribed. A principal criterion is that of location. The title page of a book is, of course, uniformly located at or near the beginning of the sequence of pages. In extending this criterion to nonbook media, code makers have sought to identify equivalent sites with the same quality of consistent location. Criteria based on location usually prescribe that information from the item itself be preferred to information from an outside source, since the label found on a source such as a disc or cassette will typically remain with the item longer than the container or accompanying material.

A second major criterion accords precedence to the source providing the most complete or comprehensive information. Often this will conflict with the criterion of location; in the case of sound recording discs, space limitations on the label may not allow bibliographic details to be presented in the degree of fullness possible in sources such as the record jacket or accompanying booklet. In prescribing sources of information for nonbook materials, cataloging codes have kept the model of the title page clearly in mind, and as we have seen, those attributes of the title page deemed most attractive for this purpose are its location and its comprehensiveness. Of the two, location is clearly the dominant factor in modern cataloging convention.

An additional consideration is that access to sources of information for many nonbook media is dependent upon machinery. If a title screen is to be considered as a chief source of information for a motion picture, a cataloger must have a means of viewing the title. This might require that a cataloging agency procure the necessary hardware and the expertise to operate it. Rules that allow use of information from other sources alleviate some of these problems.

## General Material Designation

The purpose of the general material designation (GMD) is to alert the user, at an early point in the catalog record, as to the nature of the item being described. The GMD is inserted, in brackets, between the title proper and the other title information. The use of the GMD is optional.

The GMD indicates the class of material to which an item belongs, and as such is the one element of bibliographic description originally devised specifically for nonbook materials. Lacking a bibliographic precedent in the model afforded for the description of books, code framers and theorists in nonbook cataloging found no common ground for agreement in decisions to be made on the location of the GMD, on the degree of specificity to be used in its terminology, or even on its justification for existence. Controversy over the GMD has centered primarily around its function, and this major point of difference has in turn served to determine opinions on the other factors of location and specificity. Since the GMD has been made an optional feature of *AACR 2*, and can thus be included or omitted at the cataloging agency's discretion, the question as to the GMD's justification bears some consideration.

The GMD has been recognized as serving three functions:

1.  as a statement of the nature or basic format of the item cataloged and thus as a means of informing the user as to the type of material at hand

2.  as a description of the physical characteristics of the medium and as a means of alerting the user to equipment needed to make use of the item

3.  as a device to distinguish different physical formats which share the same title

These functions are particularly important when one takes into account the unique qualities of individual media and the capabilities that each type of format brings to bear in communicating its message. A musicologist who wishes to analyze the structural components of a musical composition will probably prefer a printed score to a recording of that work. A student of automotive engineering may prefer a visual representation of a mechanical process to a verbal description.

The significance of the GMD is further enhanced by the increased capabilities of online systems to allow a user to narrow a search by format. Thus, the user can restrict a search for *Hamlet* to sound recordings of the play or to videorecordings of a performance. In this way, the catalog can recognize two hitherto conflicting objectives: (1) informing the user of what the library has on a given subject or by a given author regardless of format and (2) allowing the user to limit a search to a particular kind of format.[1]

In cases where an item can be identified as belonging not only to a category defined by content, but also to another category defined by format, as in the case of a map issued on microform, the issue arises as to whether the primary purpose of the GMD should be to indicate the content (e.g., map) or format (e.g., microform, slide).

In *AACR 2*, the GMD is placed after the title proper, but before parallel titles and other title information. The requirement that the GMD be placed early in the entry poses a dilemma of sorts: The GMD must appear after the title proper; otherwise, a lengthy subtitle could relegate the GMD to a second or third line of the entry. At the same time, however, this location places the GMD in uneasy proximity to bibliographic information that has been transcribed directly from the item or other chief source of information, and also results in the interruption of a single logical unit of information, the title. Locating the GMD after the title proper was not prescribed until the General International Standard Bibliographic Description [ISBD(G)] and *AACR 2*. In earlier codes, the GMD was placed after all title information.[2]

Various alternatives to the GMD have been suggested. One involves drawing attention to the specific material designations in the physical description area through the use of underlining or capitalization. A more popular method is the provision of symbols or "media codes" which are part of the call number and indicate the particular medium type. "Color coding," the use of color in cards to indicate a specific medium, is used by some libraries but is now largely discouraged. Quite apart from other disadvantages attendant upon the use of these latter two devices is the problem that such methods are radical departures from recognized bibliographic standards, which rely upon verbal expression to indicate informational content and upon sequence of informational elements to indicate order of importance.

Two separate lists of designations are given in *AACR 2*, one for British and one for North American use. The British list contains fewer terms, and uses generic categories to group together some of the more specific formats enumerated separately in the North American list.

The terms in the North American list vary in specificity. Some media, such as sound recordings and realia, receive generic terms while terms for other media, such as flash cards, filmstrips, and microscope slides, are more specific and are, in fact, identical with specific material designations.

In the revised *AACR 2*, new GMDs have been added. The term *art reproduction* can be applied to graphic materials and to three-dimensional artefacts and realia. *Art original*, formerly used only for graphic materials, can now be applied to three-dimensional materials as well. Another term added to the list for three-dimensional materials is the GMD *toy*. Revised rule 1.1C1 has also added GMDs to designate materials for the visually impaired. The terms (*braille*), (*large print*), and *(tactile)* can be added, as appropriate, to terms in the North American list, for example, *map (tactile)* and *music (braille)*.

## Material (or Type of Publication) Specific Details Area

In *AACR 2*, the framework for the standard description of all bibliographic materials is the General International Standard Bibliographic Description [ISBD (G)]. This standard prescribes a general pattern of description for all media, while still allowing special descriptive elements essential for particular media to be accommodated within the ISBD (G) without damage to the integrity of the framework. This is accomplished by setting aside the "Material (or Type of Publication) Specific Details Area" (area 3) to be used only "for details that are special to a particular class of material or publication." *AACR 2* originally recognized serials and cartographic materials as requiring such an area. Subsequent revised rules also included area 3 provisions for music scores and computer files.

## Publication Area

Publication information is an obvious requirement for the description of both print and nonbook materials. However, it is equally manifest that the concepts of publisher and publication will have to be defined so that they are appropriate for the description of nonbook materials.

The concept of publisher must be extended to include the different types of functions and activities that may occur in the production and distribution of nonbook materials. A variety of functions are subsumed under the rubric "publication, distribution, etc., area" in *AACR 2*, and the data for this publisher-analog can include the names of persons or organizations such as distributor, publisher, producer, and production company. In *AACR 2*, the responsibilities of the producer can go beyond the mere issuance or release of an item. Producers of motion pictures can be noted in the statement of responsibility and thus can be recognized as having control over the intellectual content of the work. *AACR 2*'s glossary defines the producer of motion pictures as "the person with final responsibility for the making of a motion picture, including business aspects, management of the production, and the commercial success of the film." A greater degree of responsibility is ascribed to the production company of a motion picture, which is defined as "the company or other organization that determines the content and form of a motion picture and is responsible for its manufacture and production. If there is, in addition, a sponsor, the production company is normally responsible only for the manufacture or production of the motion picture." Similarly, in the case of cartographic materials, it is recognized that the publisher's role can go beyond publication and distribution.

## Physical Description Area

While various nonbook materials may share bibliographic characteristics such as the presence of a title, statement of responsibility, and so on, the most obvious differences lie in their physical characteristics. Therefore, rules for describing the physical characteristics of the item vary substantially depending on the type of material to be cataloged. While the cataloger will need to consult the individual chapters for specific media rather than the general rules for instructions on the formulation of the physical description area, there is an underlying framework for description, and this pattern, outlined in chapter 1, can be recognized in each of the subsequent chapters for individual media. Whatever the type of material, there are three aspects of physical description which can be provided: (1) extent of item, (2) other physical details, and (3) dimensions.

### EXTENT OF ITEM

The extent of item essentially answers the questions: What do we call this item, how many of the units are there (e.g., "2 models"), how many component parts comprise a unit [e.g., "1 model (22 pieces)"], and how extensive is the item? The term that names the item is the *specific material designation* (SMD). If the item consists of a number of components, this is specified in parentheses. For most materials, "extent" is measured in terms of physical content, but for dynamic items such as sound recordings and motion pictures, the extent is expressed in terms of duration or playing time (e.g., "53 min."), rather than measurements of the physical medium (e.g., the length of the film or tape).

## OTHER PHYSICAL DETAILS

This element contains information about physical characteristics other than extent or dimensions. Such information varies greatly according to the type of item being described; for example, for graphic items, the details regarding color are important, whereas with sound recordings, color is irrelevant but playing speed is a key detail.

Frequently, the rules for recording other physical details will require that decisions be made on questions such as the following:

Is the information important enough to include? For example, the recording density or sectoring of a computer disk, or the type of material of a three-dimensional object or a map.

Is the characteristic standard for the format? For example, the groove characteristics of a sound recording disc.

Is the information "available"? If not, how much effort is necessary to ascertain needed data?

In making these decisions, consideration must be given to the library's clientele and to what is "important" for users in a particular context or setting. Decisions as to what is "standard" for an item may require familiarity with the physical formats. Reference works will be of assistance in this regard, as well as in cases in which knowledge of technical terminology is required.

## DIMENSIONS

In recording dimensions, much depends upon what we assume to be a standard shape or size for a given format, and the number or type of dimensions given depends upon the medium. Books are typically described in terms of one dimension (height), photographs in two dimensions (height x width), and games in three (height x width x depth). For some formats, no dimensions of any kind are considered necessary. There is a trend toward recognizing standard dimensions for formats that have become relatively standardized. For some media, no dimensions are given if specific dimensions can be assumed (e.g., sound tape cassettes, slides).

## ACCOMPANYING MATERIAL

Describing accompanying material assumes that a decision has already been made that the material is indeed secondary or "accompanying," rather than primary. For items that consist of more than one media type, the cataloger must determine if one medium is predominant. If so, the other media are considered accompanying material. If on the other hand, no one medium can be considered predominant, the item is cataloged as a kit. Such decisions are sometimes straightforward, as in the case of *most* filmstrips with accompanying sound cassettes, but often the decision will be less obvious, and at times highly subjective.

Once the decision has been made as to the primary and secondary components, a further decision is required as to how accompanying material will be recorded. Four options are given:

- to create separate records for each component

- to record both components in a multilevel description

- to record the accompanying component in a note

- to record the accompanying component at the end of the physical description area that has been created for the primary item

The decision to record as a separate entry (option "a") would be followed only if it were considered important to provide full bibliographic access to the accompanying material; that is, if the accompanying material were to be considered as important as the primary material. Such instances would undoubtedly be rare. Option "b," using a multilevel description, is not being followed by LC or by most American libraries.

Most frequently, the cataloger will have to decide between options "c" and "d." The LC rule interpretations, as found in the *Cataloging Service Bulletin*, give guidelines which recommend that accompanying material be described at the end of the physical description area if the main and secondary work share a common author and publisher and if the secondary work is of use "only in conjunction with the main work, and depends on the title of the main work for identification."[3]

If the cataloger decides to describe the accompanying material as part of the physical description area, there is an option to add, in parentheses, further physical description of the item. Such information can include the extent, other physical details, and dimensions. In formulating this description, the cataloger would consult rules in the appropriate chapter for the type of material being described; for example, if the accompanying material is a sound recording cassette, chapter 6 should be consulted.

## Note Area

An important decision area is the provision of notes. In this area, the cataloger has a great deal of leeway in deciding what types of notes to include and how the notes should be formulated. The decision will be based on the policy of the individual library, which will in turn be based on the needs of the library's users and resources.

The type of notes appropriate to individual types of media will vary with the medium, and for the most part the cataloger will consult the appropriate individual chapters rather than the general chapter for guidance in constructing notes.

While the need for some notes will vary according to individual libraries, there are notes that are undoubtedly of importance to any library. One such note that is appropriate to all media is the one used to explain the source of a supplied title. Other essential notes may be specific to particular media: for example, the systems requirements note for computer files, and the publisher's number for sound recordings. Since many types of nonbook media require equipment for use, and are therefore difficult to browse, a summary note becomes especially important.

# Kits

## HOW THE CATEGORY "KIT" IS DEFINED

*AACR 2* includes rules for kits in its general chapter for description. The general chapter is used because the category of kits is independent of any given medium or type of material. For cataloging purposes, a kit can be defined as a unit comprised of more than one type of material, with no predominant medium. *AACR 2* does not use the term *kit* except in reference to the GMD.

Rules for kits are found under the section called "Items made up of several types of material" (rule 1.10). This section applies to "items that are made up of two or more components, two or more of which belong to distinct material types." This rule is considered when the item to be cataloged is a unit comprised of two different kinds of media, for example, a filmstrip and a sound recording, or a videorecording and a book.

## WHEN THE ITEM IS NOT A KIT
### Predominant Medium

Once the cataloger has determined that the unit is made up of two or more different kinds of materials, a key decision must be made: Can one of the media be identified as predominant? Rule 1.10B informs the cataloger that, if a predominant medium can be identified, the item is described in terms of that component and the subsidiary component is described as accompanying material. If, for example, the cataloger decided that the videorecording constituted the predominant medium, chapter 7 (motion pictures and videorecordings) would be used for the description of the videorecording, and the accompanying book would be described following the physical description area or in a note. There would be no further need to consult the rules for kits, since the item in question has a predominant medium and therefore is not considered as a kit.

Since *AACR 2* does not provide guidelines for deciding the question as to whether there is a predominant medium, and if so, which medium, the decision is likely to be subjective, and based on the cataloger's view of the role of each medium in the unit.

## WHICH RULES TO USE IF THE ITEM IS A KIT

The section in the general chapter (rule 1.10) will be used for the following:

1. In defining the category, and determining if this section of the rules is applicable, rules 1.10A and 1.10B are used.

2. In determining the GMD, rule 1.10C1 is applied.

3. In formulating the physical description area, rule 1.10C2 is used. If the cataloger elects to give a full description for each type of material, appropriate chapters for individual media types will need to be consulted for further detail.

While rules 1.10C3 and 1.10D address points related to notes and to multi-level description, respectively, these rules are too brief to be used on their own, and will need to be supplemented by specific rules in other parts of *AACR 2*.

In determining aspects of the record such as title, statement of responsibility, edition, series, and so on, the appropriate sections of the general chapter will need to be consulted. Choice and form of access points will be determined according to Part Two of *AACR 2*. The whole item will serve as the chief source of information. The cataloger should keep in mind that the catalog description should reflect the unit as a whole, rather than individual parts of the kit. So, for example, any titles that are specific to individual parts of the kit rather than unifying titles for the kit as a whole would not be used in the title area.

In applying the option to give further physical details for individual components of a kit, the appropriate chapters for individual media would be consulted.

## GENERAL MATERIAL DESIGNATION

Choice of the GMD will depend on whether the item to be cataloged has a collective title. In most instances, the item will have a collective title, and the GMD "kit" will be used in North American libraries. In those rare instances where the item lacks a collective title, the GMD appropriate to the type of material would be given after each title.

## PHYSICAL DESCRIPTION AREA

The cataloger is presented with three options in giving the physical description area. The three methods vary in fullness of detail.

Option "a" provides for a brief listing of each component part. The cataloger gives "the extent of each part or group of parts belonging to each distinct class of materials as the first element of description." In listing the parts, terms that are specific material designations from appropriate media chapters can be used, but the cataloger is not limited to these terms. The phrase *in container* can be used, along with the dimensions of the container, to end the description. In a revised rule, the naming of the container and its dimensions was made optional, rather than required.

The example below shows a catalog record and its corresponding OCLC MARC tagging, formulated according to option "a."

Option "a" example

Kendra and the magic cottage [kit]. --
    Chicago, Ill. : Media Associates, c1983.
      1 book, 1 sound cassette, 2 puppets, 1 activity guide ; in
container, 35 x 47 x 8 cm.

      Script, Elva Giles ; narrator, Ian King.
      Audience: kindergarten and primary grades.
      A little girl ventures into an enchanted world.

      1. Media Associates.

```
OCLC MARC Tagging

Type: o  Bib lvl: m  Govt pub:   Lang: eng  Source: d  Leng: nnn
            Enc lvl: I  Type mat: b  Ctry: ilu  Dat tp: s  MEBE: 0
Tech: n  Mod rec:     Accomp mat:
Desc: a  Int lvl: g  Dates, 1983,

1    040    xxx $c xxx
2    007    s $b s $c  $d 1 $e m $f n $g j $h 1 $i c
3    245    Kendra and the magic cottage $h kit
4    260    Chicago, Ill. : $b  Media Associates, $c c1983.
5    300    1 book, 1 sound cassette, 2 puppets, 1 activity guide ;
$c in container, 35 x 47 x 8 cm.
6    508    Script, Elva Giles ; narrator, Ian King.
7    521    Kindergarten and primary grades.
8    520    A little girl ventures into an enchanted world.
9    710 21 Media Associates.
```

Option "a" is useful when it is felt that the individual components do not merit detailed description, or are too numerous for such treatment, but yet are small enough in number to warrant enumeration of each media category.

Option "b" (see page 14) allows the cataloger to describe each component fully, using the physical description rules from appropriate media chapters to assist in the formulation of elements such as other physical details, dimensions, and so on. Each component is listed on a separate line, and the physical description detail is as full as if the component were receiving its own catalog record.

Option "b" example

Kendra and the magic cottage [kit]. --
    Chicago, Ill. : Media Associates, c1983.
      1 book (32 p.) : col. ill. ; 32 cm.
      1 sound cassette (19 min.) : analog, mono.
      2 puppets : fabric and wood, col. ; 25 cm. high.
      1 activity guide (24 p.) ; 23 cm.

      Script, Elva Giles ; narrator, Ian King.
      Audience: kindergarten and primary grades.
      In container, 35 x 47 x 8 cm.
      A little girl ventures into an enchanted world.

      1. Media Associates.

This method is used when it is felt that users would appreciate a full description of the various component parts. The fuller description is particularly valuable if the use of the item depends on details provided about its physical description, for example, running time and speed of tape cassette, mono. or stereo. Not every library has the resources for such detailed cataloging. LC will not be applying this option.

Option "c" is the least detailed description, and is to be used "for items with a large number of heterogeneous materials." In this option, the cataloger simply gives one very general term designating the unit (such as the term *various pieces*). The number of pieces is given if it can be ascertained, for example, "27 various pieces."

# Choice of Access Points

While specific chapters are provided for the description of individual media types, there is a single set of rules, in chapter 21, for choice of access points. The rules are based largely on authorship responsibility patterns and often require that a decision be made as to what constitutes authorship for a particular type of creation.

## THE CONCEPT OF *AUTHOR*

The standard concept of *author* as the person chiefly responsible for the creation of the intellectual or artistic content of a work is one that has appeared, with slight variations in wording, in established cataloging standards such as *AACR 2* and its predecessors. For certain categories of materials, it is relatively simple to decide which aspect of the work constitutes its principal intellectual or artistic content, and to identify the person chiefly responsible for this creative function. In the category of graphic materials, photographers and artists fall neatly under this straightforward definition of authorship. The concept of *author* is most accessible when the author is identified as being the person responsible for the single creative activity that forms the basis for the intellectual or artistic content of the work. In cases of authorship involving a single creative function, writers, composers, cartographers, artists, or photographers are considered as authors of the works they create. More complex are those types of works involving more than one creative activity, such as sound recordings and motion pictures.[4]

## SPECIAL RULES APPLICABLE TO NONBOOK MEDIA

While Part Two's rules for access points apply to all media types, there are still a few special rules for certain kinds of materials.

For cartographic materials, there is a section of a rule (21.1B2f) that applies only to this medium. This section is contained within a larger rule (21.1B2) for corporate body main entry. As explained further in the chapter on cartographic materials, the addition of this section to the original rule 21.1B2 results in corporate body main entry for a large number of cartographic materials.

For sound recordings, rule 21.23 applies only to this medium and contains provisions that allow main entry under performer. A large number of sound recordings will be affected by this rule. In contrast, rule 21.1B2e, which deals with motion pictures, videorecordings, and sound recordings, will apply only in rare instances, and allows main entry under performing group under certain conditions. For music sound recordings, rules from the sections on musical works, 21.18 to 21.22, may have to be consulted.

For motion pictures and videorecordings, only rule 21.1B2e (see above) deals specifically with access points for these media.

For graphic materials, rules 21.16 and 21.17 will apply in certain instances to art works that have been adapted or reproduced. These rules will affect only a limited number of materials in this category.

For microforms, computer files, and three-dimensional materials, there are no rules for choice of access points that are specific to these media.

## Form of Access Points

Chapter 22 should be consulted for form of heading for personal main and added entries; and chapter 24 gives the corresponding rules for corporate entries. No rules are specific to individual media.

## Cataloging Manuals for Specific Media

A number of manuals based on *AACR 2* have been developed to address special problems of specific media. For the most part, these manuals have been published by LC or ALA, and thus enjoy a certain degree of national official sanction. All are based on the framework of *AACR 2*, and are compatible with the latter code, although some deviations exist. Two manuals are to be used only for archival materials, while others apply to all materials within the media category. The manuals usually provide information useful for catalogers working in multimedia, nonspecialized collections as well as for specialists. However, the application of rules from the manuals may result in records that are not consistent with records formulated according to *AACR 2*, and a "two-tiered" system of cataloging may result to some degree. The cataloger using a manual will also be required to consult *AACR 2* in addition to the manual in order to address questions not covered by the manual, for example, choice of access points. This issue is discussed in greater detail in the succeeding chapters for specific media.

## Item-Level versus Collection-Level Cataloging

In many instances, the cataloger may be faced with the decision of whether to treat each item in a set individually or to deal with the set as a unit. The decision will be based on the needs of the library and its users, and the resources available. Those items receiving individual attention will be materials identified as having a particular value in their own right which would justify the expense of such treatment. Such items would also be those that, as discrete entities, have an independent value and meaning, in contrast to items that derive their meaning and importance from the collection of which they are a part. This question will be addressed in the chapters on cartographic materials, graphic materials, and microforms.

## SUBJECT ACCESS AND ORGANIZATION

Some methods of subject access, shelf organization, and classification are specific to individual media and will be discussed in succeeding chapters. We can also recognize some recurrent questions which need to be considered in the choice and application of systems for subject access and organization, and these are outlined below.

### Classification and Shelf Organization

#### BOOK VERSUS NONBOOK CLASSIFICATION SCHEMES

What should be the relationship of classification schemes for nonbook materials to the schemes used for books? Should systems established for books, such as Library of Congress Classification or Dewey Decimal Classification, be used for nonbook materials, or should special medium-specific systems be used?

The users' familiarity with the library's book classification scheme has often been a factor in determining the classification to be used for individual media. Many feel that it would be easier for patrons to use the same system throughout the library than to adjust to separate schemes for different material formats.

## CATALOG VERSUS SHELF ACCESS

Should intellectual access to the library's collection be provided primarily by means of the shelf arrangement or the catalog?

Librarians and users must be aware that shelf organization provides only one point of entry for subject access. The catalog must be used in conjunction with shelf organization, to assure retrieval of items comprised of many titles and covering many subjects, and to make retrieval possible under a variety of types of access points.

While classification schemes are thought of largely as systems for shelf organization, online public access catalogs offer potential for use of classification as a means of searching in the catalog. This potential is of particular significance for browsing nonbook media: these media have often been shelved separately from books because of their physical differences, and have thus been inaccessible for browsing by classification order. With the capability for searching by classification through the catalog, nonbook materials can now be even more fully integrated into bibliographic systems.

## SEPARATE VERSUS INTEGRATED SHELVING

Should nonbook media be physically integrated with books on the shelves? While physical characteristics of nonbook media often preclude the integration of these materials with books in shelf arrangement in most settings, arguments have been made for intershelving all materials. The principal advantage of this approach is that all materials on a given subject are grouped together on the shelves, rather than being split up into sub-collections for individual physical formats.

## BROWSING CAPABILITIES

How well do nonbook materials lend themselves to browsing? Is closed stack access justifiable? Responses to these questions may vary with the type of media considered. For some materials, the subject content may be even more accessible than is the case with books. For example, in browsing pictorial items such as photographs or sheet maps, the user is able to grasp the subject content at a brief glance. In contrast, media that require equipment for use, such as a motion picture, sound recording, or filmstrip, are far less accessible, and the browser is totally reliant upon the container or accompanying textual material for a description.

# Subject Heading Access

The questions that arise are similar to those for classification and shelf organization: Should the system for subject headings be the same as that used for books, or does the nature of the intellectual or artistic message warrant a special access system?

## ROLE OF FORM IN
## SUBJECT HEADING ACCESS

Users searching for book materials in the catalog can generally assume that items listed under subject access points are in the desired format. However, for users seeking nonbook materials, identification by type of material is likely to be of crucial importance, and in fact may serve as a basis for inclusion or exclusion. With these considerations in mind we can ask: Should items always be indexed primarily on the basis of subject content, as is done with book materials, rather than form? Should subject headings thus give the subject content as the primary entry element (i.e., as main heading) and the form of material as secondary element (i.e., as a subdivision)? Do circumstances ever warrant access solely on the basis of form? Should the equipment needed to use the item (e.g., computer hardware) serve as an initial entry point?

### FORM AS A QUALIFIER IN
### ONLINE SEARCHING

Online search capabilities enable users to search by a combination of access points of a single kind, such as two subject headings, as well as a combination of different access types, such as subject and format of material. Thus, the user can retrieve materials on the subjects of *football* and *television* as well as materials on football that are in a videotape format. In the latter search, a primary term (e.g., a subject heading) can be limited by qualifiers such as format and date. While not useful as access points in their own right, the qualifiers can assist in narrowing the search according to characteristics important to the user. Thus it is now possible for users to query the catalog using access qualifiers particularly suited to nonbook characteristics, for example by format of material, by type of equipment needed for use, and by running time, color, and similar specific attributes.[5]

# MARC

# USMARC and Its Derivatives

The USMARC format was developed by LC to provide a uniform system for communicating data in machine readable form, and thus to enable the input, storage, retrieval, and manipulation of bibliographic data by computers. Specifications for the MARC formats are given in the document called *USMARC Format for Bibliographic Data*, published by the Library of Congress.[6] There are many detailed discussions of MARC; among the most useful is Walt Crawford's book *MARC for Library Use: Understanding the USMARC Formats*.[7] For MARC as applied to nonbook materials, see Sheila Intner's chapter, "MARC Tagging for Nonbook Materials," in *Policy and Practice in Bibliographic Control of Nonbook Media*,[8] and Nancy Olson's *Cataloging of Audiovisual Materials: A Manual Based on AACR 2. Supplement: Coding and Tagging for OCLC*.[9]

The national bibliographic utilities—OCLC, RLIN, WLN, and UTLAS—have issued their own MARC formats based on LC's USMARC and designed for the use of their network members. These versions of MARC, while containing relatively minor variations from the original, are structurally compatible with USMARC. In this book, OCLC MARC has been chosen to illustrate examples of MARC tagging, since this format is the most widely used for nonbook materials.

## Coverage and Content of the MARC Formats

While the development of the MARC formats began with a standard created for books, the MARC formats presently include standards for all the nonbook materials covered in *AACR 2*: "Visual Materials" (films, two-dimensional graphic materials both opaque and intended for projection, three-dimensional materials, and kits), which still retains its earlier name, "Audiovisual," in the OCLC format; Computer files (as of this writing, still called by its earlier name "Machine-readable data files"); Maps; and Music (in OCLC this category is broken up into two separate formats for sound recordings and for music scores).

The bibliographic content, or cataloging data, of the MARC formats is derived from the prevailing bibliographic standards such as *AACR 2* (subject to interpretations determined by LC and the utility's own policy), Library of Congress Subject Headings, Library of Congress Classification, and so on. Thus the MARC formats are not to be used as substitutes for cataloging, and it is assumed that the essential bibliographic content of the record has already been determined by the cataloger. What the MARC standards do is to provide a standard for translating the cataloging data into a form that can be communicated for computer utilization.

## MARC Tagging and Coding Elements

In MARC coding, the cataloger/coder assigns each unit of bibliographic information a label, or content designator. For fields of information, the label is called a tag, or three-digit code; for example, the physical description area or field is identified by the 300 tag. In some fields, the coded information can be expressed by a fixed number of characters, for example, the "Type of Material" code uses only a single alphabetic character, and in the Visual Materials format, the category of "filmstrip" is designated by the code "f." Variable fields, on the other hand, are used for types of information whose length cannot be easily predicted; for example, the title and statement of responsibility area. For some fields, indicators, consisting of up to two characters which follow the tag, provide additional information about a field. Within each variable field, as necessary, an element of information is identified by a label called a subfield code, consisting of a single alphabetic character; for example, the dimensions are designated by the subfield code "c." Subfield codes are preceded by delimiters (some systems use a pound sign # and some a dollar sign $) to alert the computer to the fact that what follows is a code rather than bibliographic content.

# MARC as an Evolving Standard

It must be stressed that the MARC formats are constantly evolving standards, and are revised and updated by a broad-based body of representatives from the library community. Responsibility for the revision of MARC formats is shared by LC (through its MARC Development Office), by ALA (through an interdivisional committee called MARBI [Committee on Representation in Machine-Readable Form of Bibliographic Information]) comprised of representatives from the Resources and Technical Services Division, the Library and Information Technology Division, and the Reference and Adult Services Division, and by the USMARC Advisory Group, composed of MARBI, representatives from the Library of Congress, the National Library of Medicine, the National Agricultural Library, the National Library of Canada, and the four national bibliographic utilities of OCLC, RLIN, WLN, and UTLAS.

Like *AACR 2*, MARC is dynamic in nature, and the cataloger must keep current with revisions. For the same reasons, it must be recognized that rules and examples in this book will change in time as a result of revisions to MARC and to *AACR 2* (and LC rule interpretations).

# Format Integration and a
# Uniform MARC for All Media

As with *AACR 2*, one can observe aspects of MARC that reflect the commonality of bibliographic features, and that thus contain relatively uniform standards for all materials. For example, the coding for the title and statement of responsibility area and for main entry headings is essentially the same for all media. However, there are also some provisions that recognize distinctive, and sometimes unique qualities of particular media. Again, as with the *AACR 2* rules, these manifestations of uniqueness are usually most readily apparent in the case of description of physical characteristics. This is particularly evident in the case of the MARC fixed fields for coding physical characteristics, and the formats allow the cataloger or coder to specify detailed physical characteristics, many of which are not included in *AACR 2* rules.

In other cases, a MARC format may set aside a special fixed field for retrieval of information that appears only as part of the descriptive information in *AACR 2*. Examples would be the 028 field which allows retrieval of sound recordings by publisher's number, or the 034 field which serves a similar purpose for the scale information for cartographic materials. In the narrative sections of the chapters in this book, attention will be called to fields that are distinctive or unique for a particular medium.

A particularly significant development in the revision of MARC at the time of this writing is format integration. This development will provide a systematic integration of the seven USMARC bibliographic formats into a single format. As a result, for example, catalogers would be able to provide MARC coding for a serial publication in any physical format (as was already the case with *AACR 2*), rather than being faced with the choice of assigning the serial publication to either the format for serials, or to a format based on the physical type of material.

In the evolution of MARC formats, we can see a trend toward consistent treatment of all media, a trend similar to that which occurred in the development of uniform cataloging standards. John Attig explains that format specifications for certain types of material such as audiovisual materials and computer files had originally been developed in consultation with, and were primarily used by, special communities. Since these materials were originally segregated from general library collections, different cataloging conventions arose and separate bibliographic files were maintained. Thus, "for these single-format users, consistency across formats had no great significance." This situation has changed with the trends toward large integrated databases, multimedia collections and catalogs, and toward consistency in bibliographic description for all materials. Attig foresaw these trends as further arguments for and as presagers of consistency of content designation across formats, and proposed a single MARC format in his article "The Concept of a MARC Format."[10]

The cataloging examples in this book contain OCLC MARC tagging. The reader should keep in mind that: (1) other utilities and USMARC will contain differences; (2) the cataloger will need to consult the complete manual appropriate to each format for full instruction; (3) not all fields likely to appear have been included; and (4) the formats, as stated earlier, are constantly revised.

The role of the MARC formats and their utilization by bibliographic utilities cannot be overemphasized in the history of uniform standards for nonbook media. Since both MARC and the bibliographic utilities adhere to the prevailing standards for bibliographic description (e.g., at present, *AACR 2*), there is little incentive for member libraries to create and use local or special rules for nonbook media. Likewise, the availability of cataloging data for nonbook materials through the bibliographic utilities has made it possible for a far larger percentage of these materials to be brought under bibliographic control.

## NONBOOK CATALOGING RULES
## BEFORE *AACR 2*
### From Diversity to a Uniform Standard

Although the cataloging principles embodied in *AACR 2* evolved over a long period of time, relatively little attention had been paid to the development of bibliographic standards for nonbook materials until the late 1940s. The following discussion will focus on the treatment of nonbook materials in the predecessors of *AACR 2*.[11]

### Pre-*AACR 1* Codes of the 1940s and 1950s
#### ALA and LC Rules

**1949 ALA AND LC RULES**

The *A.L.A. Cataloging Rules for Author and Title Entries* (*ALACR*) were prepared by the ALA Division of Cataloging and Classification and published in 1949.[12] This publication contained rules for choice of entry and form of heading for books and a few types of nonbook materials. The *Rules for Descriptive*

*Cataloging in the Library of Congress* (*RDC*), also published in 1949, were issued by the Descriptive Cataloging Division of the Library of Congress and adopted by ALA for use in conjunction with its own rules for entry.[13] These two codes were officially recognized standards developed by the two bodies serving as national arbiters of cataloging practice.

## ALA AND LC SUPPLEMENTS FOR
## NONBOOK FORMATS

Rules for entry and description of additional materials were included in three authoritative supplements to the *RDC* and *ALACR* issued jointly by the LC and ALA. The supplement *Phonorecords* appeared in 1952,[14] *Motion Pictures and Filmstrips* in 1953,[15] and *Pictures, Designs, and Other Two-Dimensional Representations* in 1959.[16]

## SHORTCOMINGS OF THE PRE-*AACR 1* CODES

The codes that were published from 1949 to 1959 were designed and developed by cataloging specialists working in the committee structure of ALA and at LC. Thus, these codes represented the interests of only part of the constituency of libraries with media collections. Input was sought from varied authorities, but those consulted tended to be experts in specialized collections of materials typically associated with academic libraries. Little or no attention was paid to the kinds of problems dealt with in school or public libraries. In addition, the rules were designed to be used by cataloging specialists, and the formal language of the code, its detail, and the paucity of examples did not encourage use by the novice or occasional cataloger of nonbook materials.

These cataloging rules could also be criticized for placing nonbook materials in separate portions and chapters, thus emphasizing their "special" character and setting them apart from the rules for books. These shortcomings made the pre-*AACR 1* codes unacceptable to large numbers of libraries contending with the problems of nonbook materials, and eventually led to the emergence and popularity of several nonbook cataloging codes which lacked the official backing of the ALA and LC.

# *Anglo-American Cataloging Rules*

The *Anglo-American Cataloging Rules* (*AACR 1*) were published in 1967.[17] The new code represented a significant step forward by bringing together, in one volume, rules which dealt with both entry and description, and which covered books as well as the different types of specialized materials. However, while substantial revisions had been undertaken in other parts of the code, in the case of nonbook materials, little was achieved beyond incorporating the former LC supplements for nonbook materials into a single code.

The obvious result of this failure to revise and update the coverage of nonbook materials was to render this aspect of *AACR 1* obsolete at the time of its publication. Many of the newer instructional media were given scant attention in *AACR 1*, and some were omitted altogether.

The types of nonbook media covered in *AACR 1* were those that would typically form part of the collection of a research library. Although provision was made, at least in theory, for some of the newer forms of "instructional" media more likely to appear in public, school, and junior college libraries, the emphasis in any particular category or chapter was on scholarly materials. For example, the chapter on graphic media devoted much of its attention to problems in cataloging art works. Three-dimensional materials, such as games, models, and dioramas, were excluded. Media that had not yet come into prominence at the time of the preparation of *AACR 1*, notably videorecordings and computer files, were also excluded.

The new code also continued the traditional assumption that each individual type of medium required its own distinct set of rules. This was seen by some critics of *AACR 1* as compromising the idea of an integrated catalog, in that it encouraged librarians to regard nonprint media as an offshoot from the mainstream of library collections and bibliographic control.

Intense criticism of *AACR 1* emerged almost immediately upon its publication. Critics focused principally upon the failure to provide adequate rules for many of the materials commonly found in school and public library collections. Ultimately, the inadequacies of the rules for nonbook materials in the new code were to lead to further diversification of standards and to leave the library community even further away from the goal of standardization.

## Codes Developed as Alternatives to *AACR 1*

Since one of the principal grounds for the immediate criticism of *AACR 1* was its coverage, the alternative codes which followed included a much broader range of materials, primarily the newer instructional media lacking in *AACR 1*. The alternative codes also made an effort to present rules in a language and style more suited to those who are not cataloging specialists.

The need for cataloging guides suited to the requirements of school libraries had been apparent since the 1950s, but the problem became recognizably acute in the 1960s. The latter decade was marked by the development of many forms of instructional media, and by the acquisition of these media on a large scale by school libraries, often with the assistance of generous federal grants. For large research libraries whose collections remained predominantly book oriented, the problem was not nearly as severe. Similarly, those audiovisual materials acquired for the permanent collection of LC were limited both in variety and quantity. Therefore, neither of these agencies was compelled by its own internal needs to supply the leadership required to develop standards for nonbook materials.

Since no acceptable national standard had yet been established, school librarians began to produce their own manuals for the cataloging and processing of media. The later 1960s and early 1970s were marked by the proliferation of diverse cataloging codes for nonbook materials, and many, if not most, of these codes or manuals were drawn up in school library environments. Independent codes emerged as a codification of the practice of a particular school, district, or state, and thus represented a considerable degree of duplication of what was being done by others.

# Building Blocks for *AACR 2*

Some of the nonbook materials codes that had been developed in response to *AACR 1*'s inadequacies emerged as de facto interim standards and were eventually used as building blocks in the development of *AACR 2*.

## REVISED CHAPTER 12 OF *AACR 1*

The revised chapter 12 of *AACR 1* was prepared jointly by the American Library Association, the Canadian Library Association, and the Library of Congress.[18] Published in 1975, the revised chapter was officially adopted as part of the North American text of *AACR 1*.

One purpose of the revised chapter 12 was to improve the rules for two types of material included in the original chapter: motion pictures and filmstrips. Eventually, the decision was made to write an entirely new chapter with a considerably broadened scope, one that would allow the addition of rules for materials previously included in other chapters in *AACR 1* as well as rules for media that had not been included at all.

The revised chapter 12 of *AACR 1* greatly expanded the scope of the original chapter, through the introduction of new categories for three-dimensional media, kits, and videorecordings. As such, the revised chapter 12 was in fact more ambitious in its coverage than any other "chapter" in *AACR 1*, and comprised a relatively self-contained set of rules dealing with nonbook materials.

As a cataloging standard officially sanctioned by LC and ALA, the revised chapter 12 was in the strongest position of all of the newly developed codes for nonbook materials, to be adopted by national cataloging agencies and disseminators of cataloging information. In 1975, LC expanded the coverage of its MARC format for films to accommodate the audiovisual media included in the revised chapter 12. In the following year, the revised chapter 12 was implemented by LC for nonprint materials within the scope of its cataloging program. Provision for entering audiovisual media into the database of the Ohio College Library Center (now known as "OCLC Online Computer Library Center") was made possible in 1976 with the issuance of a films format derived from the MARC standard.

## REVISED CHAPTER 14 OF *AACR 1*

A revised version of *AACR 1*'s chapter on sound recordings (chapter 14) was published in 1976 in order to bring together in a single text a number of revisions announced in the LC *Cataloging Service Bulletin*.[19] This chapter, like the revised chapter 12, was seen as an interim standard, subject to further revisions in the second edition of the *Anglo-American Cataloging Rules*. However, the changes in the revised chapter 14 were not as systematic or as substantial as in the revised chapter 12. The revised rules for sound recordings remained the same as the original in terms of scope of coverage and rules for main entry.

*NON-BOOK MATERIALS: The Organization of Integrated Collections*

The preliminary edition of *Non-book Materials: The Organization of Integrated Collections* (*NBM*) was introduced in 1970 as a response to the inadequacies of rules for nonbook materials in *AACR 1*.[20] The work was written in consultation with the Technical Services Committee of the Canadian School Library Association, and was in part a culmination of the efforts of a small group of Toronto librarians with a common interest in creating a uniform system for cataloging nonbook materials. The rules reflected the principle of an integrated catalog for all media. Careful attention to the opinions of catalogers from a broad spectrum of libraries helped to make *NBM* and its successive editions widely accepted.

The preliminary edition of *NBM* was accepted as an interim guide by ALA, with the proviso that work on the subsequent edition be undertaken in concert with a permanent committee comprised of representatives from ALA and the Canadian Library Association. In the writing of the 1973 "first edition" of *NBM*, the three authors were assisted by a Joint Advisory Committee on Nonbook Materials, comprised of members from ALA, the Canadian Library Association, the Association for Educational Communications and Technology, and the Educational Media Association of Canada.[21] Whereas the preliminary edition had been written primarily with school librarians in mind, an effort was made in the first edition to serve the needs of a broad range of libraries and media centers.

The 1973 edition was subsequently accepted as a source document to be used in the revision of *AACR 1*. Since this revision was still years from completion, many libraries adopted *NBM* as their unofficial interim guide. A second edition of the rules appeared after the publication of *AACR 2*.[22]

*NON-BOOK MATERIALS CATALOGUING RULES*

Another code designated for use as a source document for the revision of *AACR 1* was the *Non-Book Materials Cataloguing Rules* (*NBMCR*).[23] Prepared and published under the auspices of the (British) Library Association and the (British) National Council for Educational Technology (NCET), this code represented a combination of both "library" and "media" interests. Since the British had not had an opportunity to make a substantial contribution to the section on nonbook materials in *AACR 1*, the Library Association was eager to develop, in the revision of *AACR 1*, a set of guidelines consistent with standards of its own making.

Designed with the objective of achieving a single national bibliographic standard for nonbook media, the *NBMCR* was intended for collections of nonbook materials in all types of libraries, including specialized film and record libraries. A notable feature of this code was its coverage of film materials, some of which was eventually made a part of *AACR 2*.

*STANDARDS FOR CATALOGING NONPRINT MATERIALS*, **4TH EDITION**

The *Standards for Cataloging Nonprint Materials*, 4th edition, written by Alma Tillin and William J. Quinly, and published by the Association for Educational Communications and Technology in 1976, also served as a foundation for the revision of rules for nonbook materials in *AACR 2*.[24] The first edition had been published in 1968 and the various editions enjoyed widespread popularity among school media centers.

## THE INTERNATIONAL STANDARD BIBLIOGRAPHIC DESCRIPTION

Another document influential not only in the development of rules for nonbook materials but for *AACR 2* as a whole was the International Standard Bibliographic Description (ISBD). The development of the ISBD grew out of the thrust for the creation of international bibliographic standards. A major impetus for this effort was the International Federation of Library Associations (IFLA). Through its program of Universal Bibliographic Control, IFLA helped bring about the ISBD, a set of requirements designed to delimit elements of description, their order of presentation, and punctuation. In 1975, work was begun on an "umbrella" ISBD for all materials – the General International Standard Bibliographic Description [ISBD (G)]. This standard was developed to serve as a framework for the description of all types of media, as well as to serve as the basis for specialized ISBDs, such as the ISBD for cartographic materials and the ISBD for nonbook materials.[25]

## *Anglo-American Cataloguing Rules, Second Edition*

In the years that followed the publication of *AACR 1* in 1967, significant steps were undertaken to improve bibliographic standards for nonbook materials, and, as discussed earlier, two of *AACR 1*'s chapters on nonbook materials were issued in revised versions. Still, these and other important changes made to the 1967 text had been achieved on a piecemeal basis, and it became apparent that a more systematic and comprehensive revision was needed.

In 1974, a meeting was held to discuss the preparation of a new edition of *AACR 1* which would reconcile the British and North American texts and incorporate revisions already adopted. It was at this time that the Joint Steering Committee for Revision of AACR was formed to coordinate the revision efforts. Eventually, the initial objectives for preparation of the new edition were expanded, and a more ambitious revamping of the code was the result.

*AACR 2*'s publication in 1978 was not without controversy. Although the code in general has been adopted as a standard for the description of both book and nonbook media, the rules for computer files and for microforms were found inadequate by many in the library community. Reasons for these controversies and the emergence of alternative sets of rules are discussed in succeeding chapters.

## Anglo-American Cataloguing Rules, Second Edition, 1988 Revision

The Joint Steering Committee for the Revision of AACR (JSC), comprised of representatives from the United States, the United Kingdom, Canada, and Australia, is the official body authorized to approve changes to *AACR 2*. Three sets of revisions of *AACR 2* approved by the JSC were approved after this time.[26] The decision was made to issue a consolidated edition of *AACR 2* which would incorporate all revisions made to the code since its initial publication. Most of these revisions were communicated to the library community well in advance of the publication of *AACR 2*, 1988 rev. in late 1988.

This book reflects the 1988 revision of *AACR 2*. The most notable changes affecting nonbook materials are the new provisions for microcomputer software, digital sound recordings, and materials for the visually impaired. Many of the issues which led to significant changes in the rules will be discussed in later chapters.

The *Anglo-American Cataloguing Rules, Second Edition, 1988 Revision* do not reflect a radical change from the rules in the original *AACR 2* in 1978.[27] Instead, *AACR 2*, 1988 rev. integrates into a single volume the complete text of the 1978 edition, with corrections, and all changes authorized since 1978 by the Joint Steering Committee for Revision of AACR. Most of these changes were made known to librarians through the published revisions approved by the JSC and through LC's *Cataloging Service Bulletin*.

Even with the publication of *AACR 2*, 1988 rev., bibliographic standards will continue to change and develop. Since cataloging standards and their interpretation are constantly evolving, the cataloger should keep current with new developments through LC's *Cataloging Service Bulletin*. The rule interpretations published in CSB are also issued by LC in a cumulated set in looseleaf form, with quarterly updates.[28]

## NOTES

[1]Carolyn O. Frost, "Nonbook Materials in the Online Public Access Catalog," in *Policy and Practice in Bibliographic Control of Nonbook Media*, ed. Sheila S. Intner and Richard P. Smiraglia (Chicago: American Library Association, 1987), 86.

[2]International Federation of Library Associations and Institutions, Working Group on the General International Standard Bibliographic Description, *ISBD(G), General International Standard Bibliographic Description*, annotated text. (London: IFLA International Office for UBC, 1977).

[3]Library of Congress, *Cataloging Service Bulletin* 15 (Winter 1981): 10.

[4]For an excellent discussion of authorship in nonbook materials, see Martha Yee, "Integration of Nonbook Materials in AACR 2," *Cataloging & Classification Quarterly* 3 (Summer 1983): 1-18.

[5]Frost, "Nonbook Materials in the Online Public Access Catalog," 85.

[6]Library of Congress, *USMARC Format for Bibliographic Data* (Washington, D.C.: Cataloging Distribution Service, 1988).

[7]Walt Crawford, *MARC for Library Use: Understanding the USMARC Formats* (White Plains, N.Y.: Knowledge Industry Publications, 1984).

[8]Sheila S. Intner and Richard P. Smiraglia, eds. *Policy and Practice in Bibliographic Control of Media* (Chicago: American Library Association, 1987).

[9]Nancy B. Olson, *Cataloging of Audiovisual Materials: A Manual Based on AACR 2. Supplement: Coding and Tagging for OCLC* (Mankato, Minn.: Minnesota Scholarly Press, 1985).

[10]John Attig, "The Concept of a MARC Format," *Information Technology and Libraries* 2:7-17 (March 1983).

[11]Parts of this discussion are based on the author's chapter, "The Development of Bibliographic Standards for Nonbook Materials: A Historical Survey," in *Cataloging Nonbook Materials: Problems in Theory and Practice* (Littleton, Colo.: Libraries Unlimited, 1983), 13-32. For an additional survey, see Jean Weihs's chapter, "A Taste of Nonbook History: Historical Background and Review of the State of the Art of Bibliographic Control of Nonbook Materials," in Intner and Smiraglia's *Policy and Practice in Bibliographic Control of Media*, 3-14.

[12]*A.L.A. Cataloging Rules for Author and Title Entries* (Chicago: American Library Association, 1949).

[13]Library of Congress, Descriptive Cataloging Division, *Rules for Descriptive Cataloging in the Library of Congress* (Washington, D.C.: The Library, 1949).

[14]Library of Congress, Descriptive Cataloging Division, *Rules for Descriptive Cataloging in the Library of Congress: Phonorecords* (Washington, D.C.: The Library, 1952).

[15]Library of Congress, Descriptive Cataloging Division, *Rules for Descriptive Cataloging in the Library of Congress: Motion Pictures and Filmstrips* (Washington, D.C.: The Library, 1953).

[16]Library of Congress, Descriptive Cataloging Division, *Rules for Descriptive Cataloging in the Library of Congress: Pictures, Designs and Other Two-Dimensional Representations* (Washington, D.C.: The Library, 1959).

[17]*Anglo-American Cataloging Rules, North American Text* (Chicago: American Library Association, 1967). (*AACR 1* was issued in two editions: the North American text and the British text.)

[18] *Anglo-American Cataloging Rules, North American Text; Chapter 12 Revised: Audiovisual Media and Special Instructional Materials* (Chicago: American Library Association, 1975).

[19] *Anglo-American Cataloging Rules, North American Text; Chapter 14 Revised: Sound Recordings* (Chicago: American Library Association, 1976).

[20] Jean Riddle (Weihs), Shirley Lewis, and Janet Macdonald, *Non-book Materials: The Organization of Integrated Collections*, Preliminary ed. (Ottawa: Canadian Library Association, 1970).

[21] Jean Riddle Weihs, Shirley Lewis, and Janet Macdonald, *Nonbook Materials: The Organization of Integrated Collections*, 1st ed. (Ottawa: Canadian Library Association, 1973).

[22] Jean Weihs, Shirley Lewis, and Janet Macdonald, *Nonbook Materials: The Organization of Integrated Collections*, 2d ed. (Ottawa: Canadian Library Association, 1979).

[23] *Non-Book Materials Cataloguing Rules*. NCET Working Paper No. 11 (London: National Council for Educational Technology with the Library Association, 1973).

[24] Alma Tillin and William J. Quigly, *Standards for Cataloging Nonprint Materials: An Interpretation and Practical Application*, 4th ed. (Washington, D.C.: Association for Educational Communications and Technology, 1976).

[25] International Federation of Library Associations and Institutions, Working Group on the International Standard Bibliographic Description for Non-Book Materials, *ISBD(NBM), International Standard Bibliographic Description for Non-Book Materials* (London: IFLA International Office for UBC, 1977); International Federation of Library Associations and Institutions, Joint Working Group on the International Standard Bibliographic Description for Cartographic Materials, *ISBD(CM), International Standard Bibliographic Description for Cartographic Materials* (London: IFLA International Office for UBC, 1977); *Anglo-American Cataloguing Rules, Second Edition* (Chicago: American Library Association, 1978).

[26] *Anglo-American Cataloguing Rules, Second Edition. Revisions.* (Chicago: American Library Association, 1982); *Anglo-American Cataloguing Rules, Second Edition. Revisions 1983* (Chicago: American Library Association, 1984); *Anglo-American Cataloguing Rules, Second Edition. Revisions 1985* (Chicago: American Library Association, 1986).

[27] *Anglo-American Cataloguing Rules, Second Edition, 1988 Revision*, edited by Michael Gorman and Paul W. Winkler for the Joint Steering Committee for Revision of AACR (Chicago: American Library Association, 1988).

[28] Library of Congress, *Library of Congress Rule Interpretations* (Washington, D.C.: L.C. Cataloging Distribution Service, 1988- ).

# GENERAL REFERENCE SOURCES FOR
# CATALOGING NONBOOK MATERIALS

Berman, Sanford, ed. *Cataloging Special Materials: Critiques and Innovations.*
Phoenix, Ariz.: Oryx Press, 1986.
Nine essays, in an approach that is "variously critical, practical, and
creative" discuss materials including films and videos, computer software,
Spanish-language works, comic books, children's literature, serials, fine arts,
music, and government documents. Covers descriptive and subject cataloging as
well as classification.

Blixrud, Julia C., and Edward Swanson. *A Manual of AACR2 Examples Tagged
and Coded Using the MARC Format.* Lake Crystal, Minn.: Soldier Creek
Press, 1982.
Examples give catalog records and corresponding OCLC MARC coding and
tagging. Covers the formats for books, serials, maps, scores, sound recordings,
audiovisual media, manuscripts, and microforms.

Daily, Jay E. *Organizing Nonprint Materials.* 2d ed. New York: Marcel Dekker,
1986.
Part 1 contains chapters that discuss cataloging, classification, and the use of
nonprint materials. Gives consideration to aspects of "Material Cataloged by
Content" (maps, pictures), and "Material Cataloged by Identifying Features"
(sound recordings, motion pictures, videotapes). One chapter includes guidelines
for developing procedural manuals. Part 2 contains examples of bibliographic
entries, with explanations. The examples for sound recordings depart from
*AACR 2* in that a special area has been created to include performer information.
Approximately half of the book is comprised of an alphabetical list of subject
headings followed by Dewey Decimal Classification numbers, along with a
corresponding classified list of subject headings followed by Dewey numbers.

Ellison, John W., ed. *Media Librarianship.* New York: Neal-Schumann, 1985.
Thirty-four chapters cover issues in media-services management, including
cataloging and the physical organization of nonprint materials.

Ellison, John W., and Patricia Ann Cody, eds. *Nonbook Media: Collection
Management and User Services.* Chicago: American Library Association,
1987.
Covers a wide range of media, including maps, phonograph records, films,
videodiscs, videotapes, art reproductions, holographs, original art, photographs,
slides, overhead transparencies, flat pictures, posters, charts, study prints,
machine-readable data files, models, realia, holographs, and microforms. Each
chapter looks at the medium itself (history, characteristics, advantages and disadvantages); selection (criteria, review sources); and maintenance and management
(storage and care, management issues). The management sections include brief
discussions of organization and arrangement of materials.

Fleischer, Eugene. *A Style Manual for Citing Microforms and Nonprint Media*. Chicago: American Library Association, 1978.

"Designed to be a companion to any one of the style manuals for the writing of research papers and theses." Provides the writer with a set of rules for citing sound recordings, motion pictures, and other media that may have been excluded from the other manuals. "Written to produce citations which will be compatible with the established footnote and bibliographic forms and so become an integral part of the style of the paper."

Fleischer, Eugene, and Helen Goodman. *Cataloguing Audiovisual Materials: A Manual Based on AACR II*. New York: Neal-Schumann, 1980.

Gives eighty-one cataloging problems covering cartographic materials, sound recordings, motion pictures and videorecordings, graphic materials, three-dimensional artefacts and realia, and kits. For each example, there is a pictorial representation and description of the item to be cataloged, bibliographic records for all three levels of descriptive cataloging, and discussion of cataloging decisions made. Also includes introductory narrative sections.

Intner, Sheila S. *Access to Media: A Guide to Integrating and Computerizing Catalogs*. New York: Neal-Schumann, 1984.

The first part of the book focuses on current and past practices and developments in the bibliographic control of nonprint materials. Includes a history of the development of media collections, and looks at administration and organization of media in libraries. Presents findings of research on current bibliographic practices in providing access to nonprint collections in U.S. public libraries, as well as bibliographic practices in other libraries. Describes the author's 1981 national survey of attitudes of public librarians toward bibliographic treatment of nonprint materials. Continues with recent research involving bibliographic practices in academic and school libraries. Part Two presents a strategy for improving access to media through integrated online bibliographic systems.

Intner, Sheila, and Richard Smiraglia, eds. *Policy and Practice in Bibliographic Control of Nonbook Media*. Chicago: American Library Association, 1987.

Part One, "Background, theory, and management concerns," includes chapters on history and theory of bibliographic control for nonbook materials, online public access catalogs, subject access, and current and future needs of the catalog. Part Two includes chapters on the cataloging of individual media: music and sound recordings, motion pictures and videorecordings, two- and three-dimensional materials, and microcomputer software. A concluding chapter discusses MARC tagging for nonbook materials.

Lamy-Rousseau, Francoise. *Classification des Images, Materials et Donnees = Classification of Images, Materials and Data*. 2d ed. Longueuil (Quebec): M. F. Rousseau, 1984.

Presents a classification system developed for nonbook materials. Allows categorization by various aspects of subject content and form, and by specific physical material and media format. Illustrations of the different formats. In French and English.

*OLAC* [Online Audiovisual Catalogers] *Newsletter.* [Various places]: Online
 Audiovisual Catalogers, 1981- . Quarterly.
 Essential reading for all catalogers of audiovisual materials. Reports on
developments of interest in the field, presentations, meetings, and others. The
"Questions and Answers" sections address problems raised by practicing
catalogers.

Olson, Nancy B. *Audiovisual Material Glossary.* Dublin, Ohio: OCLC, 1988.
 Gives 724 definitions of terms relating to materials covered in *AACR 2*'s
chapters 3, and 5-11. Illustrations accompany many of the definitions.

_____. *Cataloging of Audiovisual Materials.* 2d ed. Mankato, Minn.:
 Minnesota Scholarly Press, 1985. [second printing, January 1986 with minor
 corrections].
 Chapters on sound recordings, motion pictures and videorecordings, graphic
materials, microcomputer software, three-dimensional artefacts and realia,
microforms, audiovisual serials, and kits. For each type of material there is an
outline and commentary of relevant *AACR 2* rules, numerous examples with
photograph of item to be cataloged, and *AACR 2* catalog records. Introductory
chapters provide an overview of *AACR 2*, and brief coverage of subject access,
and various considerations to be made in the process of cataloging audiovisual
materials. A companion volume provides MARC tagging (OCLC format) for the
examples given in the main volume.

Olson, Nancy B., and Edward Swanson. "The Year's Work in Nonbook Processing, 1986." *Library Resources & Technical Services* 31 (October/December
 1987): 356-63.
 Survey of developments in standards, selection, and cataloging, and
classification and subject access. Update of 1987 developments is in press.

Rogers, JoAnn, with Jerry D. Saye. *Nonprint Cataloging for Multimedia Collections: A Guide Based on AACR 2.* 2d ed. Littleton, Colo.: Libraries Unlimited, 1987.
 Covers cartographic materials, sound recordings, graphic materials, motion
pictures and videorecordings, computer files, three-dimensional materials, and
microforms. Gives detailed explanations of *AACR 2* rules and considerations in
their implementation; includes relevant LC rule interpretations and revised rules.
Explanations are enhanced by information on the physical and other
characteristics of the various formats. Also helpful are the numerous examples
with explanations of rules used.

Weihs, Jean. *Accessible Storage of Nonbook Materials.* Phoenix, Ariz.: Oryx
 Press, 1984.
 Based on the premise that nonbook materials should be intershelved in
"patron-oriented circulating libraries." Discusses managerial concerns affecting
staff and patrons, and storage and handling considerations affecting the
materials themselves. Individual chapters on the care, handling, and storage of
individual media are given for the formats of sound discs, magnetic tapes, film
media, two-dimensional opaque materials, three-dimensional and boxed
materials, and microcomputer disks. Illustrations show shelving devices and
methods appropriate to each type of format.

Weihs, Jean, Shirley Lewis, and Janet Macdonald. *Nonbook Materials: The Organization of Integrated Collections.* 2d ed. Ottawa: Canadian Library Association, 1979.

Designed as a "companion volume" to *AACR 2*. The rules selected have been paraphrased for simpler reading. The format consists of a brief set of general rules followed by rules for the entry and description of individual media formats. There are sections on subject analysis and guidelines for the care, handling, and storage of different kinds of media. Rules are illustrated by sample catalog records. There are a number of rules that are slight modifications of *AACR 2*, or provide special provisions for some types of media such as technical drawings.

# 2

θθθθθθθθθθθθθθθθθθθθθθθθθθθθθθθθθθθθθθθθθθθθθθθθθθθθθθθθθθθθθθθθθθθθθθθθθθθθθθθθθθθθθθθθθθ

# *Cartographic Materials*

θθθθθθθθθθθθθθθθθθθθθθθθθθθθθθθθθθθθθθθθθθθθθθθθθθθθθθθθθθθθθθθθθθθθθθθθθθθθθθθθθθθθθθθθθθ

## DECISION AREAS IN
## DESCRIPTIVE CATALOGING

### Scope

**DEFINING *CARTOGRAPHIC***
**Content and Format**

The category of cartographic materials in *AACR 2*'s chapter 3 includes media that share the basic characteristic of "[representing] the whole or part of the earth or any celestial body." Among these media are atlases, globes, navigational charts, a wide variety of two- and three-dimensional maps, and even aerial photographs, if they have a cartographic purpose.

**FORMAT**

*AACR 2* distinguishes between two categories of cartographic formats:

1. A cartographic item in its original form (e.g., a photograph, or three-dimensional artefact). Such items are governed by the rules for cartographic materials in chapter 3.

2. A cartographic item whose original form has been *reproduced* in another format; for example, a map reproduced as a microform or slide. Such an item is governed by the rules for the format in which the map has been reproduced. *AACR 2* requires that the starting point for the description in such cases is the format of the reproduction, that is, the physical item in hand; a map that has been reproduced as a microform would be cataloged using chapter 11 for microforms. However, chapter 3 would still be used to note cartographic aspects of the item, such as scale information.

Contrary to *AACR 2*, LC has adopted a different approach. While *AACR 2* prescribes that microform reproductions be described according to the characteristics of the physical item in hand, that is, the microform reproduction itself, the

LC policy is to describe the microform reproduction according to the original publication. (See chapter 8.) For cartographic materials, this policy of describing the original may pose some particular problems, since it may be difficult for the cataloger to gain access to the original, and since there may be no cataloging copy for the original.[1]

## CONTENT

There are additional questions of categorization that are not dealt with directly by *AACR 2*. Some materials, while containing cartographic content, may not be essentially cartographic in purpose. For example, a map puzzle designed to teach geographic concepts may be considered by some catalogers as essentially instructional in purpose, and more appropriately treated as a game covered by the rules for three-dimensional materials. LC's Geography and Map Division, however, treats cartographic items in any form as maps. A similar problem is posed by computer software capable of producing computer-generated maps. In this instance, it is probably best to use the chapter for computer files, since the computer characteristics of the item will probably be of essential interest to the user.

## PREVIOUS RULES

*AACR 1*'s chapter on maps was limited to maps, map sets, and series. In contrast, *AACR 2*'s chapter on cartographic materials is much wider in scope, and goes beyond maps to include atlases, aerial photographs, views, and space remote sensing images.

## CARTOGRAPHIC MATERIALS: A Manual of Interpretation for AACR2

In cataloging maps, specialized subject expertise in the area of cartography becomes invaluable. Many terms and concepts referred to in *AACR 2*'s chapter 3 are probably unfamiliar to the nonspecialist. A manual prepared by the Anglo-American Cataloguing Committee for Cartographic Materials should provide much-needed assistance: *Cartographic Materials: A Manual of Interpretation for AACR2* (hereafter referred to as *CM*).[2] The manual elaborates on *AACR 2*, and provides considerable background information necessary for the cataloging of cartographic materials. Included are detailed illustrations, numerous examples of rule applications, and a glossary. Special attention is given to map series. The manual covers the same type of materials included in *AACR 2*'s chapter 3; that is, it is not limited to maps of a particular kind, such as archival maps.

In the following presentation of *AACR 2* rules for the descriptive cataloging of cartographic materials, appropriate supplementary rules from *CM* have been included. This inclusion is selective, and is intended to outline those rules which represent a substantial departure from *AACR 2*, or provide significant clarification or augmentation of rules in many problem areas.

# Sources of Information

## LACK OF A TITLE-PAGE EQUIVALENT

The preferred chief source of information for cartographic materials is defined as the item itself. For many cartographic items, all the information—both cartographic and bibliographic—is presented on a single sheet. For a single sheet map, the rules treat the whole item as the chief source; thus, if variant information exists, the cataloger will not be able to use location as a criterion for selecting the chief source. Information may appear on the upper or lower, right- or left-hand corner, with no preferred location established. This is in contrast to media that have an identifiable title-page analog, such as the title frames of a film or filmstrip, or the title screen of a computer file.

# Title and Statement of Responsibility Area

## CHOOSING AMONG VARIANT TITLES

Since the chief source is the entire item, a map will often contain more than one title. *AACR 2*'s rule 3.1B3 refers the cataloger, in such a case, to rule 1.1B8, which deals with titles in two or more languages or scripts. If this is not applicable, the title is to be selected according to the order of the titles or the layout appearing on the chief source. If these criteria are insufficient to make the choice, the most comprehensive title is chosen.

*Cartographic Materials* provides further directives on choice of title, if there is doubt as to which of the titles should be chosen as the title proper. Selection should be according to the following table:

- a title located within the neat line or border of the main map, etc.

- a title located on the recto of the item outside the neat line or border of the main map, etc.

- a panel title [folded title, located on either the] (recto or verso)

- a title located on the verso of the item

- a title located on a cover, container, etc.

In considering titles occurring in the locations above, preference is given to titles that include both area and subject.[3] *Cataloging Government Documents: A Manual of Interpretation for AACR2 (GD)* explains further that if, for example, the title within the neat line of a thematic (subject-oriented) map includes only the name of the geographic area, and the panel title includes both the area and the subject, the cataloger should select the panel title as the title proper; the title within the neat line should be recorded as a variant title in a note. If both titles on the map indicate the geographic area and subject content, the title proper should be chosen strictly on the basis of location.[4]

## IMPORTANCE OF GEOGRAPHIC AREA
## IN TITLES

The *AACR 2* rules make it clear that the geographic area must always be included in the title. Titles transcribed from the item must give some indication of the geographic area being covered. If the title lacks this information, the cataloger should add a word or brief phrase indicating the area covered. This should appear as other title information and is enclosed in brackets, for example, Vegetation [GMD] : [in Botswana] (3.1E2).

If an item lacks a title, the cataloger should supply one as instructed in 1.1B7, and the supplied title should include the name of the geographic area covered (3.1B4). *CM* suggests that, when relevant, the supplied title also include the primary subject content of the item.

## ITEMS WITHOUT A COLLECTIVE TITLE

Cartographic items that lack a collective title can be cataloged either as a unit or with individual bibliographic records for each separately titled part (3.1G4). If the item consists of a large number of physically separate parts, the cataloger also has the choice of supplying a collective title (3.1G5). Rules for other formats covered in *AACR 2* allow the option to treat the item either as a unit or as separate entities, but only in the case of cartographic materials is the cataloger given the additional choice of supplying a collective title.

The decision made on the unit to be cataloged will determine most aspects of the bibliographic record; therefore, this decision should be the first one made in the cataloging process. LC normally applies the option in 3.1G4 (to make separate bibliographic descriptions) only when the item consists of a number of physically separate maps. For example, if the item consists of a number of maps on one sheet, LC will either describe the item as a unit, or will consider one of the maps to be predominant and thus catalog it as the main map.[5]

## GENERAL MATERIAL DESIGNATION

### GENERIC VERSUS SPECIFIC

The Anglo-American Cataloguing Committee for Cartographic Materials voiced disapproval for the GMD terms *map* and *globe* on the North American list, while preferring the more generic term *cartographic material* on the British list. It was the opinion of the committee that the North American terms were too specific and limiting, and that many other materials that might fall within the category of cartographic materials would not be comprehended by the terms *map* and *globe.*[6]

Two arguments can be made in support of the British preference for generic terms: (1) A clear distinction is made between general and specific material designations, and (2) general terms, embracing a wider range of categories, are less confining than a list of specific terms which may not fit the item in hand.

## THE GMD FOR MAP REPRODUCTIONS IN ANOTHER FORMAT

In cases in which the cartographic item is a reproduction of a work originally produced in another format such as microform or a slide, the GMD will be assigned on the basis of the physical entity being cataloged, rather than the original content that has been reproduced. A "cardinal principle" in *AACR 2* requires that the starting point of description is the physical item in hand, rather than an original that has been reproduced by the item. Karrow points out that "this practice may help the librarian who wants to know whether a given description should be sent to the map room or the microform room, but a reader looking for maps of Idaho will not be helped by finding a collection of old maps on microfilm under 'Historic Idaho [microform].' " Karrow thus raises a legitimate question concerning the basic purpose of the GMD as an "early warning device." He contends that "library users generally care less about the format of a work than its content and most users (including reference librarians) would prefer to see 'Historic Idaho [map]' and worry later about whether they need a microfilm reader to use it." He thus proposes that the GMD be reserved for the specification of content, leaving the specific material designation to serve the function of recording the actual physical form.[7] The issue is whether the GMD's primary purpose is to describe the content or the format of the item.

*AACR 1* did not allow a GMD for maps. While the Library of Congress will not apply *AACR 2*'s optional rule to display the GMD for cartographic materials, the cataloger might consider the advantages that the GMD offers in alerting the user to the type of information described.

## STATEMENT OF RESPONSIBILITY

### ROLES OF INTELLECTUAL RESPONSIBILITY

In determining what information on the item constitutes a statement of responsibility, the cataloger may encounter a variety of roles to be considered. Statements of responsibility can be made for persons such as cartographers, compilers, engravers, illuminators, revisers, scientific editors, and government mapping agencies.[8]

### LOCATION OF STATEMENT OF RESPONSIBILITY INFORMATION

Since presentation of cartographic information is not as standardized as title-page layout for books, statements of responsibility will often be located on the item separate from the main title. They may be found, for example, in the upper or lower margin of the map, near the legend, following a variant title (e.g., panel title), or on a cover or other container.[9]

# Mathematical Data Area

For cartographic materials, *AACR 2*'s area 3 is the "mathematical data area," and is comprised of statements for scale, for projection, and for coordinates and equinox. This information is grouped together into a separate area which appears in a prominent part of the catalog record, between the edition and the publication areas. (In *AACR 1*, all scale information was relegated to a note.)

## SCALE INFORMATION

The importance of the scale information can be seen from the fact that it is required (1) even in a Level One description, (2) even if the scale is already recorded as part of the title information, and (3) even if the scale information is not found on the chief source.

## THE REPRESENTATIVE FRACTION AS THE STANDARD FORM OF SCALE EXPRESSION

The presentation of scale information is highly standardized, and whenever possible, the scale is given as a representative fraction expressed as a ratio (1: ), preceded by the word *scale*. If the scale is expressed on the item in another form, such as a bar graph, or as a verbal statement (e.g., "one inch to four miles"), the cataloger is still required to translate the scale information into the standardized representative fraction.

## COMPUTING A REPRESENTATIVE FRACTION FROM VERBAL SCALE STATEMENTS

*Cartographic Materials* provides guidance on the computation of a representative fraction from a verbal scale statement. If the scale on the map is given in miles to the inch, the representative fraction is calculated by multiplying the number of miles per inch by 63,360 (the number of inches in one mile).[10]

## COMPUTING SCALE INFORMATION FROM AN OUTSIDE SOURCE

If the scale information has been taken from outside the chief source, it is given in square brackets. If no statement of scale can be found on the item itself, its container, case, or accompanying material, *AACR 2* prescribes computing a representative fraction from a bar graph or grid, or by comparison with a map of known scale. In this case the scale is preceded by *ca*. *CM* considers the latter method of computation as "one of the least accurate ways of calculating [a representative fraction]" and suggests that the comparison with a map of known scale be used only as a last resort.[11]

*Cartographic Materials* also gives instruction on how to compute a representative fraction from a bar scale (preferring this term to *AACR 2*'s *bar graph*). This computation can be accomplished by using a device called a natural scale indicator, which allows the cataloger in most cases to read the representative fraction directly from the indicator.[12]

## WHEN SCALE CANNOT BE GIVEN AS A
## REPRESENTATIVE FRACTION

Some statement regarding the scale must always be given, even in cases in which the scale cannot be determined, or the scale information varies, or an item is not drawn to scale. Only if the scale cannot be determined by any of the aforementioned means should the cataloger give the statement "Scale indeterminable" (3.3B1). LC's policy, however, will depart somewhat from this directive: LC prefers *Scale not given* to *AACR 2*'s phrase *Scale indeterminable*. The latter term is reserved for cases in which efforts made to determine the scale of an item by comparing it with other maps have been unsuccessful.[13]

Chapter 3's insistence on some sort of statement regarding the scale is similar to chapter 1's requirement that a date always be provided. In both cases, if the necessary information is not available from the item, the cataloger must attempt to provide an estimate.

In other cases the cataloger may be confronted with the opposite problem: a range of scale information. Rules 3.3B3 to 3.3B6 provide for cases in which the scale varies within one item, for cases in which there is a multipart item with two or more scales, and for items in which all the main maps are of one or more scales. While *AACR 2*'s 3.3B5 and 3.3B6 call for use of the phrase *Scales vary*, LC in certain instances is using *Scales differ* instead.[14]

There are some instances in which scale information is not appropriate and a scale need be given only if the information appears on the item. This occurs with celestial maps, maps of imaginary places, views (bird's-eye views or map views), and maps with nonlinear scales. The cataloger can indicate that the item is "Not drawn to scale" (3.3B7).

## PROJECTION INFORMATION
### Level of Detail

While the statement of projection is given if found on the item or other prescribed sources, the cataloger has the option to include in addition, associated phrases connected with the projection statement (3.3C2). LC is applying the option to add these associated phrases if they are given on the item.[15]

## COORDINATES INFORMATION
### A Means for Online Access

Another option provides for a statement of coordinates and equinox (3.3D1), and gives specific guidelines for the sequence of the coordinates and for the way in which the coordinates are to be formulated. LC is recording the coordinates or equinox if the information is readily available (e.g., if the coordinates are printed on the item.)[16]

*AACR 2*'s provision for a statement of coordinates has major ramifications for online subject access to cartographic materials. Numerical parameters such as the latitude and longitude boundaries, scale, and date enable a means of retrieval which is independent of the ambiguities of language, and which allows a precise and unequivocal identification of geographic entities. Names of areas can change, as political governance changes; names can be expressed in several languages; at times, the geographic area on a map may encompass multiple jurisdictional boundaries. But by expressing the geographic area in terms of coordinates, such problems of identification are bypassed. At present, the RLIN bibliographic utility provides the capability of searching via coordinates, and other systems will probably find this type of access of value in the future. LC's decision to include a statement of coordinates whenever latitude and longitude are shown on a map will substantially increase the prospect of improved retrieval of maps.[17]

## OCLC MARC MAPS FORMAT

The MARC format makes it possible for essential cartographic information to be used as retrieval elements or qualifiers in an online search. In addition to providing for the verbal expression of *AACR 2*'s mathematical data area, the MARC Maps format also requires that this information be represented in a coded form in field 034. This control field contains information about scale, coordinates, and equinox. It is not intended for display on the catalog record, but to provide standardized online retrieval by coordinates.

In the OCLC "Base" fixed field for base map elements, coding for thirty types of map projections and for prime meridian can be indicated. Another type of cartographic information is provided for in the "Relief" fixed field, which contains codes for relief types. The eleven types of relief codes (e.g., "contours," "shading," "gradient tint") are listed and defined. No specific instructions for indicating relief types are given in *AACR 2*.

# Publication Area

## UNDATED PUBLICATIONS

*Cartographic Materials* gives guidelines for inferring the date of publication if the date is not stated as such on the item (3.1F1). The inferred publication date should be derived from other dates on the item, such as those appearing in the title information, statement of responsibility, edition statement, or printing or publisher's code. However, certain information found on the item should not be considered when inferring a date of publication; for example, dates of boundaries ("cease-fire lines as of 1967") and dates in base map notes (e.g., "based on the 1972 Forest Service class A map").[18]

## ROLE OF THE
## GOVERNMENT AS MAP PUBLISHER

Larsgaard reminds us that "the U.S. government is the largest publisher in the world," and that "almost any agency can, and at some time may, produce maps." Through the federal depository system, many of the estimated 160 million sheet maps per year distributed by the federal government will make their way into libraries. Since "easily 75%" of cartographic collections will be government documents, a familiarity with reference sources in this area may assist in verifying publication data.[19]

# Physical Description Area

## CHANGES IN RULES FOR THE
## SPECIFIC MATERIAL DESIGNATION

Rule 3.5B1 lists nine different specific material designations which can be used to record the number of physical units of a cartographic item. The original *AACR 2* had a list of twenty-six terms, many of them technical. The new list of nine terms is derived from a list provided in *CM* as an alternative to the list in the original *AACR 2*.[20] *CM*'s terms were used by LC in its application of the original *AACR 2*.[21]

New rules now allow the description of materials for the visually impaired, e.g., "1 map (braille)," and "1 map (print and tactile)."

## *MAP* AS PHYSICAL AND CONTENT UNIT

Some ambiguity exists in *AACR 2*'s use of the term *map*. In rule 3.5B2, the cataloger is asked to specify if there is more than one map on a sheet (e.g., "6 maps on 1 sheet"). In this case, the term *map* appears to indicate subject content rather than a physical entity. The same use of the term appears later in reference to the converse situation in which a single map entity consists of a number of physical sections. (Note: LC is using the phrase "on ... sheets" instead of "in ... sections" as indicated in *AACR 2*; e.g., "1 map on 4 sheets," not "1 map in 4 sections.") In other rules, however (3.5B1 and 3.5B4), *AACR 2* uses the term *map* to refer to the physical unit.[22]

## OTHER PHYSICAL DETAILS

In addition to the physical details (color, mounting, and material) given in *AACR 2*, LC is indicating whether the item is printed on both sides of a sheet (e.g., "1 map : both sides"), whether the item is a manuscript (e.g., "1 map : ms."), or is a photoreproduction (e.g., "1 map : photocopy").[23]

## DIMENSIONS

There is only one rule covering dimensions, 3.5D1, but it contains eight paragraphs of detailed instructions and twenty examples that illustrate the diverse situations possible. The rule provides for items that are circular, irregularly shaped, have no neat lines, or have bleeding or damaged edges. Also covered are single maps printed on both sides of a sheet at a consistent scale, and maps printed with panels designed to appear on the outside when the sheet is folded. The sections of rule 3.5D1 are difficult to scan since they are not labeled or further subdivided. The illustrated examples provided in *CM* are of enormous help in clarifying the different sections of rule 3.5D1; for example, the graphic representations make clear the distinction between such concepts as "one map on both sides of one sheet," "one map printed in segments on one sheet," and "one map on two or more sheets," as well as the difference between the neat line, border, and margins.[24]

The Library of Congress is exercising the option in rule 3.5D5 for adding the dimensions of any container of the item. According to *GD*, types of containers for cartographic items include covers, cases, slipcases, envelopes, and portfolios.[25]

## OCLC MARC MAPS FORMAT

The Physical Description Fixed Field (007) in the OCLC MARC Maps format makes it possible to code information that replicates and to some extent extends, the data provided in *AACR 2*'s physical description area. Subfield codes are given for general material designations, specific material designations, color, physical medium, type of reproduction, production/reproduction details, and polarity. A separate fixed field is given for microform maps.

In the "Form" fixed field (Special Format Characteristics), codes allow identification of specific formats such as manuscripts, picture or post cards, calendars, puzzles, Braille or tactile materials, games, wall maps, and playing cards.

## PREVIOUS RULES

*AACR 1* required that items be measured according to the border or margin, in contrast to the present rules which measure according to the neat lines; the latter are lines, usually grid or graticule, that enclose the detail of a map. Thus the new rule requires the cataloger to measure the dimensions relative to the geographic content.

# Note Area

The Library of Congress and *GD*, the manual for cataloging government documents, have provided guidelines for the use of notes having special relevance for cartographic materials:

The Nature and Scope note (3.7B1) is the place to record the date relating to cartographic information (e.g., "Shows the main battles of 1944-1945"), particularly if that date differs from the date of publication. This information is recorded here, rather than in the publication note.

The source of title proper (3.7B3) is being recorded by LC when the title proper is taken from the verso of the item or from its container (e.g., cover) or when the title proper is a panel title (folded title).

The physical description note is not used by LC to indicate if the item is a photoreproduction (i.e., photocopy); this is contrary to *AACR 2*'s rule 3.7B10. Instead, LC is indicating this information, as mentioned earlier, in the "other physical details" section of the physical description area. The method of reproduction, however, will be recorded in a note.

Important numbers for cartographic items include stock numbers, order numbers, plate numbers, classification numbers, and any other number or alpha-numeric code which would further identify or distinguish the item (3.7B19).

If a reproduction of a map has been reduced or enlarged from the original, the scale will be affected. In such cases, the scale of the reproduction is recorded in the statement of scale area. The scale of the original item is recorded in a note if it is known or can be determined.[26]

# Choice of Access Points

## DEFINING PERSONAL AUTHORSHIP

*AACR 2*'s general principles for main entry prescribe that works of personal authorship are entered under the name of "the person chiefly responsible for the creation of the intellectual or artistic content of a work." The original *AACR 2* specifically stated that cartographers are regarded as the authors of the maps they create.

*Cartographic Materials* saw limitations in the original *AACR 2*'s concept of personal authorship for cartographic materials, and would qualify this definition of authorship in the original rule 21.1A1 to read "cartographers *may* be the authors of their maps." In its "Guidelines for Choice of Access Points," *CM* argues that "the intellectual responsibility of cartographers can vary from complete responsibility for the cartographic item as a whole to only partial responsibility that may in some cases be no more than photographic or mechanical duplication or tracing of an existing base map."[27]

## CORPORATE ENTRY

Rules for corporate entry are of particular significance for cartographic materials, since according to Ristow, "it is estimated that 80% of all maps issued in the world are maps and charts by federal, state, county and municipal surveying and mapping agencies."[28]

## REACTION TO THE ORIGINAL *AACR 2* RULES FOR CORPORATE ENTRY

The chapter on choice of access points in the original *AACR 2* contained no rules specific to cartographic materials. Under the original rule 21.1B2, only a small percentage of cartographic materials would have qualified for main entry under corporate body. The rules thus would have had the effect of placing the majority of cartographic materials under title main entry. Map librarians at the Geography and Map Division at LC and other institutions raised the objection that large numbers of title main entries in maps would be inappropriate in view of the fact that so many map titles are nondistinctive.

Strong opposition to the original 21.1B2 was voiced also by the Anglo-American Cataloguing Committee for Cartographic Materials. The committee was successful in convincing the National Library of Canada and the Library of Congress to accept an interpretation of the original 21.1B2 which would "permit entry under corporate body for a large body of cartographic materials currently excluded from corporate main entry by *AACR 2*."[29] This "interpretation" eventually appeared as a rule revision.

## EXPANDING THE RULES TO INCLUDE CORPORATE RESPONSIBILITY

Category "f" was added to rule 21.1B2 in the 1982 revisions of *AACR 2* approved by the Joint Steering Committee for Revision of AACR. With the addition of this category, a cartographic work is entered under the heading for the appropriate body if it emanates "from a corporate body other than a body that is merely responsible for the publication or distribution of the materials."

It may be difficult at times to determine the nature of the corporate publisher's degree of responsibility. *CM* suggests that the cataloger take into account the publication history of the corporate body and whether it is known to be a map-making organization which normally originates and issues maps. If these conditions apply, the corporate body could be considered as having responsibilities beyond the mere publishing of the cartographic material.[30]

In some cases, the map publisher's responsibility may be fairly obvious. For example, the idea of the corporate body's mapping activities may be conveyed by its name, for example, Hellenic Military Geographical Service. In other cases, the cartographic responsibility of the publisher may be less clear from its name, for example, the Solomon Islands' Ministry of Agriculture and Lands. In these instances, the cataloger might look for indications of responsibility from statements on the map such as "prepared by ..." or "compiled, drawn, and printed by ..."[31]

## CONCEPTS OF AUTHORSHIP IN
## PREVIOUS RULES

The 1949 ALA rules considered the following persons or corporate bodies as responsible for the intellectual content of maps and atlases: cartographers, editors, publishers, government bureaus, societies or institutions, engravers, if known to be mapmakers, and copyright claimants (rule 10).

Likewise, *AACR 1* extended and modified the concept of intellectual responsibility for cartographic materials in a separate set of rules for determining main entry for maps. Among persons and corporate bodies considered as principally responsible for the geographic content of a work were "1) the individual whose survey provided the basis for the cartography, 2) the cartographer, 3) the engraver, if known to be also a cartographer, [and] 4) the corporate body, including a map publisher, that prepared the map" (rule 211B).

# Form of Heading

*AACR 2*'s chapter 23 gives rules for the formulation of headings for geographic names and thus is to be used for main and added entry headings for names of places. Geographic subject headings are also based on this chapter.

# Cataloging Maps Individually or as Sets

The question of what level of bibliographic description is appropriate for a series or set is a perennial problem area in the bibliographic control and organization of such items as maps, graphic materials, and microforms. These materials may be issued in large sets or collections which are capable of being organized and described either individually or as a set. For cartographic materials, such collections of related materials often occur as map sets or map series. As with microform collections, such sets may comprise the majority of the library's collection for this medium. Larsgaard notes that "in the majority of cartographic materials collections, at least 60% of the holdings, and sometimes as much as 90%, will be map series."[32]

*AACR 2* provides some guidelines for cataloging map series, but more detailed assistance can be found in *CM*, which contains two appendices on this subject. Appendix D describes series maps as well as "multi-sheet maps." Appendix E includes guidelines for cataloging a map series.

### DEFINITION AND CHARACTERISTICS OF
### MAP SERIES

A collection of maps is often referred to as a "map set" or more recently as a "map series," and is not to be confused with a "monographic series" (see *AACR 2*, appendix D), although there are some similarities between them. While the number of maps in a map series can vary widely, common unifying characteristics include the following:

Format—A uniform size, format, scale, and projection, and a common system of cartographic symbolization.

Distinctiveness as a bibliographic entity—Each map within the series is complete and can be used independently. Each map has its own sheet title or designation and also contains the collective or series title, authorship and publication information, and legend data.

Publication—Usually produced and published by one government body. May be issued simultaneously or over a period of time, with some large series issued over many years.

Content—Each map of a series covers a specific area (e.g., quadrangle area, administrative unit). While most map series cover a contiguous geographic area (e.g., city, state, country, the world) in a systematic arrangement, a series may also consist of maps covering a common geographic area with each map displaying a different or related theme or subject.[33]

## CATALOGING A MAP COLLECTION AS A WHOLE OR AS SEPARATES

Rule 3.0J allows the cataloger the choice between describing a collection of maps as a whole or describing each map individually and giving the name of the collection as a series. This choice should be made according to the needs of the cataloging agency. If the decision is made to catalog the collection as a whole, the cataloger is directed to chapter 13, "Analysis," which gives guidelines for "preparing a bibliographic record that describes a part or parts of an item for which a comprehensive entry has been made." Various options for analysis are presented: analytics of monograph series and multipart monographs, display of parts in the note area, analytical added entries, "in" analytics, and multilevel descriptions.

Given the large number of individual items likely to be found in a map series, the provision of catalog records on an individual basis may be an overwhelming task. According to Moore, "few map collections in America are completely cataloged, with the heaviest priorities given to unique, research materials such as foreign topographic series."[34] *CM* suggests that in determining whether to describe a map collection as a whole or separately, the cataloger consider the number of maps in a collection, and the frequency with which they are revised. In addition, consideration should be given to the availability of alternative bibliographic tools to provide access to the collection. In many situations, adequate access to individual maps may be provided by an "index map," defined in *CM*'s glossary as "an index, usually based on an outline map, which shows the layout and numbering system of map sheets which cover an area." Some index maps appear on the margin of an individual map sheet, while others may be found on a separate leaf.

# Classification

Among the predominant schemes used for the classification of maps, three—Library of Congress, Dewey Decimal, and Universal Decimal—are parts of comprehensive systems designed to cover all subjects. Two others—Boggs and Lewis and American Geographic Society—were specifically developed for maps. Since area rather than subject is the key point of interest for most map users, the schemes use geography or area as the focal point of organization, with the possible exception of Dewey. Merrett points out that most map classification schemes are organized around division of continents into countries; the resulting approach is politically oriented, but has cartographic warrant, since most maps are published by government agencies which produce maps of areas within their jurisdictions. A major limitation of this approach of course is the possibility that political divisions will change.[35]

## BOGGS AND LEWIS

The Boggs and Lewis classification system is exclusively devoted to maps, and was developed to meet the needs of the U.S. State Department's Map Library.[36] Intended for cataloging as well as classification, it used area as main entry followed by subject, date, cartographer, and title. While many map librarians have argued that geographic area should be the primary basis for the organization of maps, the 1949 ALA Committee on Classification rejected Boggs and Lewis' scheme on the grounds that maps should be classified according to the same principles as books. ALA refused to publish the scheme because it did not conform to established practices. It was not until several years later that the scheme was published by the Special Libraries Association.[37]

The Boggs and Lewis system is based on a numerical schedule for areas and an alphabetic list for subjects. The classification notation consists of four elements: (1) three or more decimal numerals representing area, with continents divided by countries; (2) one or more lower-case letters representing subject, with ten main classes further subdivided by 500 specific terms specially devised for maps, and a notation for form; (3) the date of the situation portrayed on the map; and (4) the initials of the author or publisher.

Map librarians have given the Boggs and Lewis system high praise for its subject and area notations, logical development, well-balanced allocation of numbers, and freedom from a North American bias. The scheme is enhanced by an area index and index map. A major criticism has been that the scheme, issued in 1945, has never been updated and is thus of limited usefulness when classifying maps from rapidly changing areas of the world.

## AMERICAN GEOGRAPHICAL SOCIETY

Like Boggs and Lewis, the American Geographical Society classification scheme is also exclusively devoted to cartographic materials. The first edition appeared in 1947; revisions were issued in 1952 and again in 1969.[38] A further similarity to Boggs and Lewis is the use of a numeric notation to represent area, and an alphabetic notation to identify broad subject classification, followed by a date. The primary classification is by continent, with further groupings for countries. The United States has its own primary notation, and is thus treated as a continent. The subject classification is comprised of twelve map-oriented classes. As with Boggs and Lewis, AGS provides that the date be the date of the situation portrayed on the map. Criticism of the AGS system has centered on its very broad classification scheme, while some find the simplicity of the scheme to be an advantage. Merrett finds the scheme best suited to "medium to large distinct collections requiring simpler classification than Boggs and Lewis or Universal Decimal Classification."[39]

## DEWEY DECIMAL CLASSIFICATION

The Dewey Decimal Classification (DDC) is a classification scheme designed primarily for books.[40] In the 19th edition of Dewey, published in 1979, all maps (except historical maps) are classified under the number 912: "graphic representations of surface of earth and extraterrestrial worlds." To this base number are added numbers for subject and/or area taken from the main schedules or from an auxiliary area table. The primary classification is by continent, with regional groupings for countries.

Numerous criticisms have been leveled against DDC's area classification. There is insufficient distinction between countries and regions; for example, the Republic of South Africa has the same notation as Southern Africa (-68). As in many other parts of the schedule, one finds categories with odd groupings; for example, there is a category that groups together the countries of the Netherlands, Belgium, Switzerland, Greece, Romania, and the Balkans. The scheme is heavily weighted in favor of the United States (again, characteristic of the scheme as a whole); the United States comprises 63 percent of the 235 main notational divisions in DDC.[41] Those who feel that location should be the primary basis for a map classification object to the fact that in DDC, many maps are classed according to subject categories, thus relegating location to a secondary subdivision (via the area tables).

DDC's advantages lie in its familiarity to users, its revision at regular intervals, and its adaptability, allowing it to be expanded locally.

## UNIVERSAL DECIMAL CLASSIFICATION

Based on DDC, the Universal Decimal Classification (UDC) resembles its predecessor in its decimal notation, general structure, and its book orientation.[42] As in DDC, the notation 912 is used for maps, and is refined by standard area subdivisions. As in DDC, there are unevenly grouped categories, and the definition of regions is often less than satisfactory, but as an international scheme, it is less biased toward the United States. Subject categories can be taken from anywhere in the schedules, and combined with 912 and an area notation. It is also possible, through a notation for form, to indicate the way in which a map is produced, for example, as a pocket map or profile map. Different approaches are possible: A map can be classed first by area and then theme, or the reverse. Because of the complexity of its notation, it may be best suited to environments such as scientific or research libraries.

## LIBRARY OF CONGRESS CLASSIFICATION

The Library of Congress Classification (LCC), like DDC, is essentially a scheme designed for books.[43] The LCC "G" Schedule groups maps together with geography, anthropology, and recreation. Numerical notation is used to classify maps by major geographical, political, or cultural units, which can be further subdivided according to major countries or regions. The notation assigns blocks of numbers to areas, and within an area, maps are hierarchically arranged by subject or region. Following the numerical notations, major topics can be designated by alphabetic characters. Each of these subjects in turn is divided numerically.

The seventeen subject categories are specifically designed for maps, for example, political geography, economic geography. Following the area and subject code, LCC adds the date (for single sheet maps) or truncated scale (for series maps). As with Boggs and Lewis and AGS, the date in the LCC system is usually the date of the situation portrayed on the map, or an approximate date if the exact date cannot be determined. An exception is made for historical geography, in which case the date is that of the map's publication.

LCC enjoys widespread acceptance and use by map librarians. Its defenders argue that LCC is capable of meeting the requirements of any large general map collection, while remaining flexible enough to accommodate change or expansion if required by specialized libraries, and that it is frequently and regularly updated.[44] Critics of LCC point out that it is still primarily a book scheme that has been adjusted to accommodate maps, that it is not revised often enough to keep up with geopolitical changes, and that it has an Anglo-American bias.

## COMPARISON OF THE MAJOR SCHEMES

Each of the four classification schemes for maps has its strengths and limitations. Boggs and Lewis is strong both in terms of area and subject assignment; its disadvantages are that many of its political assignments are now out of date and that its use of a series of letters to represent subject may be confusing to users. The strength of AGS is its simplicity and ease of use, but this is also the source of its major weakness: Its subject classification may be considered too broad and does not permit the precise classification of maps with specialized subjects. Dewey's strengths are its very detailed Areas Table which allows for the notation of small area subdivisions and its "number-building" features which allow for detailed subject notation. Among its drawbacks are its uneven distribution of geographic categories, and its tendency to produce long and unwieldy numbers when a map represents a specialized subject or small region. LCC is strong in both area and subject representation, although its area assignment schedule is much stronger for the United States than for other countries.

Since most large academic libraries now use LCC for their book collections, and since most major map collections are in large academic or research libraries, it seems likely that LCC will remain the most widely used map classification scheme in the United States.

## ALTERNATIVE SYSTEMS FOR ORGANIZATION

Besides geographic classification, maps may be organized by subject, date, accession number, provenance, or size. Organization by size can allow for more effective utilization of space: Folded formats such as road maps are frequently relegated to a vertical file, and large items such as wall maps may require storage in special holders.[45]

Organization by accession number has been advocated as a way of avoiding the cost and effort of classification. In the absence of a classification system, however, the catalog assumes the burden of the retrieval functions and thus the money and time saved may be lost in additional costs of extensive cataloging, as well as loss of retrieval effectiveness.

## Bibliographic Control

The LC Geography and Map Division (LCG&M) was established in 1897, and began providing geographic name, date, and author information for maps ("titling") around 1910. LCG&M's first extensive cataloging of maps did not occur until after World War II; after the war, LC began providing cards for Army Map Service depository maps.[46] It was some time, however, before a nationally recognized bibliographic standard for cartographic materials gained a foothold within the library community. The 1949 ALA rules did not win the acceptance of the map librarians, and *AACR 1* was also met with criticism.[47] Undoubtedly, the development of the MARC format for maps in 1968, and the emergence of nationwide online bibliographic networks such as OCLC and RLIN, contributed enormously to the adoption of a single bibliographic standard for cartographic materials. As of 1980, LCG&M was cataloging approximately eight thousand titles per year on MARC Map, and has recently begun to accept manual records from other libraries for inclusion in the *National Union Catalog*.[48] Automated bibliographic networks can also be cited as a primary factor in increasing the number of maps cataloged in map libraries' collections.

## NOTES

[1]Mary Lynette Larsgaard, *Map Librarianship: An Introduction*, 2d ed. (Littleton, Colo.: Libraries Unlimited, 1987), 159.

[2]Anglo-American Cataloguing Committee for Cartographic Materials, *Cartographic Materials: A Manual of Interpretation for AACR2* (Chicago: American Library Association, 1982).

[3]*Cartographic Materials*, 24.

[4]American Library Association, Documents Cataloging Manual Committee, *Cataloging Government Documents: A Manual of Interpretation for AACR2* (Chicago: American Library Association, 1984).

[5]*Cataloging Government Documents*, 58.

[6]Minutes of the first meeting of the Anglo-American Cataloguing Committee for Cartographic Materials, Ottawa, 1-5 October 1979, 5, 6.

[7]Robert W. Karrow, "Innocent Pleasures: ISBD(CM), *AACR2*, and Map Cataloging," *Special Libraries Association, Geography and Map Division, Bulletin*, no. 126 (December 1981): 8.

[8]*Cartographic Materials*, 34.

[9]*Cataloging Government Documents*, 55.

[10]*Cartographic Materials*, 166, 167.

[11]Ibid., 170, 171.

[12]Ibid., 167, 170.

[13]*Cataloging Government Documents*, 61.

[14]Ibid., 61.

[15]Ibid., 63.

[16]Karrow, 7.

[17]OCLC, *Maps Format*, 2d ed. (Dublin, Ohio: OCLC, 1986).

[18]*Cartographic Materials*, 77-79.

[19]Larsgaard, *Map Librarianship*, 53.

[20]*Cartographic Materials*, 88-91.

[21]*Cataloging Government Documents*, 68.

[22]Ibid., 69.

[23]Ibid., 74.

[24]*Cartographic Materials*, 92-94.

[25]*Cataloging Government Documents*, 77.

26Ibid., 79-87.

27*Cartographic Materials*, 164.

28W. W. Ristow, *The Emergence of Maps in Libraries* (Hamden, Conn.: Linnet Books, 1980), 108.

29*Cataloging Service Bulletin* 7 (Winter 1980), 3.

30*Cartographic Materials*, 164.

31Patricia A. Moore, "Topographic Maps in US Libraries." *International Library Review* 19(3) (1987): 213, 214.

32Larsgaard, 153.

33*Cataloging Government Documents*, 70, 71.

34Moore, "Topographic Maps in US Libraries," 221.

35C. E. Merrett, *Map Classification: A Comparison of Schemes with Special Reference to the Continent of Africa*, Occasional Paper, no. C54 (Urbana, Ill.: University of Illinois Graduate School of Library and Information Science, 1982), 6.

36S. W. Boggs and D. C. Lewis, *The Classification and Cataloging of Maps and Atlases* (New York: Special Libraries Association, 1945).

37Merrett, *Map Classification*, 16.

38Roman Drazniowsky, *Cataloging and Filing Rules for Maps and Atlases in the Society's Collection*, rev. ed. (New York: American Geographical Society, 1969).

39Merrett, *Map Classification*, 28.

40*Dewey Decimal Classification and Relative Index*, 19th ed., ed. Benjamin Custer (Albany, N.Y.: Forest Press, 1979).

41Merrett, *Map Classification*, 12, 13.

42International Federation for Documentation, *Universal Decimal Classification, UDC 9: Geography, Biography, History*, 4th ed. (London: British Standards Institute, 1972).

43Library of Congress. Subject Cataloging Division. *Classification, Class G: Geography, Maps, Anthropology, Recreation*, 4th ed. (Washington, D.C.: Library of Congress, 1976).

[44]Larsgaard, *Map Librarianship*, 119.

[45]Ibid., 115.

[46]Ibid., 143.

[47]Karrow, 2, 3.

[48]Larsgaard, *Map Librarianship*, 143.

# DESCRIPTIVE CATALOGING EXAMPLES

## Items to Be Cataloged

1. Sheet map

One map, colored, plastic; 57 x 88 centimeters, with no border or neat line; folds to 22 x 14 centimeters.

Upper right hand corner and panel:

TRAVEL U.S.A.
Wisconsin, Michigan and The Great Lakes

Produced by the Cartographic Division
of the Geographical Society of America

Alvin T. Brynne, Chief cartographer
James R. Flint, Assistant chief cartographer

Lower right:

Albers Conical Equal-Area Projection
Scale: 1:1,570,000 or 24.8 miles to the inch.
c1982

Lower left corner:

Copyright 1982
Copies of this map may be purchased from the Geographical
Society of America, Washington, D.C. 20036.

2. Route map

One route map, colored. Size of sheet: 88 centimeters x 57.3 centimeters. Neat line: 86 centimeters x 55.3 centimeters. Folds to panel 22 x 9.7 centimeters.

One mile in units of the bar scale measures two inches with a ruler. If a natural scale indicator is consulted, the scale is computed to be 1:31,680.

Bus routes are color coded.

Front panel: The Ride Guide

A handy, all-around-town travel guide to the routes and services of the Clear Bay Transportation Authority.

Map front:   The Ride Guide
Clear Bay, Texas

Effective date 9/16/84
Copyright 1984
The Clear Bay Transportation Authority.

Reverse side of map gives description of Clear Bay transit services, routes, fares, hours of operation.

Also on reverse:
Copyright 1984 / Clear Bay Transportation Authority.
Prepared by The Graphic Group, Inc.
Clear Bay Transportation Authority

16226 Seahorse Boulevard
Clear Bay, Texas 77264

3. Globe

One globe of the world, colored, wood, mounted on a metal stand, 31 centimeters in diameter. Ten study guides are included.

From accompanying publisher's brochure:

Student's International Globe    42786

Cooper Globe Makers
Designers of quality globes since 1932.
Winston Salem, North Carolina
c 1972

Stamped on globe:

Student's World Globe
Scale: 1:41,849,600
c 1972    Cooper Globe Makers
42786

4. Relief model

One relief model, colored, plastic. Map dimensions, 75 x 66 centimeters (height x width), with depth of 3 centimeters, in container, 80 x 71 cm.

Lower left corner:     Hanson & Associates

Container:                    Arkansas Relief Map
                              Prepared by Hanson & Associates

                         1:600,000
                         Vertical exaggeration 1:10

                         c1985  Hanson & Associates
                              Pine Bluff, Arkansas

# *AACR 2* Records and OCLC MARC Tagging

## 1. SHEET MAP

Geographical Society of America. Cartographic Division.
    Wisconsin, Michigan and The Great Lakes / produced by the Cartographic Division of the Geographical Society of America ; Alvin T. Brynne, chief cartographer ; James R. Flint, assistant chief cartographer. -- Scale 1:1,570,000. 1 in. to 24.8 miles ; Albers conical equal-area proj. -- Washington, D.C. : The Society, c1982.
    1 map : col., plastic ; on sheet 57 x 88 cm. folded to 22 x 14 cm. -- (Travel U.S.A.)

    I. Brynne, Alvin T. II. Flint, James R. III. Title. IV. Series.

OCLC MARC Tagging

| Type: e | Bib lvl: m | Lang: eng | Source: d | Form: | Relief: a |
|---------|-----------|-----------|-----------|-------|-----------|
| RecG: a | Enc lvl: I | Ctry: dcu | Dat tp: s | Govt pub: | Indx: 0 |
| Desc: a | Mod rec: | Base: ca | Dates: 1982, | | |

```
1  040      xxx $c xxx
2  007      a $b j $d c $e e $f n $g z $h n
3  034 1    a $b 1570000
4  110 2    Geographical Society of America. $b Cartographic
Division.
5  245 10   Wisconsin, Michigan and the Great Lakes / $c produced by
the Cartographic Division of the Geographical Society of America ;
Alvin T. Brynne, chief cartographer ; James R. Flint, assistant
chief cartographer.
6  255      Scale 1:1,570,000 $b Albers conical equal-area proj.
7  260 0    Washington, D.C. : $b The Society, $c c1982
8  300      1 map : $b col., plastic ; $c on sheet 57 x 88 cm.
folded to 22 x 14 cm.
9  440 0    Travel U.S.A.
10 700 10   Brynne, Alvin T.
11 700 10   Flint, James R.
```

## *AACR 2* applicable rules

### Chief source of information

**3.0B2:** Chief source of information is cartographic item itself.

### Area 1

**3.1B1:** Record title proper as in 1.1B.

**3.1C1:** GMD. LC will not apply option for GMD for maps.

**3.1F1:** Record statements of responsibility as in 1.1F.

**1.1F6:** Record multiple statements of responsibility in order indicated by sequence.

### Area 3

**3.3B1:** Give scale as representative fraction expressed as a ratio (1: ). Precede ratio by word *scale*.

**3.3B2:** Optionally, give additional scale information found on item (such as statement of comparative measures). Use standard abbreviations. Precede information by full stop.

**3.3C1:** Give statement of projection if found on item. Use standard abbreviations.

**Area 4**

**3.4C1, 3.4D1, 3.4F1:**
　　　　Place, name, and date as in 1.4.

**1.4D4:**　　Name of publisher shortened since already in statement of responsibility area.

**1.4F6:**　　Copyright date in absence of publication date.

**Area 5**

**3.5B1:**　　Record number of physical units and SMD.

**3.5C3:**　　Indicate if colored.

**3.5C4:**　　Record material if considered to be significant (e.g., if map is printed on substance other than paper).

**3.5D1:**　　Give height x width for two-dimensional cartographic items. If map has no neat lines, give the greater dimensions of the map itself. If map lacks one or more of its borders, give the height x width of the sheet specified as such. If sheet contains a panel or section designed to appear on the outside when the sheet is folded, give the sheet in folded form as well as the size of the map.

**Area 6**

**3.6B1:**　　Record series statement as in 1.6.

**Choice of access points**

**21.1B2f:**　Enter under heading for corporate body if cartographic item emanates from corporate body responsible for more than publication or distribution.

**21.1B4:**　Enter under heading for subordinate unit if responsibility of subordinate unit is stated prominently.

**21.30B:**　Collaborating author added entries.

**21.30J:**　Title added entry.

**21.30L:**　Series added entry.

**Form of heading**

**24.13, Type 1:**
　　　　If subordinate unit of corporate body contains a name that by definition implies that it is part of another, enter the subordinate unit as a subheading of the name of the higher body.

## 2. ROUTE MAP

Clear Bay Transportation Authority (Clear Bay, Tex.)
The ride guide : Clear Bay, Texas / prepared by The Graphic
Group, Inc. -- Scale [ca. 1:31,680]. -- Clear Bay, Tex. : Clear
Bay Transportation Authority, c1984.
1 map : col. ; 86 x 56 cm. folded to 22 x 10 cm.

Effective date, Sept. 16, 1984.
Text on verso.
Color coded bus routes.
Gives routes, fares, hours of operation.

I. Graphic Group. II. Title.

OCLC MARC Tagging

```
Type: e     Bib lvl: m    Lang: eng    Source: d  Form:    Relief:
RecG: a     Enc lvl: I    Ctry: txu    Dat tp: s  Govt pub: 1 Indx:0
Desc: a     Mod rec:      Base: ^^     Dates: 1984,
```

```
1    040    xxx $c xxx
2    007    a $b j $d c $e a $f n $g z $h n
3    034 1  a $b 31680
4    110 2  Clear Bay Transportation Authority (Clear Bay, Tex.).
5    245 14 The ride guide : $b Clear Bay, Texas  / $c prepared by
The Graphic Group, Inc.
6    255    Scale ca.[1:31,680]
7    260 0  Clear Bay, Tex. : $b Clear Bay Transportation Authority,
$c c1984.
8    300    1 map : $b col. ; $c 86 x 56 cm. folded to 22 x 10 cm.
9    500    Effective date, Sept. 16, 1984.
10   500    Text on verso.
11   500    Color coded bus routes.
12   500    Gives routes, fares, hours of operation.
13   710 21 Graphic Group.
```

### *AACR 2* applicable rules

**3.0B2:**   Chief source is item itself.

**Area 1**

**3.1B1:**   Title proper.

**3.1B3:**   If chief source bears more than one title, choose title on basis of
sequence or layout; if these are insufficient to enable decision, choose
most comprehensive title.

**3.1C1:**   LC will not assign GMD.

**3.1E1:**    Record other title information as in 1.1E.

**3.1F1:**    Statements of responsibility.

**Area 3**

**3.3B1:**    Scale as representative fraction.
If no statement of scale is found on item, compute representative fraction from a bar graph. Give scale in square brackets preceded by *ca.*

**Area 4**

**3.4C1, 3.4D1, 3.4F1:**
Name, place, and date.

**Area 5**

**3.5B1:**    Number of units and SMD.

**3.5C3:**    Color.

**3.5D1:**    Give measurements of face of map measured between the neat lines. Give sheet size in folded form as well as size of map.

**Area 7**

**3.7B9:**    Additional publication information.

**3.7B10:**    Additional physical description.

**3.7B18:**    Make notes describing contents.

**Choice of access points**

**21.1B2f:**    Emanates from corporate body responsible for more than publication or distribution.

**21.30E:**    Added entry for prominently named corporate body with functions beyond distribution and manufacture.

**21.30J:**    Title added entry.

**Form of heading**

**24.4C1:**    If two or more corporate bodies have same name, add word or phrase as instructed in 24.4C2-24.4C9.  Optional to add, even if no need to distinguish.

**24.4C3:**    Add name of local place (see 24.4C4-24.4C7) in which body is located.

**24.4C4:**    For bodies located outside British Isles, add name of smallest or most specific political jurisdiction (e.g., name of city).

## 3. GLOBE

Cooper Globe Makers.
    Student's world globe. -- Scale 1:41,849,600. -- Winston
Salem, N.C. : Cooper Globe Makers, c1972.
    1 globe : col., wood, mounted on a metal stand ; 31 cm. in
diam. + 10 study guides.

    Title in brochure: Student's international globe.
No. 42786.

    I. Title.

```
OCLC MARC Tagging

Type: e Bib lvl: m Lang: eng  Source: d Form:      Relief:
RecG: d Enc lvl: I Ctry: ncu  Dat tp: s Govt pub:   Indx: 0
Desc: a Mod rec:    Base: ^^  Dates: 1972,

1  040    xxx $c xxx
2  007  d $b c $d c $e b $f n $g z $h n
3  034 1  a $b41849600
5  110 2  Cooper Globe Makers.
6  245 10 Student's world globe.
7  255    Scale: 1:41,849,600
8  260 0  Winston Salem, N.C. : $b Cooper Globe Makers, $c c1972.
9  300    1 globe : $b col., wood, mounted on a metal stand ; $c 31
cm. in diam. + $e 10 study guides.
10 500    Title in brochure: Student's international globe.
11 500    No. 42786.
```

### *AACR 2* applicable rules

**3.0B2:**    Chief source of information is cartographic item itself, second in preference is the cradle and stand of the globe. If information is not available, take it from accompanying printed material (e.g., brochure).

### Area 1

**3.1B1:**    Title proper. Title from globe is preferred over title in brochure.

**3.1C1:**    LC will not display GMD for globes.

### Area 3

3.3B1:    Scale as representative fraction.

### Area 4

**3.4C1, 3.4D1, 3.4F1:**
    Place, name, and date.

**3.0B3:** Accompanying material can be prescribed source for publication area.

**Area 5**

**3.5B1:** Number of physical units and SMD.

**3.5C3:** Color.

**3.5C4:** Material.

**3.5C5:** Indicate if item is mounted.

**3.5D4:** Give diameter, specified as such, for globes.

**3.5E1:** Record name of accompanying material.

**Area 7**

**3.7B4:** Indicate titles on the item other than the title proper. (Rule extended here to include variant title on brochure.)

**3.7B19:** Important numbers.

**Choice of access points**

**21.1B2f:** Work emanates from corporate body. Statement from brochure suggests that Cooper's responsibility includes the design of the globe, and thus extends beyond mere publication and distribution.

**21.30J:** Title added entry.

## 4. RELIEF MODEL

Hanson & Associates.
Arkansas relief map / prepared by Hanson & Associates. -- Scale 1:600,000. Vertical exaggeration 1:10. -- Pine Bluff, Ark. : Hanson, c1985.
1 relief model : col., plastic ; 75 x 66 x 3 cm. in container, 80 x 71 cm.

Title from container.

I. Title.

OCLC MARC Tagging

```
Type: e Bib lvl: m Lang: eng Source: d  Form:    Relief: h
RecG: a Enc lvl: I Ctry: aku Dat tp: s  Govt pub:  Indx: 0
Desc: a Mod rec:  Base: ^^  Dates: 1985,
```

```
1  040    xxx $c xxx
2  007    a $b q $d c $e e $f n $g z $h n
3  034    a $b 600000
4  110 2  Hanson & Associates.
5  245 10 Arkansas relief map / $c prepared by Hanson & Associates.
6  255    Scale 1:600,000.
7  255    Vertical exaggeration 1:10
8  260 0  Pine Bluff, Ark. : $b Hanson, $c c1985.
9  300    1 relief model : $b col., plastic ; $c 75 x 66 x 3 cm. in
container, 80 x 71 cm.
10 500    Title from container.
```

### *AACR 2* applicable rules

**3.0B2:** Sources of information include: (1) item itself, and (2) container. Container is used as chief source, since item itself gives only publisher's name.

### Area 1

**3.1B1:** Title proper. It could be argued that the title proper is "Arkansas," with "relief map" as subtitle (other title information), but the layout suggests the three words constitute one unit.

**3.1C1:** LC will not assign GMD.

**3.1F1:** Statement of responsibility.

### Area 3

**3.3B1:** Scale as representative fraction.

**3.3B8:** For relief models, give vertical scale after the horizontal scale if it can be ascertained (example in rule: "Vertical exaggeration 1:5").

### Area 4

**3.4C1, 3.4D1, 3.4F1:**
Place, name, and date.

**1.4D4:** Publisher's name in shortened form.

### Area 5

**3.5B1:** Number of physical units and SMD.

**3.5C3:** Color.

**3.5C4:**    Indicate material.

**3.5D3:**    For relief models, give height x width in centimeters as in 3.5D1, and optionally add depth.

**3.5D5:**    Optionally, add dimensions of container, specified as such. LC will apply option.

**Area 7**

**3.7B3:**    Rule calls for source of title proper to be indicated, if title was not taken from chief source. Although container serves as "substitute" chief source in this example, a note is recorded since title is not taken from preferred chief source, that is, item itself.

**Choice of access points**

**21.1B2f:**    Corporate body's responsibility extends beyond publication.

**21.30J:**    Title added entry.

# REFERENCE SOURCES

## Cartography and Geography

Birch, T. W. *Maps: Topographical and Statistical.* 2d ed. Oxford: Oxford University Press, 1964.
    Describes modern maps and the methods employed in their production. Includes various kinds of statistical maps and graphs and their construction, as well as photographs, diagrams, and charts. Coverage includes plans, equipment, measurements, projections, modeling, and block diagrams. Explains interpretation of air photography and map landscapes.

Brewer, James Gordon. *The Literature of Geography: A Guide to Its Organization and Use.* 2d ed. Hamden, Conn.: Linnet Books, 1978.
    Bibliographic essays with annotations of specific sources give information on scope of the field and its various subfields of general geography, physical geography, and human geography. The researcher is led to studies that have produced appropriate maps and data for particular research questions. The cataloger can find in this source useful directories, almanacs, glossaries of terms and place names, and cartographic resources.

Burnside, C. D. *Mapping from Aerial Photographs.* 2d ed. New York: John Wiley and Sons, 1985.
    Presents mathematical concepts in deriving topographic maps from near vertical photographs. Describes how topographic information can be abstracted from basic data used in photogrammetric mapping to produce flat or three-dimensional maps.

Cuff, David J., and Mark T. Mattson. *Thematic Maps: Their Design and Production*. New York: Methuen, 1982.

Focuses on special-subject or thematic mapping. These maps are not made directly from primary work with air photos or surveys, but are compiled from existing maps. Their subject matter is a distillation of data, physical or nonphysical, taken from a wide range of sources other than maps. Examples may include rural population density, tornado patterns, or tons of coal produced. Cuff's work deals with the representation of statistical data and verbal content, layout, design, and production methods. The researcher can consult this work to learn how to interpret or create such a map, how to portray discrete or continuous data and how to map statistical measures of correlation. The cataloger can use it to learn symbols and types of displays to explain special features of maps.

Dent, Borden D. *Principles of Thematic Map Design*. Reading, Mass.: Addison-Wesley, 1985.

Gives background on the basics of design, mapping, and geography of thematic maps. Discussions of mapping techniques. Information on projections and map symbolization. A glossary and list of suggested readings are provided at the end of each chapter. Appendix lists types of maps and the agencies that publish and distribute them.

Lock, C. B. Muriel. *Geography and Cartography: A Reference Handbook*. 3d ed. London: Clive Bingley, 1976.

A 1,386-item listing of terms and individuals relating to geography and cartography. Intended for quick reference for both librarians and geographers. Includes books, periodicals, publishers, cartographic houses, commissions, societies, classification and cataloging, organizations, guides, educational institutions, and national bibliographies. Bibliographies conclude some entries. International in scope.

Monkhouse, F. J., and H. R. Wilkinson. *Maps and Diagrams: Their Compilation and Construction*. 3d ed., rev. and enl. London: Methuen, 1978.

Covers the materials, tools, techniques, and methods used in the production of maps. Includes relief, climatic, economic, population, and settlement maps. Terms, symbols, and uses are explained. Includes numerous charts, diagrams, and other illustrations.

Traces the history of cartography, cartographic measurements such as coordinates and scale, types of data compiled to create a map, and how this data is symbolized, processed, and transferred into graphic form. Examines the part that aerial photography plays in this process. Different types of maps and the various kinds of data that can be represented are discussed and examples provided. Projections and various aspects of map design and construction are covered.

Muehrcke, Phillip C. *Map Use: Reading, Analysis, and Interpretation*. 2d ed. Madison, Wis.: JP Publications, 1986.

Essential reference work for both the specialized and general map user. Divided into three sections: map reading, map analysis, and map interpretation. Muehrcke's explanations of map symbols and map types are especially helpful. Appendixes contain information on map scales, remote sensing, map projections, and direction-finding instruments.

Robinson, Arthur H., Randall D. Sale, Joel L. Morrison, and Phillip C. Muehrcke. *Elements of Cartography.* 5th ed. New York: John Wiley and Sons, 1984.

Part 2, "Theoretical Principles," explains basic measurement concepts such as scale projection, coordinates, the various forms in which these mathematical statements occur, and the descriptions of various graphics options. Part 3, "Data Manipulation," discusses remote sensing technology and strategy, data classification for analysis, and use of area symbols. Includes glossary.

Tooley, Ronald Vere. *Tooley's Dictionary of Mapmakers.* New York: Alan R. Riss, Inc., 1979.

List of 21,450 mapmakers. Alphabetical arrangement by name, giving dates of birth and death, titles of honor, addresses and changes of addresses, dates of editions, and notes relating to historical significance of a work. Also includes variant spellings of names and complete names needed to distinguish relatives. Scope includes philosophers, geographers, astronomers, explorers, surveyors, engravers, and lithographers.

## Directories and Sourcebooks

Cobb, David A., comp. *Guide to U.S. Map Resources.* Chicago: Map and Geography Roundtable, American Library Association, 1986.

Describes over 900 collections. Types of libraries represented include academic, public, geoscience, state, federal, historical societies, and private research libraries. Geographical breakdown by state with libraries listed alphabetically within. For each collection, the guide provides address, telephone number, names of staff, and information on cataloging, interlibrary lending, circulation, and the nature and scope of the collection. Introductory tables identify the largest collections of printed maps and aerial photographs and the largest collections by type of library. Additional tables include summaries of staff hours, cataloging and classification operations, and federal depository collections.

Field, Lance. *Map User's Sourcebook.* London: Oceana Publications, Inc., 1982.

A directory of map sources to aid users in obtaining current maps of specific areas. Begins with a review of cartographic materials, mapping agencies, institutes, and geographic surveys worldwide. Discusses the basic types of maps, measurement used in cartography, the accuracy of maps, and care and storage. The list of sources is divided into four areas: private, public, federal, and international. Listing is alphabetical by state and by city within each state for the U.S., and alphabetical by country within each major region for international sources. Addresses are provided for commercial map makers, retail map sources, map reference libraries, and state, federal, and international map sources. Includes a bibliography and a glossary of selected cartographic terms.

Wolter, John A. *World Directory of Map Collections.* 2d ed. IFLA Publications 31. New York: K. G. Saur, 1986.

Information on collections worldwide. Subject areas, size of holdings by type, amount cataloged, contact people, and public services.

# Dictionaries and Glossaries

*Columbia Lippincott Gazetteer.* Edited by Leon E. Seltzer. New York: Columbia University Press, 1962.

A comprehensive gazetteer which gives places of the world including countries, regions, provinces, states, counties, cities, islands, lakes, mountains, deserts, and other types of geographical areas and features. The Geographic Names of the Department of Interior and the Swiss Topographic Agency as well as numerous government agencies and libraries have verified a wide range of data including spelling variations and altitudes. Helps the cataloger and researcher verify variant spellings, relate places to features or history, find transliterations, locate coordinates for longitude and latitude, check place names, changes, and dates when changes occurred.

*Glossary of Geographical Names: In Six Languages (English, French, Italian, Spanish, German, and Dutch).* Compiled and arranged by Gabriella Lana, Liliana Iasbez, and Lidia Meak. Amsterdam: Elsevier Publishing Company, 1967.

A glossary of place names and geographic features including rivers, lakes, oceans, cities, and countries. Assists map/geographer researchers in interpreting features and names on maps. Helps the cataloger to translate maps, correct spellings of place names, and document variant spellings.

International Cartographic Association. *Multilingual Dictionary of Technical Terms in Cartography.* Wiesbaden, Germany: Franz Steiner Verlag, 1973.

Terms cover topics about cartography and its branches, mathematical cartography, various cartographic expressions (symbols, colors, concepts, lines, and dots), compilation and editing, practices, reproductions, products, and distribution. Arrangement is by subject groups. Equivalent words or phrases are given in five languages: German, English, Spanish, French, and Russian. An alphabetical index of main terms, auxiliary terms, and synonyms is provided for each of fourteen languages. The cataloger can find words for *publisher, copyright, scale, projection*, and *atlas* to help in translating data on a map.

*Rand McNally Commercial Atlas and Marketing Guide.* New York: Rand McNally, 1876- . Annual.

LC advises using this guide for establishing U.S. geographic headings [*CSB* 18 (Fall 1982):61]. Includes U.S. and Canadian metropolitan area maps, and U.S. maps and indexes by state.

Room, Adrian, comp. *Place-name Changes since 1900: A World Gazetteer.* Metuchen, N.J.: Scarecrow Press, 1979.

The entries include names that have been officially changed by governments and do not include alternate spellings, temporary renamings, and alternate names in different languages. Each entry consists of the current place name, the identification (village or city, etc.) location, former name, and year of renaming. Helps both cataloger and researcher explain name changes on maps and calculate the approximate date for a work. Cross references are given from former names to the full entries.

U.S. Defense Mapping Agency. Topographic Center. *Glossary of Mapping, Charting, and Geodetic Terms.* 3d ed. Washington, D.C.: U.S. Government Printing Office, 1973.

Comprehensive dictionary with brief definitions. Terms unique to a specific profession are identified with the discipline. Certain types of terms have been excluded: map feature names, units of measure, basic mathematical terms, and general terms not unique to mapping, charting, or geodesy.

*Webster's New Geographical Dictionary.* Springfield, Mass.: Merriam-Webster, 1984.

Essential information on spelling, pronunciation, location, population, size, economy, and history for over 47,000 places. Special features include a list of geographical terms in various languages and their English equivalents, a brief explanation of map projections, and maps to supplement the text. One of the most useful items of information is the history of countries and name changes.

## Map Librarianship

Association of Canadian Map Libraries. *Bulletin.* Ottawa: ACML. 1974- . Quarterly.

*base line: A Newsletter of the Map and Geography Round Table.* Chicago: American Library Association. 1980- . Six issues per year.

Draniowsky, Roman. *Map Librarianship: Readings.* Metuchen, N.J.: Scarecrow Press, 1975.

A compilation of forty-eight selected articles on maps, their history, classification and cataloging, acquisition, storage, and preservation. Various elements of maps are explained, including grids, contours, projections, scale symbols used on maps, colors used in map printing, and production of maps. Among the different types of maps discussed are topographical, nautical, and aeronautical. Uses of maps are explained. Bibliographic essays consider cartographic periodicals, literature reporting map exhibits, and guides to the use of atlases. Includes an extensive bibliography.

Larsgaard, Mary Lynette. *Map Librarianship: An Introduction.* 2d ed. Littleton, Colo.: Libraries Unlimited, 1987.

Three chapters are particularly useful for the cataloger. Chapter 2, "Classification," summarizes primary classification schemes. Chapter 3, "Cataloging and Computer Applications," traces the history of map cataloging, current developments, important organizations involved, rule changes made, problem areas, and online trends and computer applications for catalog records. Covers various standards for map cataloging, including *AACR 2*, ISBD (CM), and *AACR 1*. Chapter 6, "Reference," suggests reference works useful for map catalogers, and is valuable for both researcher and cataloger in its definition of terms and concepts (e.g., scale, projection, grids, and graticules).

Larsgaard's book is both informative in content and lively in style. Her bibliography is impressive; there are sixty pages of works cited in her text, and an additional forty-one-page bibliography of specialized works.

Nichols, Harold. *Map Librarianship.* 2d ed. London: Clive Bingley, 1982.

Covers many aspects of map librarianship: acquisition, storage and retrieval, classification and cataloging, reference and information services, and care and preservation of maps. Discusses various classification schemes, highlighting the advantages and disadvantages of each; also, entry, description, and filing arrangement of catalog records. Includes examples and an extensive reading list.

Special Libraries Association. Geography and Map Division. *Bulletin.* [Various places]: The Division, 1947- . Quarterly.

Information about conferences and new publications. Feature articles about cataloging changes, issues, and solutions.

Western Association of Map Libraries. *Information Bulletin.* Santa Cruz, Calif.: WAML. 1969- . Three issues per year.

Information about new publications, new indexes to maps, and map collections. Articles about cataloging issues, rule changes, and solutions to problems in map cataloging.

## Map Cataloging and Classification

*Bibliographic Guide to Maps and Atlases.* Boston: G. K. Hall. 1979- . Annual.

Purpose is to "bring together publications compiled by research libraries of the New York Public Library and the Library of Congress." For each title, descriptive bibliographic data and classification notation are provided. Access is by main entry, and added entries for coauthors, editors, compilers, titles, series titles, and subject headings.

*Cartographic Materials: A Manual of Interpretation for AACR2.* Prepared by the Anglo-American Cataloguing Committee for Cartographic Materials. Chicago: American Library Association, 1982.

Essential manual for the map cataloger. The rules in chapter 3 of *AACR 2* are stated, reworded for clarification when necessary, and provided with examples. The "applications" sections supply interpretations of rules. When options are available, policy alternatives are given, including the policies of the national libraries and archives of Australia, New Zealand, Great Britain, Canada, and the United States.

The manual instructions are supported by informative graphics when appropriate. For example, the rules for chief source of information are explained verbally and illustrated by pictures of terms such as *cover, portfolio,* and *tube.* An illustration is included to explain graphically what is meant by the *cartographic item itself* and the *container.* The mathematical data area section contains detailed instructions on scale and coordinates, with helpful illustrations. Appendix B explains in detail various procedures for determining the representative fraction scale of a map. One of the most useful features in the book is the explanation of the physical description area. Numerous illustrations are provided to show the many ways the extent of the item may be described. Since *AACR 2* gives no directions for the description of map series, and since a large proportion of any map collection is composed of these, the manual includes an appendix on the treatment of map series. Rule applications for map series are also provided throughout the text. Includes examples of catalog records, lists of abbreviations, a glossary of cartographic terms, and a comprehensive index.

*Cataloging Government Documents: A Manual of Interpretation for AACR2.* Chicago: American Library Association, 1984.
Shows how pertinent *AACR 2* rules are applied to various forms of government documents including maps. Especially important since the majority of cartographic materials produced today are government documents. *AACR 2* rules are explained and guidelines and examples provided. Indicates if the Library of Congress or Government Printing Office practice differs from the *AACR 2* rule. Suggests tools for further reference. Selected terms are defined in the discussion of the rules.

Christy, Barbara. "Map Classification: Basic Considerations and a Comparison of Systems." *Western Association of Map Libraries Information Bulletin* 4 (March 1973): 29-42.
Compares six map classification systems, giving a brief characterization of each, and noting advantages and disadvantages for large map collections. Those examined are ones developed by: The American Geographical Society, Army Map Service, Bibliotheque Nationale, Boggs and Lewis, Dewey Decimal Classification, and Library of Congress.

*Dewey Decimal Classification.* 19th ed. Albany, N.Y.: Forest Press, 1979. (See earlier discussion.)
Maps and cartography subjects are found in the pure and applied science sections with geographic area and combined topics provided by number building. Cartography is found in the section on Mathematical Geography, "Graphic representations of surface of earth and extraterrestrial worlds."

*ISBD(CM): International Standard Bibliographic Description for Cartographic Materials,* recommended by the Joint Working Group on the International Standard Bibliographic Description for Cartographic Materials set up by the IFLA Committee on Cataloging and the IFLA Sub-section of Geography and Map Libraries. London: IFLA International Office for UBC, 1977.

Library of Congress. *Classification, Class G: Geography, Maps, Anthropology, Recreation.* 4th ed. Washington, D.C.: Library of Congress, 1976. (See earlier discussion.)
Comprehensive, regularly updated and revised, this classification system for maps is the most widespread in use. Schedule G covers atlases, globes, and maps. The geography categories include cartography, oceanography, anthropogeography, and human ecology.

_____. *Library of Congress Catalog: A Cumulative List of Works Represented by Library of Congress Printed Cards: Maps and Atlases.* Washington, D.C.: Library of Congress, 1953-55. 3v.

_____. *National Union Catalog, Cartographic Materials.* Washington, D.C.: Library of Congress, 1983- . In microfiche only.
Gives indexes for names, titles, subject headings, series, and geographic classification codes.

_____. Processing Services. *National Level Bibliographic Record—Maps.* Prepared by Phyllis A. Bruns. Washington, D.C.: Library of Congress, Cataloging Distribution Service, 1981.

Contains specifications for data elements to be included in machine-readable cataloging records intended to be contributed to a nationwide database. The content of both full and minimal level bibliographic records is specified. Based on *AACR 2* and the MARC format. Provides tables which label content of fixed and variable fields and subfields for each designator and which indicate what information is mandatory, optional, or not used.

Map Online Users Group. *Newsletter.* [Various places]: The Group, 1979- .

Moore, Barbara N. *A Manual of AACR2 Examples for Cartographic Materials.* Lake Crystal, Minn.: Soldier Creek Press, 1981.

Provides twenty-two examples of catalog records for a wide range of cartographic materials. Each example contains reproductions of chief source data, a catalog record, and citation of *AACR 2* rules used. Gives index to rule numbers used for examples in the manual.

Moore, Patricia A. "Topographic Maps in US Libraries." *International Library Review* 19, no. 3 (1987): 201-23.

Discusses problems of cataloging topographic map series. Examines guidelines in *AACR 2* and *Cartographic Materials.*

Schreiber, Robert E. "Defining Map Areas in Cartographic Cataloging." *Western Association of Map Libraries. Information Bulletin* 18 (November 1986): 29-33.

Addresses problem of incomplete and inconsistent description of map coordinates. Schreiber suggests ways of standardizing map coordinate cataloging and proposes a mandatory note area explaining what coordinate statements represent and when and how they were supplied from other sources. Argues that, as computer searching by coordinates becomes more feasible, the accurate rendering of coordinates will become increasingly essential.

Studwell, William E. "A Simple and Successful Method to Enhance Map Subject Access." *Western Association of Map Libraries. Information Bulletin* 16 (June 1985): 357-58.

Proposes method for increasing number of subject headings with area as their initial element. Suggests automatically supplying subject headings using the pattern "(Area) #X Maps" whenever the areas involved are not covered by subjects beginning with a geographical area.

_____. "Inconsistency in Library of Congress Policy for Some Place Names as Subjects: A Problem for Map Catalogers." *Western Association of Map Libraries. Information Bulletin* 17, no. 3 (July 1986): 224-34.

Maintains that consistent subject headings for geographic areas are important to map catalogers and map users. Takes issue with the "jurisdiction with territorial changes" rule of *LCSH.*

———. "Map Libraries and a Subject Heading Code." *Western Association of Map Libraries. Information Bulletin* 18 (March 1987): 157-58.

Reviews recent indicators in the literature that a comprehensive theoretical code of *LCSH* is being formulated. Studwell feels that map libraries would gain more from such a code than other types of libraries since maps historically have received less attention in cataloging matters than monographs and serials.

# 3

øøøøøøøøøøøøøøøøøøøøøøøøøøøøøøøøøøøøøøøøøøøøøøøøøøøøøøøøøøøøøøøøøøøøøøøøøøøøøøøøøøøøøøøøøøøøøø

# *Sound Recordings*

øøøøøøøøøøøøøøøøøøøøøøøøøøøøøøøøøøøøøøøøøøøøøøøøøøøøøøøøøøøøøøøøøøøøøøøøøøøøøøøøøøøøøøøøøøøøøø

## DECISION AREAS IN
## DESCRIPTIVE CATALOGING

### Scope

**DEFINING THE MEDIUM: Distinguishing Features
and Possible Formats**

*AACR 2*'s chapter 6 provides rules for the description of sound recordings in a variety of media formats, including discs, open reel-to-reel tapes, cartridges, cassettes, and piano and other rolls. Sound recording media covered by the chapter must be limited to sound. Accordingly, sound track films are included as long as the film is not accompanied by visual material. If visual images do accompany the sound recording, the rules for motion pictures and video-recordings are applied, as is also the case for music videos.

If a sound recording accompanies a visual or other medium, as, for example, a tape cassette and filmstrip unit, the cataloger must decide which medium is predominant. Typically, the visual medium is predominant, and the item is cataloged using the rules for graphic materials, with the sound recording treated as accompanying material. However, such decisions should be made on a case-by-case basis. Depending on which medium is judged to be predominant, the unit could be cataloged as a sound recording, as graphic material, or as a kit.

Recordings in other forms, such as wires and cylinders, or in "various experimental media" are not specifically covered by chapter 6, but the rules for physical description, along with special notes, can be used. For sound recordings of musical works, the cataloger will need to consult chapter 5 on music scores and, in many instances, chapter 25 on uniform titles.

The medium of sound recordings includes a wide range of materials which can differ not only in physical format, but in their intellectual or artistic content. Sound recordings can include different types of musical works (e.g., classical, popular, folk, jazz), spoken recordings (e.g., readings of literary works, materials for instruction in foreign languages), and sound effects (e.g., recordings of the sound of thunder, train whistles).

# Sources of Information

## LABEL AS CHIEF SOURCE

In many cases, a sound recording will contain a number of possible sources from which cataloging information could be transcribed: sound data from the recording itself, the disc label, the front and back sides of a container, and accompanying material. *AACR 2*'s preferred source is the label permanently affixed to the item. Rule 6.0B1 gives the chief source of information for the major formats of sound recordings. In each case, the label is a key part of the source, and sometimes the only source. For discs and rolls, the chief source is the label itself; for reel-to-reel tapes, the reel and label; for tape cassettes, the cassette and label, for tape cartridges, the cartridge and label; and for a sound recording on film, the container and label.

Labels affixed to sound discs, cartridges and tape cassettes are preferred over containers such as disc sleeves and boxes. Sometimes, usually because of space limitations, the disc will not contain information as complete as that given on other sources such as the container. Containers, as well as accompanying material, may serve as a chief source when these sources alone describe the item as a collective unit, or if information is not available from the label itself. *AACR 2*'s consistent pattern of preference for information from the item itself represents a change from *AACR 1*, which preferred the container of a sound recording as a principal source even if data were to be found on the disc.

Textual data are preferred to sound data. "For example, if a sound disc has a label and also information presented in sound form on the disc, prefer the label information." This is in contrast to *AACR 2*'s rules for computer files, where information from the item itself takes precedence over information on the label. For other materials such as motion pictures, videorecordings, filmstrips, and microforms, the chief source will likely be found on the item itself, as a part of the message being communicated by the medium. The difference for sound recordings, of course, lies in the fact that the information within the item itself is not in textual form. An advantage for the cataloger is that playback equipment will not be needed to gain access to information from the item.

# Title and Statement of Responsibility Area

## TITLE PROPER FOR MUSICAL SOUND RECORDINGS

For titles in musical sound recordings, rule 6.1B1 directs the cataloger to the corresponding rule in the chapter for music, 5.1B (revised), since similarities exist in the cataloging of music scores. A key problem in this area is the distinction between the title proper and other title information. The first step in this process involves deciding if the title in question is distinctive or generic (i.e., the name of a type of composition). To determine this, the cataloger removes certain identifying elements from the title. These elements are the medium, key, date of composition, and the serial, opus, or thematic index number. If what is left is the name of a type of composition, such as "Symphony" or "Sonata," then the title is considered as generic; the identifying elements are added back on as part of the title proper; for example, "Sonata, in E flat major for viola and piano, op. 142." If, on the other hand, the "stripped down" title consists of something other than the name of a type of composition, then any indications of medium, key, and so on, are considered as other title information; for example, "An evening's effort: for soprano, flute, and piano, op. 150." Reference sources may need to be consulted to determine what terms are names of types of compositions.

## SUPPLIED TITLES

Noncommercial recordings will often lack a title on the item. As in similar situations with other recordings and other types of materials, the cataloger will construct a title proper in such cases.

If it is necessary to supply a title for a musical work (5.1B2), the rules require that the supplied title be formulated using guidelines from the rules for uniform titles for music, as outlined in rules 25.25 to 25.35 in the chapter on uniform titles. The formulation of uniform titles will require some familiarity with music terminology and concepts, as well as the consultation of reference works.

## ITEMS WITHOUT A COLLECTIVE TITLE

A sound recording containing a collection of works is a common occurrence, since the physical formats of discs, cassettes, and cartridges contain a fixed amount of space, and the works recorded on these formats vary in length. Often, this collection of separate works contained on the same physical item will lack a collective title.

For sound recordings lacking a collective title, the cataloger has a choice of describing the recording as one unit or of providing separate bibliographic records for each of the works. LC will describe the item as a unit[1] The decision made on the unit to be cataloged will determine most aspects of the bibliographic record; for example, the title proper, physical description and notes will differ according to whether the record describes the recording as a unit or as separates. Such decisions may be determined by factors such as adherence to LC policy, space considerations (since a unit approach will result in fewer records), and ease of use for the patron seeking a discrete bibliographic work.

## GENERAL MATERIAL DESIGNATION
### Placement

Determining the placement of the GMD will require careful attention in the case of sound recordings without a collective title, since the outcome will depend on whether the unit has one author or different authors. If uniform titles are involved, another decision will have to be made on whether to include the GMD in the uniform title. LC will not apply this option.

## PARALLEL TITLES

Parallel titles will occur frequently in musical sound recordings, since music transcends language, and one publication may be issued for several language audiences. The cataloger is referred to rule 1.1D for instruction on the formulation of parallel titles.

## STATEMENT OF RESPONSIBILITY AND THE ROLE OF THE PERFORMER

Statements of responsibility are recorded for writers of spoken words, composers of performed music, and collectors of field material, but not necessarily for performers. *AACR 2* requires the cataloger to make a judgment as to the nature of the performer's contribution. Rule 6.1F1 stipulates that a statement of responsibility be recorded only if "the participation of the person(s) or body (bodies) ... goes beyond that of performance, execution, or interpretation of a work (as is commonly the case with 'popular,' rock, and jazz music)." No statement of responsibility is to be given 'if the participation is confined to performance, execution, or interpretation (as commonly the case with 'serious' or classical music and recorded speech)." In such instances, the statement of responsibility is given in a note.

Some types of performers are relatively easy to categorize. For example, the work of jazz artists involves a considerable degree of improvisation to the point that the contribution of the performer may be equal to that of the composer. Performers of classical music and recorded speech, for the most part, perform the work as written by the composer or author. Less straightforward is the case of "popular" music: some performers "arrange" the music moderately to suit their style, while other performers lend their own unmistakable stamp to their performances. In such cases it is difficult to determine whether the contribution goes beyond mere interpretation.

The Library of Congress has decided to allow statements of responsibility for performers "only in the most obvious cases," that is, for non-"classical" music.[2] From a practical standpoint, the argument can be made that such restrictions are necessary in the interests of saving space (catalog records for sound recordings are, on the average, the lengthiest of all). However, some argue, as does C. P. Ravilious, that "from the standpoint of pure aesthetics there is no such thing as a 'neutral' performance: the performer can never be a transparent medium, and this fact might just as well be recognized in the structure of catalogue entries."[3]

In addition, we can consider the position of some music theorists that even in the realm of "serious" music, there is a growing recognition that performances often go beyond execution and interpretation, especially in the case of music written before the 19th century. It can be said of some types of "early music" that performances can pass over the line that separates interpretation from arrangement — or even virtual recomposition.[4]

# Publication Area

## RECORDING THE PLACE OF PUBLICATION

For published sound recordings, as with other materials, *AACR 2* requires the cataloger to record the place of publication. This is in contrast to *AACR 1*, in which place of publication was omitted for most sound recordings, and where exceptions were made if companies were not known primarily as record publishers. For nonprocessed sound recordings, however, no place of publication is given (6.4C2, new).

While *AACR 2* requires that both the place of publication and name of publisher be given, it is often no easy matter to uncover this information. If no place of publication is given on the recording, the cataloger must decide whether to indicate the name of the probable country of publication, or try to locate the place of publication in reference sources.

## TRADEMARK NAMES

In the sound recording industry, the trademark name may often be considered as sufficient for identification in a national context. The importance accorded to the trademark name is still evident in *AACR 2*, which prefers the trade name, brand name, or subdivision used by the company if the recording bears both the name of the publishing company and the trade name, and so on (6.4D2).

It may be difficult at times to distinguish a trade name from that of a series (e.g., "Disney Storyteller. Walt Disney Productions"). Rule 6.4D3 prescribes that in case of doubt, the cataloger should treat the name as a series title. Familiarity with the sound recording industry and consultation of appropriate reference works will assist in this decision.

## DISTRIBUTORS

The cataloger has the option to record the name of the distributor in addition to the name of the publisher (6.4D1). In light of the special significance that the distributor plays in the sound recording industry, this information may be particularly valuable.

## PREVIOUS RULES

In *AACR 1*, the manufacturer's catalog number was typically included in the publication area for sound recordings. In *AACR 2*, this information is given in the area of the bibliographic record assigned to identifying numbers. While this placement of the manufacturer's number is in accordance with the ISBD pattern of description, there may be some disadvantage for the users who have come to regard the trademark name and catalog number as an inseparable unit of information.

## COPYRIGHT DATES—"C" OR "P"?

Sound recordings frequently bear two kinds of copyright dates: The copyright for the recorded sound is designated by "p," whereas the copyright for the textual data, such as program notes, is indicated by "c." It has apparently been difficult for cataloging decision makers to agree on whether to record the date as "p" or "c." In *AACR 1*, the decision was for "p," while *AACR 2*, when first published, used the "c" date, so that the transcription of publication data for sound recordings would be consistent with other materials. Currently, the LC interpretation is to use "p," and this is now reflected in an example in the revised *AACR 2*.[5]

## PUBLICATION DATA FOR
## UNPUBLISHED SOUND RECORDINGS

Publication data are indicators as to where, by whom, and when an item has been produced or distributed, but such information is not appropriate for works that have been issued in single copies and were never intended for distribution. An example is the category of nonprocessed sound recordings, defined in *AACR 2* as "non-commercial instantaneous recordings, generally existing in unique copies." They include items such as oral history interviews, and recordings of lectures. While place, name, and date of publication are required for commercially produced sound recordings, the publication area for unpublished, or nonprocessed recordings includes only the date of recording. The recording date is formulated according to the rules developed for another type of unpublished material, manuscripts (4.4B1). In the original *AACR 2* (rule 6.11C) no publication data of any kind were given in the publication area for these materials; instead, the date of recording was given in the note area. Rules 6.11A to 6.11.D, dealing with nonprocessed sound recordings, have since been replaced by rules 6.1B1 for the title proper, 6.4C2, 6.4D4, and 6.4F3 for the publication area, and 6.7B7 for the note area.

## DATE OF RECORDING IN
## PUBLISHED MATERIALS

If the date appearing on a published sound recording is a date of recording rather than publication, it is given in the edition and history note. In the OCLC MARC Sound Recordings Format, a separate fixed field (033 Capture Date and Place) allows coding of information about the recording date and/or place.[6]

## SOUND RECORDING COPIES

A different kind of "noncommercial" recording occurs when copies are made of recordings that were issued originally in a commercial format. Frequently, these copies also involve a transfer to another physical medium, as in a tape copy of a disc original. *AACR 2* does not address this question directly, but does indicate in its cardinal rule that the cataloger should describe the physical format in hand.

# Physical Description Area

## EVOLVING FORMATS

By "disc recordings," the original *AACR 2* had in mind the older audio formats of 33⅓ rpm, 45 rpm, and 78 rpm. The digital, laser-scanned format of compact discs was not introduced to the audio industry until well after the publication of *AACR 2*. Thus, revised rules were added in order to describe digital formats, and to make a distinction between digital and analog types of recordings. In contrast, the formats of sound cassettes and sound cartridges had already been standardized for some time when the *AACR 2* rules were published. The rules recognize standard specifications for certain characteristics: For example, standard dimensions have been established for cassettes and cartridges; a standard number of tracks exists for cartridges and cassettes; tape widths are standardized for reels, cartridges, and cassettes. Revised rules also acknowledge that playing speeds are standard for tape cassettes and digital discs.

## DURATION – HOW AND WHEN TO INDICATE

The rules prescribe that the total playing time be indicated. Frequently, however, no indication will appear on the item, or only the playing times for individual pieces will be listed. The rules allow a statement of the playing time if it can be readily established, or optionally, an approximate time. LC recommends that the separately stated durations on a single item be added together and given as a total; it also advises the cataloger against approximating durations of an item from the physical characteristics of the item, for example, from the number of sides of a disc, or type of cassette.[7]

In the original *AACR 2*, rules for recording the duration were found only in the specific media chapters for which this indication was appropriate: sound recordings, and motion pictures and videorecordings. In the revised rules, basic provisions for duration are given in the general chapter in rule 1.5B4.

In the OCLC MARC Sound Recordings Format, a separate field (306) is provided to indicate the running time of a sound recording in hours, minutes, and seconds. Unlike its counterpart in the physical description field, this information does not display on the catalog record. If this field were made searchable, duration could be used as a retrieval element.

## OTHER PHYSICAL DETAILS:
### Recent Revisions

Revised rule 6.5C2 now provides for the addition of an important bit of information in the other physical details section. It is now possible to make a distinction between analog and digital recordings, for example:

1 sound disc (45 min.) : analog.

1 sound disc (56 min.) : digital.

Another revised rule (6.5C7) prescribes that the number of sound channels (i.e., whether mono., stereo., or quad.) be given "if the information is readily available," thus recognizing that this information is frequently difficult to determine.

The 007 fixed field in the OCLC MARC Sound Recordings Format provides for a coded representation of information found in textual form in the physical description area, and also allows the provision of additional detail for archival materials.

## Note Area

Notes of particular relevance for sound recordings include the following:

Statements of responsibility—Names of performers who did not qualify for inclusion in the statement of responsibility area can be given here, along with the corresponding medium of performance (6.7B6). Alternatively, performers' names can be combined with the contents note if appropriate.

Edition and history—For nonprocessed sound recordings, the cataloger can give the available details of the event (revised 6.7B7).

Physical description—Durations can be included for items without a collective title which have been described as a unit (6.7B10). It is important to remember that the term *compact disc* can be given here. This term is relatively well known to the public, whereas earlier clues, such as the designation *analog* and the disc size (4¾ in.), may not convey that the item is a compact disc.

Contents—Since many sound recordings contain multiple titles, this note will often be used to list individual works contained on the item, statements of responsibility, and durations of individual pieces (6.7B18).

Publishers' numbers—The publisher's number is considered an essential piece of information by music librarians, and in *AACR 1* was included as part of the publication area. Considerable opposition was voiced to the placement of this information as the nineteenth note in *AACR 2*, which has established a uniform pattern for the order in which notes are presented. In view of the unique importance of this number for sound recordings, LC has recorded the publisher's number as the first note, and in revised rule 1.7B a note may be given first if it is of primary importance.

In the OCLC MARC Sound Recordings Format, a separate fixed field (028) is provided for giving the publisher's number in coded form, thus making it possible to search for sound recordings by this field. The same information appears on the catalog record in noncoded form in a notes field generated from the coded version.

"With" notes—This note will be essential for sound recordings that lack a collective title and have been described in separate records. The note begins "With:" and lists the other separately titled parts of the item in the order in which they appear (6.7B21).

## Choice of Access Points

### AUTHOR OR PERFORMER MAIN ENTRY?

Chapter 21 (Choice of access points) contains a special set of rules for sound recordings. These rules, like their counterparts in chapter 21, are based on authorship responsibility patterns. Throughout, the key questions to be addressed in consulting the rules are: Is there more than one work? If multiple works, are they by the same person? If by more than one person, is there a principal performer? If more than one principal performer, are there more than three?

Broader theoretical questions include: What is the primary artistic content of the work and who is responsible for this content? What persons—performers or composers—will the patron associate with a particular recording?

### CONCEPT OF AUTHOR IN SOUND RECORDINGS

The concept of author in sound recordings is particularly complex. Involved here is the theoretical issue of the effect of transferring an intellectual or artistic idea from one medium to another. Phonograph recordings may document simultaneously the intellectual or artistic idea found in a music score and also the performance of it.

In *AACR 2*'s rules for the entry of sound recordings, implicit recognition is made of two types of authorship contributions: the creation of the written form of a work—music, text, and so on—and the rendering of that work in a recorded performance. Primacy is accorded to the first type of contribution, and thus a sound recording of one work or of two or more works by the same person is entered "under the heading appropriate to that work." Accordingly, entry is under the heading that the work would receive if it appeared in written form—for a musical work, this would be the heading for the composer, and for a literary text, the author (21.23A).

In the case of collections written or composed by different authors, the rules for sound recordings allow for a "substitute" author to be considered as primarily responsible for the collection. Main entry in this case is given to the person or corporate body represented as principal performer (or the first named, if there are two or three principal performers). Recognition is accordingly made of the unity which a single performer or performing group can impart to the collection.

In some cases, a corporate main entry can be given to the performing group if the sound recording "[results] from the collective activity of a performing group as a whole where the responsibility of the group goes beyond that of mere performance, execution, etc." (21.1B2e). This rule applies to similar situations for films and videorecordings. The LC rule interpretation gives as an example "an acting group that performs by means of improvisation" and in which the "development of the drama proceeds entirely on the basis of improvised dialogue."[8]

As we have seen, the performing person can be given the main entry for a sound recording only if the individual has recorded works by different composers or authors and is indicated as principal performer. A performing group can be given main entry under the same conditions, and in both instances, the cataloger's decision is based on factors other than the nature of the performer's contribution. However, in a contrasting situation, performing groups can also be given main entry if their responsibility goes beyond execution and performance of the work, a criterion similar to that used by the cataloger in deciding whether to include a performer (person or corporate body) in the statement of responsibility area.

## TREATMENT OF AUTHORSHIP IN PREVIOUS CODES

In the Phonorecords supplement to the 1949 ALA rules, and in *AACR 1*, the author or person primarily responsible for the intellectual or artistic content of a recording was the composer or author of the work in its printed form. Performers were never regarded as authors, or regarded as candidates for main entry.

## ADDED ENTRIES

Frequently, a sound recording will name a large number of performers who might be possible added entries. There are LC rule interpretations that give assistance in deciding what added entries should be made for performers named on a sound recording. Considerations include the role of the performer, the number of works contributed, the degree of prominence given on the chief source, and whether the person is a member of a corporate body that has been given a heading. A conductor or accompanist would not be considered such a member, however. Other exceptions worthy of their own headings are individual performers of jazz ensembles.[9]

# Form of Heading

Even the casual observer of contemporary popular music is aware that many performing groups have names that do not convey the idea of a corporate body. When such names are given as main or added entries, the cataloger must consider whether to add a general designation in parentheses according to rule 24.4B. There are LC rule interpretations that assist in this decision. The designation "Musical group" is added "if the name is extremely vague, consisting primarily of single, common words (e.g., Circle, Who, Jets) or the name has the appearance of a personal name (e.g., Jethro Tull)," but not "if the name contains a word that specifically designates a performing group or a corporate body in general (e.g., band, consort, society) or contains a collective or plural noun (e.g., Ramblers, Boys, Hot Seven)." Further directives are included.[10]

# SYSTEMS FOR ORGANIZATION

## Closed Stack Systems

A library's choice of system for the physical organization of materials may well be determined by the type of access that is to be provided to the collection. Many libraries argue that classification is too expensive for sound recordings, preferring instead that they be shelved in accession number order. Security considerations may also lead to a decision for a closed stack collection. In some libraries, the sound recordings themselves may be in a closed stack area, while containers such as disc jackets and boxes for cassettes and compact discs may be displayed openly for browsing. Even if the library does decide to classify its recordings, it may still be necessary to house these materials separately, because of their fragility and the difficulty of integrating them with print materials on the shelves. The decision made as to type of physical organization will have ramifications for the type of catalog or surrogate access to be provided. For example, if a closed stack collection is arranged solely by simple accession number order, adequate access must be provided through the catalog or index.

### NUMERICAL SCHEMES

Most closed stack collections are organized by a numerical system. Since there is no browsing, and since the primary purpose of the organization is to provide a unique identification for each item in the collection, any numerical system may suffice, such as an accession number or other sequential, uncoded type of number.

Another basis for organization is the numbering system provided by sound recording publishing companies. Recordings can then be organized first by publishing company and then by catalog number. One advantage to this system is that such numbers may be obtained from such sources as reviews, sales charts, and discographies.

## Open Stack Systems/Classification

In selecting an organization for an open stack system, consideration should be given to certain characteristics of sound recordings that will determine the effectiveness of schemes devised for their organization and classification.

### SCOPE AND CONTENT OF SOUND RECORDINGS

A major consideration is that the medium of sound recordings encompasses both musical and nonmusical content. It includes recordings of events, literary works, instructional materials, and sound effects. Most of the standard systems for classifying sound recordings, such as Dewey Decimal Classification or Library of Congress Classification, deal only with music, and must be manipulated to include other types of recordings.

## MULTIPLE TITLES ON ONE PHYSICAL ITEM

Most classification schemes are unable to deal adequately with the fact that sound recordings are commonly issued in a multititle format, with more than one work included in a recording. Sometimes the separate works share some characteristics, such as the same composer, or the same medium of performance, but more often than not, recordings contain more than one type of composition or works by more than one composer. Whatever the basis for a scheme's organization — whether by form, medium, stylistic period or composer — the class number can only be based on one of the works on the recording, unless one assigns a disproportionately high number of records to a collection or anthology category. The physical recording itself is a single entity that can only be placed in one location on a shelf, but the contents of the recording might logically fall in several different places. Therefore, patrons who rely on browsing alone may not be able to find in one place all the recordings of a single composer or performer, or similar groupings.

## ACCESS BY PERFORMER

Until recently, classification schemes have primarily been concerned with organizing materials in the Western "classical" music tradition. Many libraries, however, now have substantial holdings in "popular" idioms such as rock, country and western, jazz, folk, or in non-Western musical forms. For these traditions the elements of form, medium, or composer are often a less important means of identifying recordings. Solo or group performers in particular may be a more meaningful identifier than composer or lyricist. Even in Western classical music, the performer may be a key retrieval point for the user.

The emerging field of early classical music has also not been adequately dealt with in classification schemes. The phenomenon of multiple works and composers on a single recording is particularly noticeable in these recordings. In addition, early musical works were often not specifically assigned to a particular medium; thus, a work might be recorded as a vocal or instrumental interpretation or a combination. If a collection is arranged primarily by medium of performance, this could result in recordings of the same work being scattered throughout a collection.

Another consideration is that many established classification systems were prepared originally for print materials, and those schemes that were developed especially for music were based on printed music scores.

## LIBRARY OF CONGRESS CLASSIFICATION

The widespread use of the Library of Congress Classification (LCC) for book collections has often made it a de facto choice for sound recordings as well.[11] However, many limitations arise from the scheme's orientation toward books and music scores. In addition, the classification is further limited because it was developed at a time when little recognition was given to "nonclassical" genres, and when recordings were limited to one or two selections per disc. Many libraries have found LCC difficult to adapt to collections containing both classical and popular genres of music.

The two major divisions are instrumental music and vocal music. Within the instrumental category, subdivisions proceed from simple to complex instrumentation; the vocal category is divided into sacred and secular. Many of the subdivisions are further divided by format and composer or by musical form and composer. Music forms from almost all time periods are interspersed throughout the categories. This type of organization, which gives precedence to form over medium of performance, composer, and performer, will be unfamiliar to users for whom form is of secondary importance.

## DEWEY DECIMAL CLASSIFICATION

As with LCC, the popularity of the Dewey Decimal Classification (DDC) often becomes justification for use of DDC in sound recording collections.[12] DDC also shares many limiting characteristics with LCC. DDC is an enumerative system biased toward Western classical music, and while there is some recognition of popular music styles in the vocal category, jazz and early music are relatively neglected. In addition, its emphasis on form does not enable direct access to composer or performer. As McColvin points out, "It presumes ... that the reader who comes to a library for Chopin's preludes would require, in the absence of that volume, some other volume of preludes. Bach's for instance."[13]

In the 20th edition of DDC, the schedule for class 780 Music will be completely revised. The proposed revision of the DDC music schedule is more adaptable to music of non-Western and nonclassical cultures and traditions outside Western art music and makes it possible to bring together all material about a given composer.

## BLISS CLASSIFICATION

The Bliss music schedules were completely revised in 1977 to make them a fully faceted scheme, that is, a classification scheme in which the subject is broken down into its key elements.[14] These subdivisions are each assigned symbols which can be combined in a prescribed order to give a complete description of an item. Bliss is one of the few schedules that mention the possibility of sound recording applications. The new Bliss schedule also attempts to account for non-Western art music traditions, such as jazz and popular music.

## ANSCR CLASSIFICATION SYSTEM

ANSCR (Alpha-Numeric System for Classification of Sound Recordings) is a classification system specifically devised for sound recordings.[15] As such, it addresses many of the unique characteristics of sound recordings which have rendered traditional classification systems less effective when applied to this medium. Its rationale assumes that materials whose use and composition differ from books cannot fit neatly into the unified system of classification for books.

ANSCR encompasses not only musical recordings but recordings such as plays and monologs, discussions and open debates, and transcriptions of sounds (bird calls, train whistles). While designed for collections in libraries of any size or type, it is of particular value to the browser-oriented or open stack collection.

Since sound recordings often contain more than one work, ANSCR bases assignment of a given recording to a subject category on its physical measurement. If the first work on side one does not occupy one-third or more of the space on side one, the entire recording is examined to determine its classification. Popular music categories are always determined on the basis of their general content.

ANSCR is particularly well suited to popular and nonmusical collections in that it classes material first by major type of performing group or by broad type of literature and then by composer, performer, or other identifying feature. Because of the subsequent groupings under composer, performer, and author, it is easier for the library user to find the symphonies of Mozart, the latest from the singer Aretha Franklin, or the poetry of Robert Frost.

Just as ANSCR's particular strength lies in its treatment of popular and nonmusical genres, some argue that this scheme has failed to meet the needs of classical music collections. It has been criticized for its deficiencies in authority control, for its lack of consistency in the alphabetical arrangements of the composer list, and for its lack of attention to opus and thematic catalog numbers.[16]

## SEPARATE SHELVING FROM MAIN COLLECTION

There are numerous reasons why sound recordings cannot be intershelved with other library materials easily: Records and tapes do not fit well in standard library shelving, do not offer the convenience of spine labeling, and may be susceptible to heat, dust, static electricity, theft, and stress warpage.

One advantage to the arrangement of sound recording discs in open bins is that such systems make possible a "self-indexing" system by which recordings can be grouped first into broad categories, for example, by genre such as rock, country and western, and then by performer, or, in the case of classical music, by composer. Such an arrangement would be similar to those commonly found in sound recording retail stores.

## IN-HOUSE SCHEMES

In-house development of schemes often appears necessary as librarians determine that standard systems are not appropriate to their needs. The emphasis on form or medium in established schemes may lead some libraries to set up alternative schemes based on musical style, composer, or performer.

Since there is no standard system that classifies by an alphabetical arrangement of composer and/or title, many libraries have devised their own systems using this principle. Simple alphabetical order may be appropriate for closed stack collections, for specific-topic collections, and for very small browsing collections that do not require any further classed arrangement.

# NOTES

[1]*Cataloging Service Bulletin* 11 (Winter, 1981): 15.

[2]Ibid.

[3]C. P. Ravilious, "*AACR2* and Its Implications for Music Cataloguing," *Brio* 16 (Spring 1979): 11.

[4]Sue Weiland, "Sound Recordings and *AACR2*: Some Problems in Descriptive Cataloging," unpublished paper, 1985.

[5]*Cataloging Service Bulletin* 22 (Fall 1983): 16.

[6]OCLC, *Sound Recordings Format*, 2d ed. (Dublin, Ohio: OCLC, 1986).

[7]*Cataloging Service Bulletin* 33 (Summer 1986): 36.

[8]*Cataloging Service Bulletin* 14 (Fall 1981): 21.

[9]*Cataloging Service Bulletin* 34 (Fall 1986): 29, 30.

[10]Ibid., 40, 41.

[11]Library of Congress, Subject Cataloging Division, *Classification, Class M— Music*, 3d ed. (Washington, D.C.: Library of Congress, 1978).

[12]*Dewey Decimal Classification and Relative Index*, 19th ed., ed. Benjamin Custer (Albany, N.Y.: Forest Press, 1979).

[13]Lionel McColvin, *Music in Public Libraries* (London: Grafton & Co., 1924), 38.

[14]Henry Evelyn Bliss, *Bliss Bibliographic Classification*, 2d ed., ed. Jack Mills and Vanda Broughton (Boston: Butterworths, 1977- ).

[15]Caroline Saheb-Ettaba and Roger B. McFarland, *ANSCR: The Alpha-Numeric System for Classification of Sound Recordings* (Williamsport, Pa.: Bro-Dart, 1969).

[16]Richard S. Halsey, "Review of ANSCR: The Alpha-Numeric System for Classification of Sound Recordings," *Library Resources & Technical Services* 15 (Spring, 1971): 263.

# DESCRIPTIVE CATALOGING EXAMPLES

## Items to Be Cataloged

1. Sound recording compact disc—classical music

One compact disc sound recording, digital, stereo., 4¾ inches, in plastic container. Program notes in container state that playing time is 45 minutes.

Container:

COLUMBIA RECORDS<br>
W. A. Mozart<br>
Concerto for clarinet and orchestra A major (K622)<br>
F. Etienne, Clarinetist<br>
Hamilton Chamber Orchestra<br>
p 1983<br>
Columbia Records   New York, N.Y.   Columbia CD 666023

Disc label:

Mozart<br>
Clarinet Concerto A major (K622)<br>
Columbia CD 666023<br>
F. Etienne, clarinetist<br>
Hamilton Chamber Orchestra<br>
p Columbia Records  1983

2. Sound recording analog disc—popular music

One sound recording disc, analog, 12 inches, stereo., 33⅓ rpm.

Record jacket, front:

Stereo<br>
ARETHA NOW<br>
SD 8186<br>
ATLANTIC

Side label:

Stereo     ARETHA FRANKLIN     ARETHA NOW     Atlantic SD 8186

Record jacket, back:

c1968 Atlantic Recording Corporation<br>
Atlantic Recording Corporation  1841 Broadway, New York, N.Y. 10023

Disc, side one:

SD 8186<br>
Stereo<br>
ARETHA FRANKLIN<br>
ARETHA NOW<br>
Atlantic   SIDE 1   Atlantic

(Disc, side one continues on page 89.)

1. THINK (2:15) Aretha Franklin-Ted White

2. I SAY A LITTLE PRAYER (3:30)
   Burt Bacharach-Hal David

3. SEE SAW (2:42)
   Steve Cropper-Don Covay

4. NIGHT TIME IS THE RIGHT TIME (4:44)
   Lew Harman

5. YOU SEND ME (2:25)
   Sam Cooke

Distributed By Atlantic Record Sales, 1841 Broadway, New York, N.Y.

Disc, side two:                ARETHA FRANKLIN
                                  ARETHA NOW
                          Atlantic   SIDE 2   Atlantic

1. YOU'RE A SWEET SWEET MAN (2:14)
   Ronnie Shannon

2. I TAKE WHAT I WANT (2:30)
   Porter-Hodges-Hayes

3. HELLO SUNSHINE (3:00)
   King Curtis-Ronald Miller

4. A CHANGE (2:23)
   Clyde Otis-Dorian Burton

5. I CAN'T SEE MYSELF LEAVING YOU (3:00)
   Ronnie Shannon

3. Nonprocessed sound recording; cassette

One sound recording cassette: 35 minutes, monaural, 1-7/8 ips. 3-7/8 x 2½ inches (height x width); 1/8 inch tape width, 4 tracks, with accompanying typescript pamphlet.

Label, front:
   JEFFERSON-PLEASANTS FAMILY REUNION, XENIA, OHIO.

Pamphlet: 1. Olivia Pleasants Frost: "John Pleasants, 1826-1886" (20 min.)
          2. Isabel Jefferson Banks: "David Jefferson, 1843-1900". (15 min.)
          Recorded 8/13/87, Xenia, Ohio.

4. Commercial spoken sound recording; cassette

One sound recording cassette: 60 minutes, monaural, 1-7/8 ips. 3-7/8 x 2½ inches (height x width); 1/8 inch tape width, 4 tracks.
Topic deals with the importance of nutrition in achieving success.

Cassette label, front:      An RMP Audiocassette
EAT FOR SUCCESS
narrated by
McKinley R. Carter, M.D.
author of EAT FOR SUCCESS

Cassette label, back:      THE POWER SNACK
narrated by McKinley R. Carter, M.D.

RMP Audio  ES 2806
Distributed by Rogers, Minter, and Parker
Kansas City, MO

one cassette
total playing time: 60 minutes
p1986 McKinley R. Carter, M.D.      RMP Audio ES 2806

[Label indicates that Carter is the author of both works.]

## *AACR 2* Records and
## OCLC MARC Tagging

### 1. COMPACT DISC – CLASSICAL MUSIC

Mozart, Wolfgang Amadeus, 1756-1791.
   [Concertos, clarinet, orchestra, K. 622, A major]
   Clarinet concerto A major (K622) [sound recording] / Mozart. --
New York, N.Y. : Columbia, p1983.
   1 sound disc (45 min.) : digital, stereo. ; 4¾ in. + program
notes.

   Columbia CD 666023.
   Title on container: Concerto for clarinet and orchestra A major
(K622).
   F. Etienne, clarinet ; Hamilton Chamber Orchestra.
   Compact disc.

   I. Etienne, F.   II. Hamilton Chamber Orchestra.

OCLC MARC Tagging

| | | | | | |
|---|---|---|---|---|---|
| Type: j | Bib lvl: m | Lang: N/A | Source: d | Accomp mat: | |
| | Enc lvl: I | Ctry: nyu | Dat tp: s | MEBE: 1 | |
| Repr: | Mod rec: | Comp: co | Format: n | Prts: n | |
| Desc: a | Int lvl: | LTxt: | Dates: 1983, | | |

```
1  040      xxx $c xxx
2  007      s $b d $c $d f $e z $f n $g g $h n $i n $m e
3  028 02   CD 666023  $b Columbia
4  100 10   Mozart, Wolfgang Amadeus, $d 1756-1791.
5  240 10   Concertos, $m clarinet, orchestra, $n K. 622, $r A major
6  245 00   Clarinet concerto A major (K622) $h sound recording / $c
Mozart.
7  260 0    New York, N.Y. : $b Columbia, $c p1983.
8  300      1 sound disc (45 min.) : $b digital, stereo. ; $c 4 3/4
in. + $e program notes.
9  306      004500
10 500      Title on container: Concerto for clarinet and orchestra
A major (K622).
11 511 0    F. Etienne, clarinet ; Hamilton Chamber Orchestra.
12 500      Compact disc.
13 700 10   Etienne, F.
14 710 20   Hamilton Chamber Orchestra.
```

### *AACR 2* applicable rules

**Uniform Title**

For most works of classical music, it will be necessary to construct a uniform title, since a single work can appear under many different titles. The uniform title will bring together all versions of a single work in the catalog, regardless of the differences that would appear in individual title page titles. In *AACR 2*, 1988 rev., the rules for music uniform titles will be re-ordered to reflect the sequence in which they are applied. In locating information needed for constructing the uniform title, the cataloger will probably need to consult reference sources.

**25.1A:** Uniform titles provide the means for bringing together all the catalog entries for a work when various manifestations have appeared under various titles.

**25.2A:** "Enclose the uniform title in square brackets, and give it before the title proper."

**25.25:** "Formulate a uniform title for a musical work as instructed in 25.26-25.31."

**25.29A1:**   Use accepted English form of name if the title of the work consists solely of the name of one type of composition and if there are cognate forms in English, French, German, and Italian.

**25.30B1:**   Add medium of performance if title consists solely of the name of a type of composition.

**25.30B4:**   Use English terms for medium of performance.

**25.30B7:**   In indicating medium of performance, use name of solo instrument followed by name of accompanying ensemble.

**25.30C4:**   Use thematic index numbers as identifying element for certain composers, if title consists solely of name of composition. Precede number by initial letter of bibliographer's name (e.g., "K" for Mozart's bibliographer Ludwig Köchel).

**25.30D1:**   Include statement of key for pre-20th-century works. Indicate if major or minor.

### Chief source of information

**6.0B1:**   Chief source of information for disc is permanently affixed label.

### Area 1

**6.1B1:**   [revised] "For data to be included in titles proper for musical terms, see 5.1B."

**5.1B1:**   [revised] For titles consisting of name of type of composition, record medium of performance, key, and numbering, as part of title proper.

**6.1C1:**   GMD as in 1.1C1, *sound recording*, following title proper, in brackets.

**6.1F1:**   Statement of responsibility for composer. Performer not included here since his or her participation is limited to performance, execution, or interpretation.

### Area 4

**6.4C1, 6.4D1, 6.4F1:**

Place of publication, name of publisher, date as in 1.4C, 1.4D, 1.4F. LC rule interpretation for 1.4F5: "Transcribe copyright dates other than a phonogram copyright date preceded by a lowercase 'c'; transcribe the phonogram copyright date preceded by a lowercase 'p'." [CSB 25 (Summer 1984): 30]

**1.4F6:**   Give copyright date in absence of publication date.

**Area 5**

**6.5B1:** Record number of physical units and SMD *sound disc.*

**6.5B2:** [new] Give playing time as instructed in 1.5B4.

**1.5B4:** [new] Give playing time as stated on item.

**6.5C2:** [new] For a disc or tape, give the type of recording, that is, the way in which sound is encoded on the item; for example, digital.

**6.5C3:** [new] Omit playing speed of a digital disc if it is 1.4 meters per second.

**6.5C7:** Give number of sound channels (stereo).

**6.5D2:** Give dimension of disc in inches.

**6.5E1:** Accompanying material.

**Area 7**

**6.7B19:** Publisher's number. LC rule interpretation: LC records the publisher's number as the first note. [CSB 11 (Winter 1981): 15]

**6.7B4:** Titles that vary from title proper.

**6.7B6:** Statements of responsibility for performers and their medium of performance.

**6.7B10:** Important physical details.

**Choice of access points**

**21.23A:** For sound recording of one work, give main entry appropriate to that work. Main entry under single personal author (that is, composer).

**21.23A:** Added entries under principal performers.

**21.30J:** No added entry for title proper if a conventionalized uniform title has been used in entry for a musical work.

**Form of heading**

**22.1A:** Name by which commonly known.

## 2. POPULAR MUSIC – ANALOG DISC

    Franklin, Aretha, 1942-
      Aretha now [sound recording] / Aretha Franklin. -- New York, N.Y. : Atlantic, c1968.
      1 sound disc (29 min.) : analog, 33⅓ rpm, stereo. ; 12 in.

      Atlantic: SD 8186.
      Program notes by Jack Springer on record jacket.
      Contents: Think -- I say a little prayer -- See saw -- Night time is the right time -- You send me -- You're a sweet sweet man -- I take what I want -- Hello sunshine -- A change -- I can't see myself leaving you.

      I. Title.

```
OCLC MARC Tagging

Type: j  Bib lvl: m  Lang: eng    Source: d   Accomp mat:
         Enc lvl: I  Ctry: nyu    Dat tp: s   MEBE: 1
Repr:    Mod rec:    Comp: pp     Format: n   Prts: n
Desc: a  Int lvl:    LTxt:        Dates: 1968,

1  040    xxx $c xxx
2  007    s $b d $c  $d b $e s $f m $g e $h n $i n
3  028 02 SD 8186 $b Atlantic
4  100 10 Franklin, Aretha, $d 1942-
5  245 10 Aretha now $h sound recording / $c Aretha Franklin.
6  260 0  New York, N.Y. : $b Atlantic, $c c1968.
7  300    1 sound disc (29 min.) : $b analog, 33 1/3 rpm, stereo. ;
$c 12 in.
8  306    002900
9  500    Program notes by Jack Springer on record jacket.
10 505 0  Think  -- I say a little prayer -- See saw  -- Night time
is the right time -- You send me -- You're a sweet sweet man -- I
take what I want -- Hello sunshine -- A change -- I can't see
myself leaving you.
```

### *AACR 2* applicable rules

**6.0B1:**    Chief source for disc is label.

**Area 1**

**6.1B1:**    Record title proper as in 1.B.

**6.1C1:**    GMD.

**6.1F1:**    Statement of responsibility for performer whose contribution goes beyond performance, execution, or interpretation of a work, as is commonly the case with "popular" music.

**6.4C1, 6.4D1, 6.4F1:**
    Place, name of publisher, date.

**1.4F5, 1.4F6:**
    Copyright date.

**Area 5**

**6.5B1:**    Number of physical units and SMD.

**6.5B2:**    Playing time.

**1.5B4:**    LC rule interpretation: "When the total playing time is not stated on the item but the durations of its individual works are, if desired add the stated durations together and record the total, rounding off to the next minute, if the total exceeds 5 minutes." [CSB 33 (Summer 1986): 36]

**6.5C2:**    Type of recording (i.e., analog).

**6.5C3:**    [revised] Give playing speed of analog disc in revolutions per minute (rpm).

**6.5C7:**    Number of sound channels.

**6.5D2:**    Diameter of disc in inches.

**Area 7**

**6.7B19:**    Publisher's number.

**6.7B6:**    Statement of responsibility.

**6.7B18:**    Give titles of individual works. Composers and durations could also be listed. Alternatively, instead of listing the entire contents, the item could be described in a summary note.

**Choice of access points**

**21.23C:**    Entry under principal performer for sound recording containing works by different persons.

**21.30J:**    Title added entry.

## 3. NONPROCESSED TAPE CASSETTE

Jefferson-Pleasants family reunion, Xenia, Ohio
[sound recording]. -- 1987.
1 sound cassette (35 min.) : analog, mono. + 1 pamphlet.

Recorded August 13, 1987 in Xenia, Ohio.
Contents: John Pleasants, 1826-1886 / Olivia Pleasants Frost
(20 min.) -- David Jefferson, 1843-1900 / Isabel Jefferson Banks
(15 min.).

```
OCLC MARC Tagging

Type: i   Bib lvl: m   Lang: eng   Source: d   Accomp mat: i
          Enc lvl: I   Ctry: xx    Dat tp: s   Prts: n
Repr:     Mod rec:     Comp: nn    Format: n   MEBE: 0
Desc: a   Int lvl:     LTxt: b     Dates: 1987,

1  040     xxx $c xxx
2  007     s $b s $c  $d 1 $e m $f n $g j $h 1 $i c
3  245 00  Jefferson-Pleasants family reunion, Xenia, Ohio $h sound
recording
4  260 1   $c 1987.
5  300 1 sound cassette (35 min.) : $b analog, mono. + $e 1
pamphlet.
6  306     003500
7  518     Recorded August 13, 1987 in Xenia, Ohio.
8  505 0   John Pleasants, 1826-1886 / Olivia Pleasants Frost (20
min.) -- David Jefferson, 1843-1900 / Isabel Jefferson Banks (15
min.).
```

## *AACR 2* applicable rules

**6.0B1:**     Chief source of information, cassette and label.

**Area 1**

**6.1B1:**     Title proper.

**6.1C1:**     GMD.

**Area 4**

**6.4C2, 6.4D4:**
          [new] Do not record place of publication or name of publisher for nonprocessed sound recordings.

**6.4F3:**     [new] Give date of recording of nonprocessed sound recording.

**Area 5**

**6.5B1:**     Number of units, SMD.

**6.5B2:**     Playing time.

**1.5B4:**     Playing time; LCRI: Add stated durations.

**6.5C2:**     Type of recording (i.e., analog).

**6.5C3:** Give playing speed of tape in inches per second (ips).

**6.5C3:** [revised] Omit playing speed if it is standard for the item (e.g., 1-7/8 inches per second for a tape cassette).

**6.5C6:** Omit number of tracks for cassettes if standard for item (i.e., 4 tracks).

**6.5C7:** Number of channels: mono.

**6.5D5:** Omit dimensions for cassette if standard for item (3-7/8 x 2½ in.).

**Area 7**

**6.7B7:** [revised] Give available details of the event, for nonprocessed sound recordings.

**6.7B18:** Titles, statements of responsibility, and durations of individual works.

**Choice of access points**

**21.23C1:** Title main entry for sound recording containing works by different persons having no principal performer.

## 4. COMMERCIAL SPOKEN RECORDING, CASSETTE

Carter, McKinley R.
   Eat for success ; The power snack [sound recording] / narrated by McKinley R. Carter. -- Kansas City, MO : Distributed by Rogers, Minter, and Parker, p1986.
   1 sound cassette (60 min.) : analog, mono. -- (An RMP audiocassette)

RMP Audio ES 2806.
Describes the importance of nutrition in achieving success.

I. Title.   II. Title: The power snack.

OCLC MARC Tagging

```
Type: i  Bib lvl: m  Lang: eng   Source: d    Accomp mat:
         Enc lvl: I  Ctry: mou   Dat tp: s    Prts:  n
Repr:    Mod rec:    Comp: nn    Format: n    MEBE: 1
Desc: a  Int lvl:    LTxt: i     Dates: 1986,
```

```
1  040     xxx $c xxx
2  007     s $b s $c  $d 1 $e m $f n $g j $h 1 $i c
2  028 02  ES 2806 $b RMP Audio
3  100 10  Carter, McKinley R.
4  245 10  Eat for success ; The power snack $h sound recording /
$c narrated by McKinley R. Carter.
5  260 0   Kansas City, MO : $b Distributed by Rogers, Minter, and
Parker, $c p1986.
6  300     1 sound cassette (60 min.) : $b analog, mono.
7  306     006000
8  490 0   An RMP audiocassette
9  520     Describes the importance of nutrition in achieving
success.
10 740 41  The power snack.
```

## *AACR 2* applicable rules

**6.0B1:**  Chief source of information, cassette and label.

**Area 1**

**6.1B1:**  Record title proper.

**1.1G3:**  Item lacks collective title. Record individually titled parts, separated by semicolon if parts are by same person.

**6.1C1:**  GMD.

**6.1F1:**  Record statements of responsibility relating to writers of spoken words.

**1.1F7:**  Omit titles from names of persons in statement of responsibility.

**Area 4**

**6.4C1, 6.4D1, 6.4F1:**
Place, publisher, date.

**1.4D3:**  Include phrases indicating function of publisher.

**1.4F5, 1.4F6:**
Copyright date.

**Area 5**

Same as in example #3.

**Area 6**

**6.6B1:**    Series title.

**Area 7**

**6.7B19:**    Publisher's number.

**6.7B17:**    Summary.

**Choice of access points**

**21.23B:**    Enter two or more works by the same person under the heading appropriate to those works.

**21.4A:**    Enter works by one personal author under heading for author.

**21.30J:**    Added entry for title different from title proper.

# REFERENCE SOURCES

## Discographies

**MUSIC MATERIALS**

*Bibliography of Discographies. Vol. 1: Classical Music 1925-1975.* Compiled by Gerald D. Gibson and Michael H. Gray. New York: Bowker, 1977.
Information on more than 3,000 discographies of classical music published in American and European journals between 1925 and 1975.

*Bibliography of Discographies. Vol. 2: Jazz.* Compiled by Daniel Allen. New York: Bowker, 1981.
Over 3,000 jazz discographies from publications between 1935 and 1980.

*Bibliography of Discographies. Vol. 3: Popular Music.* Compiled by Michael H. Gray. New York: Bowker, 1983.
Entries arranged alphabetically under LC Subject Headings as well as under personal names. Includes matrix numbers, release date, and place and/or date of recording.

Cohn, Arthur. *Recorded Classical Music: A Critical Guide to Compositions and Performances.* New York: Schirmer Books, 1981.
Exhaustive coverage of classical recordings and a critical guide to the compositions and performances on those recordings. From pre-Baroque to 20th-century avant-garde; includes all performing media. Arranged alphabetically by composer, the entries include medium of performance, record information, and

critical comments. Index of record labels and numbers. Each entry has an annotation and a recommended recording. Alphabetical by composer with subheadings by medium of composition (piano, orchestra, etc.). Exhaustive record label index. Cassettes and tapes not included.

Cooper, David Edwin. *International Bibliography of Discographies. Classical Music, Jazz and Blues, 1962-1972: A Reference Book for Record Collectors, Dealers, and Libraries.* Littleton, Colo.: Libraries Unlimited, 1975.
　　Arranged by period, subject, composer, and performer.

Daniels, William. *The American 45 and 78 rpm Record Dating Guide, 1940-1959.* Westport, Conn.: Greenwood Press, 1985.
　　Arranged alphabetically by record company, then by issue number. Information drawn from trade weeklies such as *Variety, Cash Box, Billboard*, and others. Focuses on popular music.

Foreman, Lewis. *Systematic Discography.* Hamden, Conn.: Linnet Books, 1974.
　　A guide to compiling discographies, intended for professional librarians, amateur discographers, and collectors. Lists sources, specialty record labels, and out-of-print materials. Includes also lists of discographies, dealers, private labels, journal literature, and sources of reviews. Gives overview of library cataloging practice for sound recordings.

Greene, Frank, comp. *Composers on Record: An Index to Biographical Information on 14,000 Composers Whose Work Has Been Recorded.* Metuchen, N.J.: Scarecrow Press, 1985.
　　Includes composers whose works have appeared on commercially available recordings.

Greenfield, Edward, Robert Layton, and Ivan March. *The Complete Penguin Stereo Record and Cassette Guide.* New York: Penguin Books, 1984.
　　A comprehensive guide to stereo records, cassettes, and compact discs of permanent music available in the United Kingdom. Also includes important issues of the major international companies, some major European domestic companies and some American digital material. Arranged by (1) composer index, (2) concerts of orchestral and concertante music, (3) instrumental recitals, and (4) vocal recitals and choir collections. Rates the quality of performance and recording.

Hoffman, Herbert H., comp. *Recorded Plays: Indexes to Dramatists, Plays, and Actors.* Chicago: American Library Association, 1985.

Holmes, John L. *Conductors on Record.* Westport, Conn.: Greenwood Press, 1982.
　　Alphabetical listing for each conductor worldwide who has performed on a sound recording. Discography also includes a brief biography and discussion of the conductor's style, importance, and place in the history of the art. Covers beginning of sound recordings to 1977. Includes tapes, 78s, 45s, and LPs. Alphabetical by name of conductor. Includes date and place of recording and names of all recording companies who have issued discs. Particularly useful for locating a particular performance of a composition.

Rust, Brian A. L. *Jazz Records, 1897-1942.* 5th ed., rev. and enl. Chigwell, Essex, England: Storyville Publications, 1982.

Lists musicians heard on disc, affiliated with jazz music and ragtime music reaching back to 1897. Blues singers are not included unless they are accompanied by jazz musicians. Arranged alphabetically by individual or group. Includes record and matrix number, date of recording, and personnel. Both American and British releases are listed.

*Schwann-1: Records and Tapes.* Boston: Schwann, 1975- . Monthly.

A "Books-in-Print" for sound recordings. Helps one determine what compositions and what performances of compositions are currently available on recordings. Entries arranged by composer, with separate sections for new listings, electronic music, collections, musicals, current popular and jazz recordings, movies, and TV shows. Lists about 50,000 available recordings from about 800 firms. Coverage includes classical, popular music, and soundtracks from musicals and films. Continues *Schwann-1. Record and Tape Guide*, 1973-1974. Originally issued as *Schwann Record Catalog*, 1949- .

*Schwann-2* is a semiannual publication, listing classical jazz and the spoken word. Also classical on lesser-known labels, monophonic, and electronic stereo. Spoken recordings category includes birdsongs and nature sounds, documentary and history, humor, "how to" and language instruction, plays, poetry, and prose. Over 10,000 entries, including 1,500 nonmusical.

*Schwann: Artists Catalog.* 1953- . Issued irregularly.

Listing of artists by name of performer. Arranged in sections by type of performance. Useful in determining whether a certain artist has recorded a particular composition.

*Schwann: Compact Disc Catalog.* 1986- . Began as a quarterly and changed to monthly in June 1986.

Compact disc new listings, recommended CD basic library, CD reviews. Main listing of available compact discs in U.S.

Smolian, Steven, comp. *A Handbook of Film, Theater and Television Music on Record, 1948-1969.* New York: The Record Undertaker, 1970.

First volume is a discography of soundtrack and/or original-cast long-playing recordings listed by show title with pertinent data. Second volume contains indexes of the record manufacturers and composers. American stage, television, and movie music.

Tudor, Dean. *Popular Music: An Annotated Guide to Recordings.* Littleton, Colo.: Libraries Unlimited, 1983.

Discography and buying guide for American popular music available on long-playing disc. Subdivided into music categories: Black (blues, rhythm and blues, soul, and reggae), Folk, Jazz, Mainstream, Popular Religious, and Rock. Recordings listed under the headings Anthologies, Innovators, and Performers. Performing artist index. Sixty-two hundred long-playing records are annotated.

## SPOKEN MATERIALS

National Information Center for Educational Media [NICEM]. *Audiocassette Finder*. Albuquerque, N.M.: NICEM, 1986.
> Lists 30,000 audiocassettes currently available. Coverage includes instructional and recreational materials: poetry, folklore, interviews, essays, documentaries, novels, plays, short stories, self improvement materials, children's stories, games, and songs. Title and subject access.

*Words on Tape 1987-88: An International Guide to Recorded Books*. Westport, Conn.: Meckler Publishing, 1987.
> Lists over 15,000 available titles of "books on cassette" from 435 cassette publishers. By author, title, and subject. Includes novels, children's fiction, plays, short stories, self-help and inspirational works, business-related coursework, poetry readings, and interviews. Provides access to individual works within a collection. Information for entries includes title, author, playing time, publisher's order number, and publisher.

# Biographical Dictionaries and Encyclopedias

Baker, Theodore. *Baker's Biographical Dictionary of Musicians*. 7th ed. Edited by Nicolas Slonimsky. New York: G. Schirmer, 1984.
> International coverage of composers and musicians, living and dead. Mostly classical musicians, but also notable jazz, pop, rock figures. Selective bibliographies and discographies.

Bane, Michael. *Who's Who in Rock*. New York: Facts on File, 1981.
> Alphabetically arranged entries on solo and group performers with commentary that includes history, notable recordings, present work, and a critical evaluation.

Kinkle, Roger D. *The Complete Encyclopedia of Popular Music and Jazz, 1900-1950*. New Rochelle, N.Y.: Arlington House, 1974.
> Covers the period 1900-1950 and the contributions of singers, orchestra leaders, musicians, arrangers, composers, and lyricists of popular music and jazz. Includes artists who began their careers before 1950, but follows their careers through the early 1970s. Covered here are the categories of Broadway and movie musicals, popular songs for each year, biographies of individuals and representative discographies. The entries are arranged by year, by type of music (Broadway, popular, etc.) and then alphabetically according to artist. Volume 4 is an index for the major categories.

*New Grove Dictionary of Music and Musicians*. 6th ed. Edited by Stanlie Sadie. London: Macmillan, 1980. 20v.
> The largest English language encyclopedia of its kind. An excellent guide to the lives of composers and lists of their works; also includes publishers and performers. Approximately 2,500 contributors. Broad scope articles about music and discussions of musical terms. Separate ethnomusicological index to all entries

dealing with non-Western and folk music. Useful for checking dates of composers and their compositions, titles, and opus numbers.

*New Grove Dictionary of American Music.* Edited by H. Wiley Hitchcock and Stanley Sadie. London: Macmillan, 1986. 4v.
Format same as *New Grove Dictionary of Music.* Authoritative material on jazz, pop, and rock.

Stambler, Irwin. *Encyclopedia of Pop, Rock, and Soul.* New York: St. Martin's Press, 1974.
Includes many terms as well as biographies. Birth and death dates. Lists of winners of various awards (e.g., Grammy, Gold Record, Academy).

Stambler, Irwin, and Grelun Landon. *The Encyclopedia of Folk, Country & Western Music.* 2d ed. New York: St. Martin's Press, 1983.
Alphabetical arrangement of entries on individual performers and performing groups. Articles and biographies, lists of awards, bibliographies.

## Sound Recordings Librarianship

Hoffman, Frank W. *The Development of Library Collections of Sound Recordings.* New York: Marcel Dekker, 1979.
Covers selection, acquisition and arrangement of phonorecords for all types of libraries. Includes a history of sound recordings in libraries, general principles of selection, criteria for selection, useful periodicals and other reviewing sources, equipment, care and preservation, and a basic collection list. Discusses descriptive cataloging, physical arrangement, and classification of sound recordings.

McWilliams, Jerry. *The Preservation and Restoration of Sound Recordings.* Nashville, Tenn.: American Association for State and Local History, 1979.
History of sound recordings and the recording media. Practical advice on storage and use requirements. Extensive bibliography and list of manufacturers and suppliers, along with the major U.S. and Canadian sound archives.

Stevenson, Gordon. "Sound Recordings." *Advances in Librarianship* 5 (1975): 286-320. New York: Academic, 1975.
Various aspects of sound recordings—for example, social and economic aspects, uses, means of control, industry producing and marketing, sound recordings in library collections.

## Dictionaries and Glossaries

Grigg, Carolyn Doub, comp. *Music Translation Dictionary: An English, Czech, Danish, Dutch, French, German, Hungarian, Italian, Polish, Portuguese, Russian, Spanish, Swedish Vocabulary of Musical Terms.* Westport, Conn.: Greenwood Press, 1978.

Polyglot dictionary useful for cataloging sound recordings with non-English labels and jacket notes. A word index leads to the main list (in table form). English is listed first.

Thorin, Suzanne E., and Carole Franklin Vidali, comps. *The Acquisition and Cataloging of Music and Sound Recordings: A Glossary.* Canton, Mass.: Music Library Association, 1984.
Helpful to librarians with little musical training. Current terminology as well as obsolete terms encountered in sources used by music librarians. Also includes a list of sources to be used with the glossary. Part 1 defines terminology used in the bibliographic description of music, while part 2 contains terms specific to sound recordings. Includes words (in English, French, German, and Italian) and abbreviations commonly found on title pages of scores and on labels and containers of sound recordings; also terms that deal with physical description.

# Cataloging and Classification

## LIBRARY OF CONGRESS CATALOGS

Library of Congress. *Music and Phonorecords: A Cumulative List of Works Represented by Library of Congress Printed Cards*, 1953-72. Washington, D.C.: Library of Congress.
LC catalog records, arranged by main entry, with subject index.

Library of Congress. *Music, Books on Music, and Sound Recordings.* Washington, D.C.: Library of Congress, 1973- .
An ongoing listing of works currently cataloged by LC. Contains entries for sound recordings of all kinds, musical, educational, literary, or political. Published semiannually with an annual cumulation (also five-year cumulations).

## BOOKS AND ARTICLES

Bowles, Garrett H. "Cataloging 78 RPM Recordings in the United States." *Brio* 20 (Summer 1983): 8-10.
Describes an attempt to create cataloging standards for archival sound recordings. The standards developed are compatible with *AACR 2* and with the MARC format, and have subsequently been approved by LC for use with their cataloging of their in-house archival collection of sound recordings.

Bratcher, Perry, and Jennifer Smith. *Music Subject Headings.* Lake Crystal, Minn.: Soldier Creek Press, 1988.
Contains all music subject headings found in *Library of Congress Subject Headings*, 10th edition, and its weekly supplements through December 1987. Reflects new format (i.e., BT, NT, RT, UF) of 11th edition. Introduction explains use of music subject headings.

Gaeddert, Barbara Knisely. *The Classification and Cataloging of Sound Recordings, 1933-1980: An Annotated Bibliography.* 2d ed. Philadelphia: Music Library Association, 1981.

Includes articles, theses, and monographs written by music librarians and scholars. Focus is on classification, but many of the listed items also deal with descriptive cataloging. Arranged chronologically, with author and topical indexes.

Kaufman, Judith. *Library of Congress Subject Headings for Recordings of Western Non-Classical Music.* Philadelphia: Music Library Association, 1983.

Argues that LC subject headings have not kept up with the development of Western nonclassical music, and offers an expansion of LC subject headings for music. Lists of suggested headings, some of which are currently not accepted by LC. Subject headings are by genre: country and folk, jazz and blues, pop, religious, and topical music.

_____. *Recordings of Non-Western Music: Subject and Added Entry Access.* Ann Arbor, Mich.: Music Library Association, 1977.

Similar approach as above entry. Points out that in the study of non-Western music, sound recordings are often more important than printed music or books, and subject headings may often be the only means of access to these recordings.

Music Library Association. *Music Cataloging Bulletin.* Ann Arbor, Mich.: MLA, 1970- . Monthly.

Essential for helping catalogers keep up-to-date with LC policy decisions on the cataloging of music and sound recordings. Purpose is to communicate LC changes quickly to music catalogers, making information available sooner than in general LC cataloging publications, such as the *Cataloging Service Bulletin.* Acts as a forum in which music catalogers can discuss problems and solutions, and communicate with LC. Covers cataloging policy decisions and interpretations on rules for descriptive cataloging, LC Subject Headings, LC Classification, authority work, and replies from LC to questions asked about their policy decisions. Also includes recent publications of interest to music and sound recordings catalogers. Annual subject and name index. A must for catalogers in libraries following LC practices and rule interpretations.

Ravilious, C. P. "*AACR2* and Its Implications for Music Cataloging." *Brio* 16 (Spring 1979): 2-12.

Discusses problems that can arise in the descriptive cataloging of music and sound recordings. Outlines changes in cataloging from the first edition of *AACR* to the second, and impact of *AACR 2* on sound recording cataloging.

Redfern, Brian L. *Organising Music in Libraries.* 2 vols. 2d ed., rev. Hamden, Conn.: Linnet Books, 1978.

Volume 1, "Arrangement and Classification" covers physical arrangement of sound recordings. Volume 2, "Cataloging," is a set of guidelines based on *AACR 2.* Compares cataloging codes and international standards.

Richmond, Sam. "Problems in Applying *AACR2* to Music Materials." *Library Resources and Technical Services* 26 (April/June 1982): 204-11.

Discusses problems in applying a generalized code to music and sound recordings, which have properties making them different from books.

Salinger, Florence A., and Eileen Zagon. *Notes for Catalogers: A Sourcebook for Use with AACR2.* White Plains, N.Y.: Knowledge Industry Publications, 1985.
Chapter 6 contains notes for sound recordings.

Simonton, Wesley, Nancy B. Olson, and Phillip Mannie. *A Manual of AACR 2 Examples for Music and Sound Recordings of Music.* Edited by Edward Swanson and Marilyn H. McClaskey. Lake Crystal, Minn.: Soldier Creek Press, 1981.
Particularly useful in pointing out comparisons between *AACR 1* and *AACR 2.* Examples illustrate major rules affecting music materials. Covers access points, uniform titles, and description. Reproduction of sources of information, list of rules used for each example, and explanations. Index to rule numbers.

Smiraglia, Richard P. *Cataloging Music: A Manual for Use with AACR2.* 2d ed. Lake Crystal, Minn.: Soldier Creek Press, 1986.
Deals with rules of descriptive cataloging for music and sound recordings. Intended as a textbook for the beginning music cataloger. Includes LC rule interpretations, and music cataloging decisions issued by the Music Section of the Special Materials Cataloging Department of the Library of Congress. Contains thirty-three complete cataloging examples with a copy of the chief source of information for the item. List of basic reference tools for music and sound recording catalogers, glossary defining music and sound recording cataloging terms, and a concordance of rule interpretations and cataloging decisions.

_____. *Music Cataloging: The Bibliographic Control of Printed and Recorded Music in Libraries.* Englewood, Colo.: Libraries Unlimited, 1989.
A comprehensive guide to cataloging music for students of music librarianship, students of cataloging, and music librarians. The guide covers full cataloging including both manual and electronic systems through descriptive and subject cataloging. Hundreds of examples and illustrations of rule applications are included.

_____. *Shelflisting Music: Guidelines for Use with the Library of Congress Classification: M.* Philadelphia: Music Library Association, 1981.
Guidelines for using LC's M Classification for music scores as well as sound recordings. Flowchart summarizes decision processes for assigning classification numbers. Glossary includes many technical terms used in cataloging and classification of sound recordings.

# 4

ฃฃฃฃฃฃฃฃฃฃฃฃฃฃฃฃฃฃฃฃฃฃฃฃฃฃฃฃฃฃฃฃฃฃฃฃฃฃฃฃฃฃฃฃฃฃฃฃฃฃฃฃฃฃฃฃฃฃฃฃฃฃฃฃฃฃฃฃฃฃฃฃฃฃฃฃฃฃฃฃฃฃฃฃฃฃ

# *Motion Pictures and Videorecordings*

ฃฃฃฃฃฃฃฃฃฃฃฃฃฃฃฃฃฃฃฃฃฃฃฃฃฃฃฃฃฃฃฃฃฃฃฃฃฃฃฃฃฃฃฃฃฃฃฃฃฃฃฃฃฃฃฃฃฃฃฃฃฃฃฃฃฃฃฃฃฃฃฃฃฃฃฃฃฃฃฃฃฃฃฃฃฃ

## DECISION AREAS IN DESCRIPTIVE CATALOGING

## Scope

### DEFINING CHARACTERISTICS OF THE MEDIUM

*AACR 2*'s chapter for motion pictures and videorecordings covers dynamic visual media. The distinguishing characteristic is that they create the illusion of motion, in contrast to static visual media, or still images. The two major media types, motion pictures and videorecordings, appear in a variety of physical formats, such as cartridges, cassettes, and reels. The category is not defined by physical features alone, since dynamic visual media share certain physical characteristics in common with projected media in still images, such as microforms, slides, and filmstrips.

The products in this category can be a single, complete, and finished entity, as well as unedited material, trailers, compilations, and stock shots (shots, incorporated into a film, which were originally made for an earlier film).

### ARCHIVAL MATERIALS

While archival materials are also covered in *AACR 2*, detailed rules for the cataloging of archival motion pictures and videorecordings are provided in a manual by Wendy White-Hensen, *Archival Moving Image Materials* (hereafter referred to as *AMIM*), issued by the Library of Congress.[1] The manual is within the framework of *AACR 2*, and covers "motion pictures and other theatrical releases, shorts, news footage (including television newscasts and theatrical newsreels), trailers, outtakes, screen tests, training films, educational material, commercials, spot announcements, home movies, amateur footage, television broadcasts, and unedited footage" (p. 1). The emphasis of *AMIM* is on descriptive cataloging, rather than name and title access. Selected rules from this manual will be cited in the following discussion.

## TRANSFER OF MEDIA FORMATS

Recent technology has made it relatively simple to transfer a motion picture to a video format. While chapter 7 is used for cataloging both formats, specific rules within the chapter recognize a distinction between motion pictures and videorecordings, and this distinction will determine aspects of the catalog record such as the general material designation and the physical description. While chapter 7 does not address this question directly, the "cardinal rule" earlier in the code makes it clear that the physical format of the item in hand, rather than the form of the original, is to be the starting point of the description.

## PREVIOUS TREATMENT

In *AACR 1*, motion pictures were grouped with filmstrips, another film-based material. Videorecordings, as a relatively new medium, were not included. When *AACR 1*'s chapter on motion pictures was revised in 1974, it was expanded to include a wide range of audiovisual media, and formed the basis for the present MARC Visual Materials format.

# Sources of Information

## ACCESSIBILITY OF THE CHIEF SOURCE

The chief source of information for motion pictures and videorecordings (rule 7.0B1) is the film itself (e.g., title frames); and the container and its label can serve as the chief source only if the container is physically attached to the piece (i.e., "an integral part"), as in a cassette or disc. While external sources such as accompanying textual material (e.g., scripts, shot lists, publicity material) and a physically separate container can also serve as a chief source, this occurs only if information is not available from the item itself. The term *available* means that information is present on the chief source: it does not refer to the availability of playback equipment to read or examine the item. Thus, a key difficulty in implementing the rules for chief source will lie in the procurement of necessary playback equipment.

## LOCATION OF THE CHIEF SOURCE

The title-page tradition is evident to some degree in motion pictures, and bibliographic information is usually found on the title frames. However, difficulties may arise in locating and then identifying the title frames. Unlike the title page of a book, the title frames of a motion picture or video are not as uniformly located at the beginning of the work. Title frames can appear toward the beginning of the film's sequence, but, as is frequently the case with some modern films, the title frames may also appear toward the end, thus requiring the cataloger to scan the entire film.

## CONFLICTING INFORMATION IN THE CHIEF SOURCE

Rule 7.0B2 states that titles are to be taken from the chief source of information. However, the rules do not provide much guidance for the selection of the title when items contain variant forms of the title within the chief source.

## DATA FROM OUTSIDE SOURCES

While in *AACR 2*, information from outside prescribed sources is to be indicated in brackets, *AMIM* departs from traditional cataloging principles in that it does not require that a distinction be made between data recorded from prescribed sources and data recorded from outside sources. As a result, no bracketing of data is required except when a word or phrase is added by the cataloger. Presumably, the rationale for this procedure is based on "the unique circumstances in the production of moving archival images," rather than the difficulty of gaining access to playback equipment (as is the case in chapter 9's relaxed rules for chief source in the case of computer files).

# Title and Statement of Responsibility Area

## DETERMINING THE TITLE PROPER FOR PHRASE TITLES

A situation frequently encountered in cataloging motion pictures and some other audiovisual materials is a phrase title linking a statement of responsibility with the title proper, such as "Walt Disney presents Cinderella." Transcribing the entire phrase results in an unwieldy and perhaps unfamiliar title to the user. While rule 1.1B2 says that such statements of responsibility are to be included in the title if they are an integral part (i.e., grammatically linked), LC rule interpretations recommend that in most instances such phrases not be considered as part of the title proper.[2] Olson recommends instead the use of a uniform title, which would allow "variant" titles to be filed under the more commonly known title and would thus not conflict with *AACR 2* rules.[3]

## SUPPLIED TITLES

In the case of some locally produced items and archival materials, the cataloger may find that there is no title on the item. Rule 7.1B2 instructs the cataloger to create a title as directed in general rule 1.1B7, and also includes more specific instructions for dealing with supplying titles for commercials, and for unedited material and newsfilm. However, more detailed guidelines for this type of material can be found in *AMIM*. For example, *AMIM* suggests the following pattern for television commercials:

[Television commercial--Coca Cola Co.]. Mean Joe Greene

[Television commercial--Miller beer]. Pit crew

If the commercial is one of a number of parts of a unit with a predominant title, it is recorded in a note:

[Title proper]     CBS News special. A Black view of South Africa
[Note]           Includes commercials for Cascade detergent, Duncan Hines cake mix, Chanel No. 5 perfume, Salvo detergent.

The rules also deal with television series and serials that have only number designations rather than episode titles, for example:

[Title proper]     General Hospital. No. 237

## WHAT TO INCLUDE IN THE
## STATEMENT OF RESPONSIBILITY AREA

Rule 7.1F1 allows the cataloger to record statements of reponsibility for persons or corporate bodies who are: (1) credited in the chief source with participation in the production of a film, (e.g., the producer, director, and animator) and (2) considered to be of major importance to the film and to the interests of the cataloging agency.

The statement of responsibility area in a catalog record for a motion picture or videorecording may contain extensive information of a type not normally found in records for book materials. In addition to including intellectual or artistic contributions, attributions can be made for technical production and a wide range of functions relating to publishing and production, since producers and production companies for motion pictures and videos may assume roles involving intellectual and artistic responsibility.

Since *AACR 2*'s rule 7.1F1 allows the cataloger to determine what information goes into the statement of responsibility, guidelines must be established for such decisions. To qualify for inclusion in this area, persons or corporate bodies must be credited with participating in the production of the item and must also be listed in the chief source. The cataloger must then make a judgment as to the importance of the contributors both in terms of the film and of the library and its users. The resulting decision will determine which contributors will be included in the statement of responsibility area, and which will be relegated to the notes area. LC rule interpretations provide some guidance by indicating which types of participants are appropriate for each area. The LC interpretations suggest that producers, directors, and writers be included in the statement of responsibility area, and that other contributors such as animators, artists, film editors, narrators, consultants, and those reponsible for music be included in a note.[4]

## AUTHORSHIP ATTRIBUTION FOR PERFORMERS

*AACR 2* rules relegate performers such as actors and singers to the notes area rather than allowing their contributions to be acknowledged in the statement of responsibility (unless they are involved in the production of the motion picture or video in additional ways). Rule 7.1F1 does not mention performers as possibilities for the statement of responsibility. However, a performer's rendition of a literary or musical work can play a key role in the artistic creation of the performed work. In contrast to *AACR 2*, the ISBD for Nonbook Materials does allow the inclusion of performers in this area.

A clarification of the performer's role would be particularly helpful in cataloging one of the newer forms of media which have emerged since the publication of *AACR 2* – music videos. An LC rule interpretation addresses the role of those responsible for the music in music video, by suggesting that "the name of a rock music performer who is the star of a performance on a videorecording may be given in the statement of responsibility even if his/her responsibility is limited to the performance," because the person's responsibility, though partial, is important in relation to the content of the work.[5]

## PUBLICATION AREA OR STATEMENT OF RESPONSIBILITY AREA?

Another decision area concerns production companies whose responsibilities encompass both "authorship" and publication roles. Should these responsibilities be recorded in the statement of responsibility or the publication area? Rules 7.1F3 and 7.4D1 allow both locations for the name of the production company. Certain corporate bodies that have not been named in the statement of responsibility may appear in the publication area if they serve publishing functions. (See later discussion on publishing roles.)

## PARALLEL TITLES

Because film is a universal medium, there will be instances in which a motion picture is originally produced in one language, and then, through the use of subtitles or dubbing, is made available for a different language audience. Rule 7.1D2 requires that if an original title in another language appears in the chief source, it is to be transcribed as a parallel title. *AMIM* gives further detail in the transcription of parallel titles.

## WORKS LACKING A COLLECTIVE TITLE

Many videos may consist of a collection of items which may or may not be the work of a single person, and which may lack a collective title. The cataloger has the option of describing the motion picture or videorecording as a unit (giving all individual titles), or of making a separate description for each separately titled work.

# Edition Area

## CONCEPT OF EDITION FOR ARCHIVAL MATERIALS

*AACR 2* provides no rules for the edition area that are unique to motion pictures and videorecordings. However, *AMIM* recognizes that in the case of archival materials, there may be "several manifestations of a work, each incomplete, ... which when taken together approximate a single whole item." To address this situation, the *AMIM* rules depart from established cataloging principles by allowing the recording of sets of multiple details. As a result, a single record may include details relating to the original, as well as details relating to later versions with minor changes. In contrast, traditional cataloging practice usually requires that separate catalog records be created for items regarded as separate editions.

*AMIM* goes on to outline a concept of edition for archival moving image material which differs substantially from the traditional concept of edition. A key part of the *AMIM* approach involves the identification of not only the *occurrence* of a change in content but also the *extent* of the change — changes which usually result from the function of editing.

# Publication Area

## DUAL ROLES OF THE PUBLISHER

Some publishing entities serve dual roles in that they are responsible for both publishing activities as well as activities relating to the artistic or intellectual creation of the film or videorecording. Therefore, as noted earlier, a publishing entity may have already been named in the statement of responsibility area. Rule 7.4D1 directs the cataloger to record in the publication area the name of a publisher, distributor, releasing agency, production agency, or producer not named earlier in the statements of responsibility.

## STATEMENT OF PUBLISHING FUNCTION

The rules allow the cataloger to add a statement of function, such as *distributor* or *production company* to the name of the publishing entity. Further direction is given in rule 1.4E. This statement is added if the function has not already been made clear from the context. In determining which term is appropriate, the cataloger will need to become familiar with the types of responsibility associated with functions such as production, distribution, and releasing agency. *AACR 2*'s glossary gives definitions for the above- named terms, but for further background, it may be necessary to consult reference sources.

## WHICH DATE?

A motion picture or video may contain a number of associated dates such as the dates of publication, distribution, release, and original production. *AACR 2* informs the cataloger which dates are recorded in the publication area and which in the note area. Dates of publication, distribution, and release, are recorded in the publication area (7.4F1). If a date of original production differs from the date of publication, and so on, it can be recorded in the note area (optional 7.4F2).

The date of production of a motion picture or video may differ significantly from the date of its release (or distribution). An LC rule interpretation offers guidance in recording copyright dates when there is a time lag of two years or more between the release and copyright dates, and prescribes that the note area be used if a date of original production differs by more than two years from the dates of publication/distribution or copyright.[6]

## DETERMINING THE PLACE OF PUBLICATION

*AMIM* remarks that "it is extremely difficult, time-consuming, and often not relevant to designate a city as the origin of a moving image work" and that, in many instances, a motion picture is released in several different cities simultaneously. In *AACR 1*, the place of publication was required only for foreign films. *AMIM* requires only the name of the country of original release (p. 88). In *AACR 2*, however, the provision for publication data for motion pictures and videorecordings is consistent with the general rules for all media, and thus some account must be made of the place of publication.

## MULTIPLE PUBLICATION FUNCTIONS

The creation of a film usually requires a collective effort involving many different kinds of authorship. Likewise, the "publication" of a film can involve many different kinds of publishing responsibilities, such as production, distribution, release, and manufacture. In some cases, the roles of authorship and publication may be blended, as in the case of many producers. Sorting out these types of publishing responsibilities can often present a challenge to the cataloger. Reference sources may assist in familiarizing the cataloger with different types of responsibility functions in the motion picture and videorecording industry.

In formulating the publication area in motion pictures and videorecordings, the cataloger may frequently find several companies in the chief source of information, each of which is involved in the publishing of the item. *AMIM* states that, for films, the agency which most nearly matches the function of publisher for books is the distributor or releasing company. For television, it is the network or local broadcasting station (p 80). *AMIM* provides a list of definitions for terms used in describing the distribution and broadcast of moving image materials. *AACR 2*'s rules recognize the functions of publisher, distributor, releasing agency, and production, and the glossary contains helpful definitions for many of these functions. The problem for the cataloger is that these functions are often not explicitly stated on the item.

## PARENT COMPANY OR SUBSIDIARY?

Due to recent trends in mergers and acquisitions, publication information for motion pictures, as with many other media, may include the name of a parent company along with that of its subsidiaries. Intner suggests that "a useful rule of thumb for catalogers is to transcribe the name or names of those bodies from whom additional copies of the item would be purchased were they desired. A library would not go to Gulf & Western (the parent company) to buy or lease a Columbia Pictures (the subsidiary) release." She recommends that the cataloger become familiar with reference tools that provide trade information to identify the relationships among motion picture and video industries.[7]

## VIDEO COPIES OF MOTION PICTURES

Another problem involving the publication area occurs with videos that are copies of motion pictures. Such items often list publication information relevant to the original version as well as the manufacturer, distributor, and so on, of the video version. LC and OCLC have come up with different approaches to this problem. LC has decided to catalog the original and use notes to describe the video format—a procedure similar to LC's policy for microforms, and one that runs counter to the basic *AACR 2* philosophy of cataloging the item in hand. Such a procedure results in placing the physical description of the motion picture in the physical description area, even though the GMD is "videorecordings"—a situation that might be confusing to the user.

OCLC allows its members the choice of treating a locally reproduced videorecording as a copy as with LC's procedure, or, alternatively, to input a new record for the videotape copy. In this latter case, the title, statement of responsibility, and publication information would be that of the original, but the GMD would be "videorecording" and the physical description would be that of the video copy. The original format would be indicated in a note (e.g., "Originally issued as super 8 mm. film cartridge"), and a note would also be given to indicate the recording date and the fact that the copy was made with permission.[8]

Multiple dates in video copies can also present a problem. *AACR 2*'s 7.4F1 and 7.4F2 indicate that the publication date of the video should be given in the publication area, and the dates relating to the original motion picture in the notes. In reality, however, there may be only two dates given in the prescribed sources—the original movie copyright, and the copyright for the packaging and art work of the video. In this case it may be difficult to determine if the latter date is the same as the actual publication date for the video.

## VIDEO COPIES OF TV BROADCASTS

A related situation involves videorecordings that are copied directly from television broadcasts. OCLC recommends treating these copies as unpublished materials "because broadcasting does not constitute publication in a legal sense or from the standpoint of cataloging theory." OCLC members may either edit an existing record for a commercially available video version of the television program, or, alternately, input a new record for the off-air copy. In this latter instance, the publication area contains only the year of the recording, and the physical description reflects the video copy. Notes are added indicating that the copy was made under license and naming the television station that broadcast the program.

## LOCALLY PRODUCED UNPUBLISHED ITEMS

Unpublished videos, or noncommercial, single-copy videos, are becoming as common as unpublished sound recordings, because of the increase in less expensive, individual-oriented video equipment. Libraries might have items such as videos of lectures, instructional materials produced in-house for staff use, local historical events, theses and dissertations in video form, or works of video art created by local residents—all of which typically contain little or no "publication" information. Originally, *AACR 2* provided no rules governing the publication area for unpublished motion pictures or videos, or for materials in general. Later, revised rules 1.4C8, 1.4D9, and 1.4F9 were added; these prescribe that no place of publication or name of publisher is recorded for unpublished items, and that only the date of production (creation, manufacture, recording) is recorded. Explicitly mentioned are "unedited or unpublished film or video materials [and] stock shots." The dates of unedited or unpublished film or video material and stock shots are formulated according to a new rule developed for manuscript material (7.4F3).

## Physical Description Area

### PROBLEMS OF TERMINOLOGY

In describing the physical format of motion pictures and videorecordings, the cataloger encounters problems found in other chapters of *AACR 2*, namely, the need to become familiar with technical characteristics and terminology peculiar to the medium and not accounted for in the *AACR 2* rules or glossary.

### FORMATS

Producers often issue the same work in a number of different physical formats, for example, as a cassette tape and as a reel. If an item being cataloged is available in two or more formats, the cataloger is to give the physical description of the format in hand according to rule 1.5A3. Optionally, a note can be made to describe other formats in which the item is available (1.7B16). Rule 1.7B20 is used to give details of other formats in the library.

In the original *AACR 2*, the cataloger could either use the term "videorecording" as the SMD and indicate the alternative form in the note area, or make a separate catalog record for each format.

A third option was also listed: that of using "multilevel description," as outlined in rule 13.6, an option not commonly followed by most cataloging agencies. It allowed the descriptive information to be divided into two or more levels, with the first level indicating information relating to the multipart item as a whole, and the second level giving information relating to an individual part.

Accordingly, the cataloger was faced with the question of whether to describe the item in hand in a generic manner that encompasses all formats, or to provide separate records for each physical format. As we have seen, a related problem occurs when the library or film user "copies" the content of one medium onto another, as is commonly the case with videorecordings of motion pictures. In both cases, the intellectual and artistic content remains the same, while the physical characteristics and publishing details have been substantially altered. *AACR 2* has addressed this issue only in part, and problem areas remain for the cataloger. While there are obvious practical advantages to "generic" descriptions, there are equally compelling reasons to provide the user with information needed for playback of the item.

## ADDITION OF A TECHNICAL SPECIFICATION

In the original *AACR 2*, a trade name or other technical specification of associated hardware could be added to the SMD for videorecordings. This occurred if the use of the item was conditional upon this information and if it was only available in that particular form. Both conditions had to apply, if the trade name was to be given in the physical description area; otherwise, the trade name appeared in the note area.

In considering whether playback of the item was limited to a particular system, the cataloger had to keep in mind that initially, a newly introduced format may be marketed for use with only one playback system, but in time, competing manufacturers may develop compatible equipment for this format. A good example is that of "U-Matic" cassettes, which at one time were capable of playback on only a single system. The trend has been toward the emergence of a certain number of industry standards for videos and the development of formats that are no longer limited to the playback equipment of a single commercial firm.

Brand names had to be specified in the physical description area if the item was "only available in that particular form." The term *available* here referred to what is obtainable from distributors. If the video was available in varying formats, this information was placed in the notes.

The Library of Congress chose to place brand name information in the notes area in every case (using a single record with a generic physical description area), while some catalogers routinely placed this information in the physical description area, in order to provide greater visibility to the patron less likely to read the notes area, or to ensure that vital playback information is not lost if the note area is omitted in an abbreviated record display.

In *AACR 2*, 1988 rev., the addition of a technical specification to the SMD has been discontinued. In the new rule 7.5B1, the trade name is no longer part of the physical description area; instead, the rule states that this specification is given in a note. The physical description note (7.7B10) is used for this purpose.

## CHANGING TECHNOLOGY AND NEW FORMATS

Several of the problems in using *AACR 2* to create the physical description area for videos result from the rapidly changing technology in videos and their associated hardware, and from chapter 7's lack of specificity in terminology. This lack of specificity is partially a result of technological advances since the writing of *AACR 2*, but even specific terms already in use when the code was written are not included. The paucity of definitions becomes particularly evident when chapter 7 is compared with chapter 2. The chapter for books and printed materials gives nearly eight pages of rules and examples in the physical description area, in contrast to the three pages in the chapter for motion pictures and videorecordings. Many terms included in chapter 7, such as *videocartridge* and *videocassette*, are not to be found in the glossary.

One example of a change in the rules arising from advances in technology can be found in the cataloging of laser videodiscs composed of still frames. With this format, the statement of total playing time is no longer appropriate. The revised rules allow duration to be given in terms of frames for videodiscs consisting of still images.

Videos available in stereo pose a similar problem. Information about this format could be placed in the notes area using rule 7.7B10a (physical description, sound characteristics), but would be more readily noticed by the user of the catalog if placed in the physical description area. Chapter 6 for sound recordings requires the statement of number of sound tracks to be included in this area (6.5C7), and this might serve as an appropriate model for videos.

### DURATION: How and When to Record

If the playing time appears on the item, it is given as stated (including seconds, if so described on the item; the original *AACR 2* allowed seconds to be given only if the playing time was less than five minutes). If the playing time is not stated on the item, and is not readily ascertainable, an *AACR 2* option allows an approximate time to be given, but LC will not apply this option. It can be argued, however, that, in view of the particular importance of this information to the user, an approximate time, like an approximate date, is better than no statement at all, and that the term *ca.* in the approximate statement alerts the user to the fact that the time is not definite.

An option is also provided, in the case of multipart items with uniform playing times, to give either the time for each work or the total duration.

In the original *AACR 2*, directions for recording the extent of playing time for motion pictures and videos were given in rule 7.5B2. Revised rules now give instructions for playing time in the general chapter.

## OTHER PHYSICAL DETAILS
### When to Record

Details such as special projection characteristics, sound, color, and projection or playing speed can be given "as appropriate," in the "other physical details" section, according to rule 7.5C. In deciding whether such information should be included, the cataloger should consider if the information is important to the user, whether or not such information would be more appropriate in a note, and whether the characteristic is standard for the item. A working knowledge of the terminology associated with special formats and their requirements will be helpful. For example, in considering terms for special projection requirements (e.g., *Cinerama, Panavision, multiprojector*), and whether the film is "anamorphic, techniscopic, stereoscopic, or multiscreen" (7.5C2), the cataloger may need to consult appropriate reference sources or glossaries.

While reels and cassettes may be relatively standardized in terms of their projection requirements, cartridges will require particular attention on the part of the cataloger. In deciding whether to record such information, the cataloger might keep in mind not only the types of equipment on which playback equipment is possible, but the equipment that is likely to be available to the users in a given setting.

## STANDARDIZATION OF FORMAT CHARACTERISTICS

As technology changes and as formats become more uniform, it is easier to ascertain which physical aspects of a format are standard for its kind. A contrast can be made between rules in chapter 6 for sound recordings — a medium that was relatively standardized at the writing of *AACR 2*, and the chapter for motion pictures and videorecordings. In chapter 6, several rules set specific standards for various physical characteristics (e.g., groove characteristics, number of tracks, dimensions of cartridges), requiring the cataloger to state such information only if it varies from the standard given. No such specific standards are given or are allowed to be assumed in the rules for the physical description for videos.

## ADDITIONAL CHARACTERISTICS FOR
## ARCHIVAL MATERIALS

In *AMIM,* far greater detail for physical characteristics can be recorded, for example, for videorecordings, one can specify playback mode and whether the item is VHS or Beta. In addition, *AMIM* allows three additional elements to the physical description area: generation, film base, and number of copies or copy number (p. 109).

## OCLC MARC AUDIOVISUAL FORMAT

In OCLC MARC, motion pictures are included in the Audiovisual Format. While the 300 variable field provides for information found in *AACR 2*'s physical description area, the fixed field 007 provides for physical description information in coded form, and provides additional detail not found in textual or uncoded form. Separate 007 fields are provided for motion pictures and videorecordings. Codes for motion pictures include indication of information such as whether the motion picture has used a standard or special presentation format, and the medium for sound. Codes for videorecordings include an indication of the videorecording format (e.g., Beta, VHS, U-Matic), and the medium for sound.

The "Leng" fixed field provides a code specifically for indicating running time for motion pictures and videorecordings. Length is recorded in minutes and is recorded as a three digit number (e.g., 027).

## Note Area

Consideration should be given to the special relevance that the following notes have for motion pictures and videorecordings:

Statement of responsibility—This note can be used to indicate cast members, such as featured players, performers, narrators, and presenters. Credits can also be given for persons other than the cast who have contributed to the artistic and technical production of the motion picture or videorecording. (Remember that rule 7.1F allowed the cataloger the choice of assigning ascription to either the statement of responsibility or the note area, depending on the importance to the users of the catalog.) Persons who have made only a minor contribution, such as assistants and associates, should not be included. Each name or group of names should be prefaced with a statement indicating their function, for example, "Script, Hiawatha Brown; commentator, Helmar Cooper" (7.7B6).

Edition and history—This information can be especially important in the case of films based on previous films or books, for example, "Based on the short story by Robert Holmes" (7.7B7). It is also useful to note the occurrence of films issued in multiple releases with different titles or sound tracks.[9] Reference sources listed later in this chapter can be helpful in uncovering information of this kind.

Publication, distribution—Information can be given such as a date of original production that differs from the date of publication, a situation not uncommon in films. (Note that for unpublished materials, the date of production, i.e., of creation, manufacture, recording, is given in the publication area.) In the OCLC Audiovisual Format, fixed field 033 (Capture Date and Place) identifies the date and place of recording or filming in coded form. In this note the cataloger can also give the country of original release if it is not stated or implied elsewhere in the description (7.7B9).

Physical description—In this note, considerable detail can be provided at the cataloger's discretion (7.7B10). This note should be used to record the type of equipment necessary to play or project the item, if this information has not been given earlier in the record. Since the physical description area does not provide a way to distinguish between Beta and VHS videocassettes, this important information should be recorded in the physical description note.[10] Some physical characteristics can be indicated that the cataloger decided not to give in the physical description area, or that go beyond the level of detail allowed in that area, especially if the item has characteristics not standard for the format.

Summary—A note giving a brief description of the content can be especially valuable for motion pictures and videorecordings, since these materials cannot be "browsed" (7.7B17). See titles later in this chapter for selected reference sources giving plot summaries for motion pictures.

In the OCLC Audiovisual Format, the fixed field code "Technique" indicates the means of creating motion used for motion pictures and videorecordings. Thus, animated films can be distinguished from live action. In *AACR 2*, indication of technique is not specifically addressed, and such information if included would be entered in the note area.

*AMIM* provides far greater detail for notes. The directives given should be useful for nonarchival materials as well. There are suggestions given for indicating awards, censorship, rating designations (e.g., "rated X"), references to published reviews, as well as detailed guidelines for statements of responsibility.

# Choice of Access Points

## DIFFUSE RESPONSIBILITY

Most motion pictures reflect the intellectual and artistic effort of a large number of individuals or "creators," each responsible for a different area of creative activity. The screenwriter responsible for the plot of the film, as well as the director responsible for key decision areas of artistic content, both play essential roles. The producer provides financial and creative support as well as general managerial direction. The cinematographer and score composer also provide creative support. In addition, the cast is responsible for artistic interpretation of both the scripts and the director's creative suggestions. This diffuse responsibility leads to problems when the cataloger tries to establish a primary intellectual or artistic area of creativity, and to identify the individual chiefly responsible for the creative content of the work.

Martha Yee has given consideration to similar questions of authorship in nonbook materials; her analysis of authorship patterns recognizes that the creation of motion pictures and videorecordings "involves carrying out multiple functions, and these functions may be carried out by different people and corporate bodies."[11]

Main entry under corporate body for motion pictures and videorecordings is possible if the responsibility of the performing group extends beyond the performance of the work, and includes responsibilities such as production, direction, and scriptwriting. A good example is the Beatles' motion picture "The Yellow Submarine."[12]

## TREATMENT IN EARLIER CODES

Earlier cataloging codes (e.g., *AACR 1*) established special main entry rules for motion pictures, and prescribed automatic title main entry, on the grounds that such "diffuse responsibility" made it impossible for the cataloger to determine primary responsibility. While a few codes acknowledged the role of the director and other creators, the primary standards adopted by most libraries dismissed the problem of film authorship by requiring main entry under title for all motion pictures. This approach discredited the efforts of individuals solely responsible for the creation of the content of media such as 8mm films or home videorecordings.

In contrast, *AACR 2*'s approach is to treat films no differently from other materials. The rules prescribe title main entry in the majority of cases where authorship is diffuse, while allowing main entry under author for cases in which one individual is clearly responsible for the primary content of the work.

Added entries provide additional means of access to key persons involved in the making of a film. Ideally, a catalog should contain access points under each name that users might associate with the work; for example, producers, directors, screenwriters, principal photographers, and principal actors of the films. Such an ideal, however, is rarely found in bibliographic records for motion pictures, nor, in most cases, would such detail be desirable.[13] Thus, supplementary sources providing additional access routes and sources of information can play an important role in serving the user with information needs relating to films. These supplementary sources are described later in this chapter.

The cataloger should keep in mind that, although many "authors" of film will not be acknowledged by main or added entry access points, there is room for attributing these roles through the statement of responsibility and notes areas. *AACR 2* gives a great deal of leeway in deciding which authors should be included in the statement of responsibility area and which in a note.

## ADDED ENTRY HEADINGS

A group of film and television cataloging experts has developed a list of relator terms to be used for added entries in the cataloging of archival moving picture images. Examples such as "Doe, John, direction," "Brown, William B., production," and similar relator terms would appear after personal names in the MARC 700 field, in subfield "e." The definitions that accompany the list of terms provide assistance in sorting out the different types of responsibilities and functions that play a role in the creation of motion picture and television media.[14]

# NOTES

[1]Wendy White-Hensen, comp., *Archival Moving Image Materials: A Cataloging Manual* (Washington, D.C.: Library of Congress, Motion Picture, Broadcasting and Recorded Sound Division, 1984).

[2]*Cataloging Service Bulletin* 13 (Summer 1981): 15.

[3]Nancy B. Olson, *Cataloging of Audiovisual Materials: A Manual Based on AACR 2*, 2d ed., ed. Edward Swanson and Sheila S. Intner (Mankato, Minn.: Minnesota Scholarly Press, 1985), 31-32.

[4]*Cataloging Service Bulletin* 13 (Summer 1981): 15; 22 (Winter 1982): 21.

[5]*Cataloging Service Bulletin* 36 (Spring 1987): 12.

[6]Sheila S. Intner, "Cataloging Motion Pictures and Videorecordings Using *AACR2* Chapter 7," in *Policy and Practice in Bibliographic Control of Nonbook Media*, ed. Sheila S. Intner and Richard P. Smiraglia (Chicago: American Library Association, 1987), 133.

[7]Ibid.

[8]OCLC, *Audiovisual Media Format*, 2d ed. (Dublin, Ohio: OCLC, 1986). All subsequent references to this format are from this edition.

[9]Intner, "Cataloging Motion Pictures," 135.

[10]Ibid.

[11]Martha Yee, "Integration of Nonbook Materials in *AACR 2*," *Cataloging & Classification Quarterly* 3 (Summer 1983): 4.

[12]Intner, "Cataloging Motion Pictures," 136.

[13]Michael Gorman, "Cataloging and Classification of Film Study Material," in *Film Study Collections: A Guide to Their Development and Use*, ed. Nancy Allen (New York: Frederick Ungar Pub. Co., 1979), 116.

[14]*Cataloging Service Bulletin* 31 (Winter 1986): 71-75.

# DESCRIPTIVE CATALOGING EXAMPLES

## Items to Be Cataloged

1. Motion picture reel

One motion picture reel, 16 millimeters; 26 minutes, sound, color. Includes guide.

Title frames:

Professional Career Series, no. 5
University of Michigan / School of Information & Library Studies
Presents
The Information Professional: Education for the Future

Produced and Distributed by
Pro-Video Productions, Inc.          c1987
Ann Arbor, Michigan

Directed by: Edward Aardvark
Script by: Consuela de los Tardes
Photography by: Kitty Line
Narrated by: Merv Goliath
Technical Advisor: Julie Tornado

Label attached to film can:
Michigan Information Professional
Duration: 26 minutes

Guide:
Students, faculty and staff from the University of Michigan School of Information & Library Studies tell about the program for education of information professionals at their school.

2. Motion picture loop

4 "super 8" loop cartridges

8 study guides for the entire topic

1 study guide for each of the four individual topics

1 teacher's manual (28 pages) in box

The cartridges have the following labels:

1. The Vietnamese Americans

2. The Chinese Americans

3. The Japanese Americans

4. The Korean Americans

Each loop is in an enclosed cartridge and has notes on its case. The notes indicate that the grade level is junior high, and that each of the film loops has a duration of four and a half minutes, is in color, and has no sound. The set as a whole describes the contributions that Asian Americans have made to American society.

Title frames for each loop and on box cover:

> Minorities in America Series
> THE ASIAN AMERICANS
> Social Sciences Association
>
> Produced by Phoenix Multimedia
> Santa Ana, Calif. 1987.

Title frame and label of each loop also include the title specific to the loop, e.g.:

> 1. THE VIETNAMESE AMERICANS

3. Motion picture cartridge

One film cartridge, 12 minutes in length, sound, color, super 8mm.

From brochure: Describes scenic, historic, and recreational attractions in Michigan. Includes information about hotels, motels, resorts, and restaurants.

Title frames:

> Gateway Productions
> Presents
>
> Tourmaster Films
> A Series for the Motor Traveler

> 6725
> DISCOVER MICHIGAN
>
> c1985 Gateway Productions
>
> Consultants
> Arthur Henley
> Michele Horner

Front label of container:

Gateway Productions
Saginaw MI

Tourmaster Films
A Series for the Motor Traveler

DISCOVER MICHIGAN          6725
Super 8mm Color

Back label of container:

Tourmaster Films          67825
Gateway Productions Saginaw MI

Discovering Michigan

4. Videotape

One videotape cassette, VHS, color, sound, 14 minutes, ½ inch tape.
The video is designed to introduce students to the use of subject heading and key-word searching in the University of Houston's card and online catalogs.

Title frames:

Searching by Subject
in the Library's Catalogs

Written and Directed
by Carolyn O. Frost, Ph.D.

Associate Professor
University of Michigan

Produced by
Houston Audiovisual Services, Inc.

c1985

This production was made possible by a grant from
The Council on Library Resources

Student played by Cherie Sutton

Videocontainer label:

Subject Searching
14 min.
Frost

## 1. MOTION PICTURE REEL

University of Michigan. School of Information & Library Studies.
    The information professional [motion picture] : education for
the future / University of Michigan, School of Information &
Library Studies. -- Ann Arbor, Mich. : Produced and distributed
by Pro-Video Productions, c1987.
    1 film reel (26 min.) : sd., col. ; 16 mm. + 1 guide. --
(Professional career series ; no. 5)

    Title on container: Michigan information professional.
    Credits: Director, Edward Aardvark ; script, Consuela de los
Tardes ; photography, Kitty Line ; narrator, Merv Goliath.
    Students, faculty and staff from the University of Michigan
School of Information & Library Studies tell about the program
for education of information professionals at their school.

    I. Pro-Video Productions.   II. Title.   III. Series.

```
OCLC MARC Tagging

Type: g  Bib lvl: m  Govt pub:      Lang: eng  Source: d  Leng: 026
         Enc lvl: I  Type mat: m  Ctry: miu  Dat tp: s  MEBE: 1
Tech: 1  Mod rec:            Accomp mat: r
Desc: a  Int lvl: f  Dates: 1987,

1  040     xxx $c xxx
2  007     m $b r $c  $d c  $e a  $f a  $g a  $ h d $i u
3  110 2   University of Michigan. $b School of Information &
Library Studies.
4  245 14  The information professional $h motion picture : $b
education for the future / $c University of Michigan,
School of Information & Library Studies.
5  260     Ann Arbor, Mich. : $b Produced and distributed by
Pro-Video Productions, $c c1987.
6  300     1 film reel (26 min.) : $b sd., col. ; $c 16 mm. + $e 1
guide.
7  440  0 Professional career series ; $v no. 5
8  500     Title on container: Michigan information professional.
9  508     Director, Edward Aardvark ; script, Consuela de los
Tardes ; photography, Kitty Line.
10 511 3  Narrator, Merv Goliath.
11 520     Students, faculty and staff from the University of
Michigan School of Information & Library Studies tell about the
program for education of information professionals at their school.
12 710 21 Pro-Video Productions.
```

*AACR 2* applicable rules

**7.0B1:** Chief source is film itself, title frames.

**Area 1**

**7.1B1:** Title proper as in 1.1B. The title proper on the item includes the name of the producer ("presenter"). A strict interpretation of 1.1B2 would result in recording the statement of responsibility imbedded in the title proper. The LC rule interpretation for rule 7.1B1 does not regard such "credits" which precede or follow the title in the chief source as part of the title proper, even though the language used integrates the credits with the title.

**7.1C1:** GMD as in 1.1C1, is *motion picture*, added after title and enclosed in brackets.

**7.1F1:** Record statements of responsibility for persons credited with film's production in the chief source and considered to be of major importance to the film. The cataloger must decide which persons or corporate bodies should be included in statement of responsibility. What is included will vary with the judgment of the individual cataloger and the needs of the constituency served by the library.

**Area 4**

**7.4C1:** Record place of publication and distribution as in 1.4C.

**7.4D1:** Record name of publisher not named in statement of responsibility. If the producer's name had been given in the statement of responsibility, it would be included in shortened form in the publication area.

**1.4D3:** Do not omit phrases indicating function performed by publisher.

**7.4F1:** Record date of publication as in 1.4F.

**1.4F6:** Give copyright date in absence of publication date.

**Area 5**

**7.5B1:** Record number of physical units and SMD *film reel*.

**7.5B2:** Give playing time as in 1.5B4.

**1.5B4:** Give playing time as stated on item.

**7.5C3:** Indicate sound with abbreviation *sd*.

**7.5C4:** Indicate color with abbreviation *col*.

**7.5D2:** Give gauge of motion picture in millimeters.

**7.5E1:** Record name of accompanying material.

## Area 6

**7.6B1:**     Record series statement as in 1.6.

**1.6G1:**     Record numbering of item within series.

## Area 7

**7.7B4:**     Note titles on item other than title proper.

**7.7B6:**     List persons not named in statement of responsibility. Do not include persons making only minor contribution.

**7.7B17:**    Give brief summary of content.

## Choice of access points

**21.1B2a:**   Corporate body main entry. Work emanating from corporate body, deals with the corporate body itself. Describes procedures and operations, staff, and resources. LC rule interpretation explains broad interpretation of term *administrative nature* and notes that some works in category 21.1B2a may be for purposes of public relations. [CSB 12 (Spring 1981): 22-23].

**21.1B4:**    Enter under heading for subordinate unit, since unit's responsibility is stated prominently.

**21.30J:**    Added entry under title if main entry is under corporate body.

An added entry could be given for the variant title, if considered important.

**21.30L:**    Added entry under series; optionally, add numeric designation.

Added entries could also be given for individuals named in the statement of responsibility or in the credits who are considered important as access points.

## Form of heading

**24.13, type 5:**

The name of a university school that simply indicates a particular field of study is entered as a subheading of the name of the parent body.

## 2. MOTION PICTURE LOOP

The Asian Americans [motion picture] / Social Sciences
   Association ; produced by Phoenix Multimedia. -- Santa
   Ana, Calif. : Phoenix, 1987.
   4 film loops (4 min., 30 sec. each) : si., col. ; super 8 mm. +
12 study guides + 1 teacher's manual. -- (Minorities in America
series)

   Audience level: junior high grades.
   Includes 8 study guides for the general topic, and one guide for
each of the 4 sections.
   Describes contributions made by Asian Americans to American
society.
   Contents: The Vietnamese Americans -- The Chinese Americans -- The Japanese Americans -- The Korean Americans.

   I. Social Sciences Association.   II. Series.


OCLC MARC Tagging

Type: g  Bib lvl: m  Govt pub:    Lang: eng Source: d  Leng: 018
         Enc lvl: I  Type mat: m Ctry: cau Dat tp: s  MEBE: 0
Tech: 1  Mod rec:          Accomp mat: r
Desc: a  Int lvl: c  Dates 1987,

1  040     xxx $c xxx
2  007     m $b c  $c  $d c $e a $f $g $h b $i n
3  049     xxxx
4  245 04  The Asian Americans $h motion picture / $c Social
Sciences Association ; produced by Phoenix Multimedia.
5  260     Santa Ana, Calif. : $b Phoenix, $c 1987.
6  300     4 film loops (4 min., 30 sec. each) : $b si., col. ; $c
super 8 mm. + $e 12 study guides + 1 teacher's manual.
6  440 0   Minorities in America series
7  500     Includes 8 study guides for the general topic, and
one guide for each of the 4 sections.
500        Audience level: junior high grades.
8  505 0   The Vietnamese Americans -- The Chinese Americans -- The
Japanese Americans -- The Korean Americans.
9  520     Describes contributions made by Asian Americans to
American society.
10 710 21  Social Sciences Association.

### *AACR 2* applicable rules

**7.0B1:**    Title frames as chief source.

**Area 1**

**7.1B1:**    Title proper. The title given is one appropriate to the item being cataloged (i.e., not for components within the item or for the series of which it is a part).

**7.1C1:**    GMD.

**7.1F1:**    Statements of responsibility considered important. The statement for Phoenix could be omitted from the statement of responsibility area, if desired.

**Area 4**

**7.4C1:**    Record place of publication.

**7.4D1:**    Although rule says to record publishers not named in the statement of responsibility, this does not mean that the cataloger should not record publishers who *have* been named. Instead, they are included, as per 1.4D4, in shortened form.

**1.4D4:**    Give publisher's name in shortened form if already named in statement of responsibility.

**7.4F1:**    Date of publication.

**Area 5**

**7.5B1:**    Number of physical units and SMD *film loop.*

**7.5B2:**    Playing time as in 1.5B4.

**1.5B4:**    If parts of multipart item have uniform playing time, give playing time followed by *each.*

**7.5C3:**    Indicate *si.* if silent.

**7.5C4:**    Color.

**7.5D2:**    Gauge in millimeters. State if super 8 mm.

**7.5E1:**    Accompanying material.

**Area 6**

**7.6B1:**    Series statement.

**Area 7**

**7.7B11:** Indicate details about the accompanying material not noted in the physical description area.

**7.7B14:** Audience level if stated on item.

**7.7B17:** Summary.

**7.7B18:** List individual works included in item.

**Choice of access points**

**21.1C3:** Entry under title for works emanating from corporate body but not falling into categories in 21.1B2 and not of personal authorship.

**21.30E:** Give added entry for publisher named in chief source whose responsibility extends beyond publishing.

**21.30L:** Series added entry.

## 3. MOTION PICTURE CARTRIDGE

Discover Michigan [motion picture] / Gateway Productions. --
Saginaw, MI : Gateway, c1985.
1 film cartridge (12 min.) : sd., col. ; super 8 mm. --
(Tourmaster films ; 6725)

Title on container: Discovering Michigan.
Credits: Consultants, Arthur Henley, Michele Horner.
Describes scenic, historic, and recreational attractions in
Michigan. Includes information about hotels, motels, resorts, and
restaurants.

I. Gateway Productions.   II. Series.

OCLC MARC Tagging

Type: g  Bib lvl: m  Govt pub:      Lang: eng  Source: d  Leng: 012
          Enc lvl: I  Type mat: m  Ctry: miu  Dat tp: s  MEBE: 0
Tech: 1  Mod rec:          Accomp mat:
Desc: a  Int lvl:    Dates: 1985,

1    040    xxx $c xxx
2    007    m $b c $c   $d c $e a $f a $g b $h  b $i u
3    245 00 Discover Michigan $h motion picture / $c
Gateway Productions.
4    260    Saginaw, MI : $b Gateway, $c c1985.
5    300    1 film cartridge (12 min.) : $b sd., col. ; $c super 8
mm.
6    440  0 Tourmaster films ; $v 6725
7    500    Title on container: Discovering Michigan.
8.   508    Consultants, Arthur Henley, Michele Horner.
9    520    Describes scenic, historic, and recreational attractions
in Michigan. Includes information about hotels, motels, resorts,
and restaurants.
10   710 21  Gateway Productions.

### *AACR 2* applicable rules

**7.0B1:**    Title frames as chief source.

**Area 1**

**7.1B1:**    Title proper appropriate to item being cataloged. See comments in
              example #1 for treatment of publisher's name included in title.

**7.1C1:**    GMD.

**7.1F1:**    Statements of responsibility considered important.

**Area 4**

**7.4C1:**    Place of publication.

**1.4D4:**    Name of publisher given in shortened form.

**7.4F1:**    Date.

**Area 5**

**7.5B1:**    Number of physical units and SMD.

**7.5B2:**    Playing time as in 1.5B4.

**1.5B4:**    Give playing time if readily ascertainable.

**7.5C3:**    Sound.

**7.5C4:**   Color.

**7.5D2:**   State if super 8mm.

**Area 6**
**7.6B1:**   Series statement.

**1.6D1:**   Include other title information only if it provides valuable information about the series. Some might feel that the subtitle provides additional information important enough to warrant its inclusion.

**1.6G1:**   Numbering.

**Area 7**
**7.7B4:**   Titles other than the title proper.

**7.7B6:**   Statements of responsibility.

**7.7B17:**   Summary.

**Choice of access points**
**21.1C3:**   Title main entry; no corporate body categories; no personal author.

**21.30E:**   Publisher added entry.

**21.30J:**   Could have added entry for variant title if considered important.

**21.30L:**   Series added entry.


## 4. VIDEORECORDING

Frost, Carolyn O.
   Searching by subject in the library's catalogs [videorecording] / written and directed by Carolyn O. Frost. -- [Houston, Tex.] : Produced by Houston Audiovisual Services, Inc., c1985.
   1 videocassette (14 min.) : sd., col. ; ½ in.

Title on container: Subject searching.
Cast: Cherie Sutton.
VHS.
Designed to introduce students to the use of subject heading and key-word searching in the University of Houston's card and online catalogs.

I. Houston Audiovisual Services.   II. Title.

OCLC MARC Tagging

```
Type: g  Bib lvl: m  Govt pub:      Lang: eng  Source:d  Leng: 014
          Enc lvl: I  Type mat: v  Ctry: txu  Dat tp: s  MEBE:1
Tech: 1   Mod rec:           Accomp mat:
Desc: a   Int lvl: f  Dates: 1985,
```

```
1     040     xxx $c xxx
2     007     v $b f $c  $d c $e b $f a $g h $h o $i u
3     100 1   Frost, Carolyn O.
4     245 10  Searching by subject in the library's catalogs $h
videorecording / $c written and directed by Carolyn O. Frost.
5     260     [Houston, Tex.] : $b Produced by Houston Audiovisual
Services, Inc., $c c1985.
6     300     1 videocassette (14 min.) : $b sd., col. ; $c 1/2 in.
7     500     Title on container: Subject searching.
8     511 1   Cherie Sutton.
9     500     VHS.
10    520     Designed to introduce students to the use of subject
heading and key-word searching in the University of Houston's card
and online catalogs.
10    710 21  Houston Audiovisual Services
```

## *AACR 2* applicable rules

### Chief source of information

**7.0B1:**   Title frames as chief source.

### Area 1

**7.1B1:**   Title proper.

**7.1C1:**   GMD.

**7.1F1:**   Statements of responsibility considered important.

**1.1F7:**   Omit titles from names of persons in statements of responsibility.

### Area 4

**1.4C6:**   If place of publication is uncertain, give probable place with question mark. If the cataloger is sure of the place, it need not be indicated with a question mark. In either case, since the information is taken from an outside source, it is enclosed in brackets.

**7.4D1:**   Give publisher not named in statement of responsibility. If the producer had been included in the statement of responsibility, it would appear in the publication area in shortened form.

**1.4D3:**    Do not omit phrase naming publisher's function.

**7.4F1:**    Date.

**Area 5**
**7.5B1:**    Number of physical items and SMD.

**7.5B2:**    Playing time.

**7.5C3; 7.5C4:**
    Sound, color.

**7.5D3:**    Give width of videotape in inches.

**Area 7**
**7.7B4:**    Titles other than the title proper.

**7.7B6:**    Statement of responsibility. Cast: List featured players.

**7.7B10:**    Give system used for videorecording.

**7.7B17:**    Summary.

**Choice of access points**
**21.1B2:**    Although the work emanates from a corporate body, it does not fall under any of the categories in 21.1B2, and thus is not entered under corporate body. If the cataloger decides that the person who wrote the script and directed the film is primarily responsible for the intellectual and artistic content of the work (see definition of personal authorship in rule 21.1A1), then the work is considered one of personal authorship, and main entry given to the personal author as in rule 21.4A. If, on the other hand, no one individual can be identified as being primarily responsible, then main entry is under title according to rule 21.1C.

**21.30E:**    Added entry for producer.

**21.30J:**    Title added entry.

**Form of heading**
**24.5C1:**    Omit terms indicating incorporation.

# REFERENCE SOURCES

## Access Routes beyond the Catalog

Patrons of the library may be interested in locating films by information not provided through catalog access points, and once found, the bibliographic record may provide only limited information about the film.

Probably one of the most important access routes not provided in catalogs is information about the cast. A user may be more interested in locating films starring Humphrey Bogart than in the films of a given producer or director. Another item of interest to patrons may be the book, play, or short story on which a film is based. This information would be of particular value to an individual who is interested in studying different film versions of a single book, or to a person who has seen and enjoyed a movie and wishes to read the book on which the movie was based. Several sources provide this and related types of information.

Many individuals may also be interested in knowing about the subject content of the film, and may find the brief synopsis found in most catalog records inadequate. Several reference sources provide this type of information in plot summaries. Critical comments or reviews of films may also be of interest to the user in selecting a film, or in film research. Several of the sources listed below provide critical comments on selected films, while others index journal and newspaper articles on film. A related bit of information is whether the film was nominated for or received awards.

The following titles provide the user with supplementary access routes for the catalog, and also serve as reference aids for the cataloger.

## Film Guides

*The American Film Institute Catalog of Motion Pictures Produced in the United States.* New York: Bowker, 1971-1976 (in progress).

Alphabetical list of film titles includes producer/distributor, release date, copyright date, type of film, number of reels, and length of film. Information on credits, cast, genre, and synopsis of plot. Credit and subject indexes.

Armour, Robert A. *Film: A Reference Guide.* Westport, Conn.: Greenwood Press, 1980.

Comprehensive look at the field of film study. Includes film production, the history of film, and sections on major actors, directors, production staff, and major films. Numerous bibliographies with an entire chapter on reference works and periodicals.

Cowie, Peter, ed. *The International Film Guide 1987.* London: Tantivy Press, 1987.

Alphabetical listing by country responsible for the production of a particular film. Within country, films are listed alphabetically, and information is given on title, producer, director, distributor, length of film, composer, actors, and synopsis.

Gifford, Denis. *The British Film Catalogue, 1895-1970: A Guide to Entertainment Films.* South Devon, England: David and Charles, 1973.
Films are organized chronologically by accession number. Up to twenty-three features of a film are listed, including length, production company, producer, director, screenplay writer, full cast listing with characters played, and summary of film's content. Subject index.

*The Great American Movie Book.* Edited by Paul Michael. Englewood Cliffs, N.J.: Prentice-Hall, 1980.
Alphabetical listing of American films with date of release, production credits, running time, and cast. Lists winners of Academy Awards. Index is divided into players, directors, and producers.

Halliwell, Leslie. *Halliwell's Film Guide.* 4th ed. New York: Charles Scribner's Sons, 1983.
Basic information on over 14,000 English language and some foreign language feature-length films. Gives English (or American) title, running time, release date, country of origin, credits, cast, short synopsis, and comments from critics. By title, with indexes for alternative and foreign titles.

_____. *Halliwell's Filmgoer's Companion.* 8th ed. New York: Charles Scribner's Sons, 1984.
International coverage, with brief information on actors, directors, and others involved with film. Includes dates for individuals, and a list of films with which the person was involved. For films, the country of origin and date are given along with a brief summary of the plot. Includes appendixes of fictional screen characters, themes explored in films, definitions of film terminology. Intended audience is the general moviegoer, rather than the film specialist.

Leff, Leonard J. *Film Plots: Scene-by-Scene Narrative Outlines for Feature Film Study.* 2 vols. Ann Arbor, Mich.: Pierian Press, 1988, 1983.
Covers classic and modern films; scene-by-scene plot summaries, location and times of action, names of major and minor characters, and selected pertinent dialogue or titles. Intended for use as a reference to a film narrative's chronology, characters, setting, and action.

Limbacher, James L. *Feature Films: A Directory of Feature Films on 16mm and Videotape Available for Rental, Sale, and Lease.* 8th ed. New York: Bowker, 1985.
Describes more than 26,000 films in 16mm (as well as 8mm and videotape), along with purchase and rental information.

_____. *Haven't I Seen You Somewhere Before? Remakes, Sequels, and Series in Motion Pictures and Television, 1896-1978.* Ann Arbor, Mich.: Pierian Press, 1979.
Provides information on thousands of titles that have been presented in the media more than once.

Magill, Frank N., ed. *Magill's Survey of Cinema.* Englewood Cliffs, N.J.:
  Salem Press, 1981.
  Ten-volume set on English language films. First series: English language
films. 1980. Second series: English language films. 1981. Foreign language films.
1985. A general reference source of representative films released after 1927.
Contains articles giving in-depth analysis of film, cast and credits information,
running time, and lengthy synopsis of plot.

Maltin, Leonard, ed. *TV Movies, 1983-84 ed.* New York: New American Library,
  1982.
  Covers over 15,000 movies shown on regular and cable TV. With over 1,500
made-for-TV movies. Alphabetical listing giving director, stars, plot, color or
black and white, original length, key songs (for musicals), concise summaries,
and reviews.

Marell, Alvin H. *Movies Made for Television: The Telefeature and the Mini-
  series, 1964-1979.* Westport, Conn.: Arlington House, 1980.
  Chronological listing of films originally shown on television. Entries include
title; date first shown; producer; director; work of fiction based on; those
responsible for photography, background music, editing; characters played by
actors; actor's real name; and synopsis. At end of book, alphabetical list of
movies, actors, and others.

*The Motion Picture Guide.* Edited by Jay Robert Nash, Stanley Ralph Ross,
  and Robert B. Connelly. New York: Bowker, 1987. 12v.
  Synopses and filmographies of feature films released 1927-1984. Volumes
1-9 give alphabetical listing by title for 35,000 American and foreign sound films.
Lists film cast and production credits, verified notations for year of release,
initial release running time, production or distribution company, variant title(s),
whether in color or black and white, genre/subject, and availability on videocassette. Volume 10 covers 13,500 silent films produced between 1910 and 1936.
Volumes 11 and 12 index the first ten volumes. Updated annually by *The Motion
Picture Guide Annual.*

Pickard, Roy. *The Award Movies: A Complete Guide from A to Z.* London:
  Frederick Muller, 1980.
  Alphabetical listing of every film named "best picture" in last fifty years by
the top nine award organizations in the United States, Great Britain, and Europe.
Part 1 lists each film with information about its awards, a synopsis, cast and
credits. Part 2 gives a history of each award organization and a chronological list
of the winners of best actor, actress, director, and so on.

Sadoul, Georges. *Dictionary of Films.* Translated and edited by Peter Morris.
  Berkeley, Calif.: University of California Press, 1972.
  Descriptions of 1,200 international films, including those from lesser-known
countries and silent films. Updated from original 1965 volume. Country of
origin, date of release, production/direction/cast credits, running time, and
critical appraisals of each film.

## EDUCATIONAL FILMS

*The Educational Film/Video Locator.* 3d ed. Consortium of University Film
   Centers. New York: Bowker, 1986. 2v.
   Lists 48,300 films and videos, with their title, date of production, duration,
whether color or black and white, sound, gauge of film, short synopsis, and
location. First volume has subject index with indication of audience level.

National Information Center for Educational Media [NICEM]. *Film & Video
   Finder.* Albuquerque, N.M.: NICEM, 1987.
   Ninety thousand citations cover documentaries, children's programs,
classics, and instructional materials available on 16mm, Beta, VHS, and optical
disk. Entries describe content, audience level, film or video format, running time,
date of release, and name and address of purchase or rental source. Title and
subject access.

# Encyclopedias

*The International Encyclopedia of Film.* Edited by Roger Manvell. New York:
   Crown, 1972.
   Covers the international history of film as an art and as an industry. More
than 1,000 entries include biographies, national film histories, general topics, and
technical terms.

Katz, Ephraim. *The Film Encyclopedia.* New York: Thomas Y. Crowell, 1979.
   Over 7,000 entries for actors, directors, producers, and screenwriters.
Covers filmmakers, filmmaking, film-related organizations and events,
techniques, processes, equipment. Includes definitions of terminology,
biographies, and filmographies of most directors and major stars.

*The Oxford Companion to Film.* Edited by Liz-Anne Bawden. New York:
   Oxford University Press, 1976.
   Short articles on all aspects of film. Includes biographies and technical
terms.

Slide, Anthony. *The American Film Industry: A Historical Dictionary.* New
   York: Greenwood Press, 1986.
   Six hundred articles on American producing and releasing companies,
technological innovations, film series, industry terms, studios, genres, and
organizations. Many articles contain an address, bibliography, and information
as to institutional holdings on the subject's films, papers, or still photographs.

# Sources Providing Access Routes
# for Film Participants

## FILM PARTICIPANTS – GENERAL

*Academy Awards: An Ungar Reference Index.* Compiled by Richard Shale. New
York: Frederick Ungar, 1978.
　　Lists Academy Award nominees and winners in all areas 1927-1977. Also
chronological listing.

*Annual Index to Motion Picture Credits.* 1978- . Westport, Conn.: Greenwood
Press, 1979- . Annual.
　　Lists credits by (1) film title (containing full list of credits for each film), (2)
type of participant or function (e.g., actor, director, producer, writer, (3) releasing company, and (4) alphabetical index of credits.

*The International Dictionary of Films and Filmmakers.* Chicago: St. James
Press, 1986- . 5v.
　　Volume 1 was originally published by Macmillan (*The Macmillan Dictionary of Films and Filmmakers. Vol. 1. Films.* Edited by Christopher Lyon.
London: Macmillan, 1984.) Later, St. James Press republished volume 1 as well
as the next three volumes, with an index volume to be published shortly. Volume
1 is a listing of approximately 750 films; each entry gives the title, director,
producer, studio, cast and credits, release date, and a short synopsis. Volume 2 is
a listing of actors and actresses, with a short biography giving birth and death
dates. Volume 3 is a listing of directors and filmmakers, with biographies and
dates. Volume 4 is a listing of writers and production staff, also giving
biographical information. Volume 5 will be a title index for the first four
volumes.

## DIRECTORS

Quinlan, David. *The Illustrated Guide to Film Directors.* London: B. T.
Batsford, 1983.
　　Alphabetical list of 570 film directors, mainly British and American. Filmog-
raphies for each.

Sadoul, Georges. *Dictionary of Film Makers.* Translated, edited, and updated
by Peter Morris. Berkeley: University of California Press, 1972.
　　Selective list of important people in cinema since 1895. One thousand entries
on directors, scriptwriters, cinematographers, art directors, composers,
producers. International in scope with entries listing a brief description of the
individual's work and filmography.

## CAST

Pickard, Roy. *Who Played Who in the Movies: An A-Z.* London: Frederick
Muller, 1979.

Alphabetically arranged by names of film characters and corresponding actor playing that character. Includes characters who were the subject of at least one major film biography. A brief paragraph on the character is followed by the details of the actor(s) who portrayed it and the film itself.

Truitt, Evelyn Mack. *Who Was Who on Screen.* 3d ed. New York: Bowker, 1983.
Alphabetical listing of about 13,000 onscreen performers who died between 1905 and 1982, including celebrities from other fields who have appeared on screen, bit players, and animal stars. Place and date of birth, films acted in, dates of films.

Weaver, John T., comp. *Forty Years of Screen Credits, 1929-1969.* Metuchen, N.J.: Scarecrow Press, 1970.
Lists names of cast with films performed in. A companion volume, *Twenty Years of Silents, 1908-1928*, published in 1971, gives similar information for this time period.

## OTHER FILM PARTICIPANTS

Enser, A. G. S. *Filmed Books and Plays: A List of Books and Plays from Which Films Have Been Made, 1928-1983.* Aldershot, Great Britain: Gower Publishing Co., 1985.
Arranged alphabetically by film title, this source tells who wrote the book or play on which the movie was based. Entries include the author's name, the title of the book or play if different from the film's and the publisher of the printed source. Also lists the entries by author and original title with the corresponding film title, distributor and date. A third section lists the original title of the book or play followed by the film title.

McCarty, Clifford. *Film Composers in America: A Checklist of Their Work.* New York: DaCapo Press, 1972.

# Dictionaries and Glossaries

Beaver, Frank E. *Dictionary of Film Terms.* New York: McGraw-Hill, 1983.
Focus on technical and cinematic terms, with illustrations. Alphabetical arrangement; also, topic index.

Geduld, Harry M., and Ronald Gottesman. *An Illustrated Glossary of Film Terms.* New York: Holt, Rinehart and Winston, 1973.
Attempts to avoid technical jargon and highly specialized terms. Besides general film terms, also definitions of terms used in film acting, film criticism, and film theory. Written for the general audience, with copious illustrations.

Konigsberg, Ira. *The Complete Film Dictionary.* New York: New American Library, 1987.
Lengthy definitions of terms used in film production, distribution, and criticism and theory.

Levitan, Eli L. *An Alphabetical Guide to Motion Picture, Television, and Videotape Production.* New York: McGraw-Hill, 1980.
Illustrations, photographs, and tables aid in the description and explanations of the processes and techniques. Avoids technical terminology.

Mercer, John, comp. *Glossary of Film Terms.* Rev. ed. The University Film Association Monograph No. 2. Houston, Tex.: University of Houston, 1979.
Technical terms, and terms from the literature of film history, theory, and criticism.

Oakey, Virginia. *Dictionary of Film and Television Terms.* New York: Barnes & Noble, 1983.
Brief definitions of technical, artistic, and business terms used in the film industry.

## Videorecordings

Note: See also listings above.

Bahr, Alice Harrison. *Video in Libraries: A Status Report, 1979-80.* 2d ed. White Plains, N.Y.: Knowledge Industry Publications, 1980.

Gothberg, Helen M. *Television and Video in Libraries and Schools.* Hamden, Conn.: Library Professional Publications, 1983.

*The International Television Almanac.* New York: Quigley, 1956- . Annual.
Includes information on television performers, producers, distributors, and feature releases.

Saffady, William. *Video-based Information Systems: A Guide for Educational, Business, Library, and Home Use.* Chicago: American Library Association, 1985.
Describes differences between various types of videocassette recording formats currently available.

*The Video Source Book.* 2d ed. Syosset, N.Y.: National Video Clearinghouse, 1979- .

## Cataloging of Motion Pictures

### LIBRARY OF CONGRESS CATALOGS

Library of Congress. *Audiovisual Materials.* 1983- . Quarterly, with cumulative indexes. Microfiche.
Contains LC records for motion pictures, videorecordings, and other audiovisual media.

_____. *Films and Other Materials for Projection*. Washington, D.C.: Library of Congress, 1973-1978.

LC catalog records for motion pictures, filmstrips, sets of transparencies, and slide sets released in the United States and Canada that have some instructional value. Entries under main and added entries, subject headings.

_____. *Library of Congress Catalog: Motion Pictures and Filmstrips*, 1953-1972. Washington, D.C.: Library of Congress.

## FILM CATALOGING MANUALS AND STANDARDS

Aichele, Joan, and Nancy B. Olson. *A Manual of AACR2 Examples for Motion Pictures and Videorecordings*. Edited by Marilyn H. McClaskey and Edward Swanson. Lake Crystal, Minn.: Soldier Creek Press, 1981.

Cataloging records, corresponding rules, explanations, rule number index.

Gartenberg, Jon. *Film Cataloguing Manual: A Computer System*. New York: Museum of Modern Art, 1979.

Developed as a result of an effort to standardize cataloging procedures in the Museum of Modern Art Department of Film.

Harrison, Helen P. *Film Library Techniques: Principles of Administration*. New York: Hastings House, 1973.

Aspects of administration covered include history and development of film libraries, selection principles, film handling and retrieval, storage and preservation, costs, and copyright. Discussion of cataloging compares several codes. Chapter on shotlisting gives principles for detailed description of a film to reduce the necessity of viewing to determine contents. Chapter on information retrieval discusses indexing systems.

International Federation of Film Archives. Cataloging Commission. *Film Cataloging*. New York: Burt Franklin, 1979.

Discusses types of cataloging systems, subject classification methods, and archival methods for handling films. Bibliography on film cataloging.

Library of Congress. *National Level Bibliographic Record—Films*. Washington, D.C.: Library of Congress, 1981- .

Defines elements to be included in records for films that might be shared with other organizations or contributed to a nationwide database. Based on the MARC films format. Replaced by *USMARC Format for Bibliographic Data*.

_____. *Moving Image Materials: Genre Terms*. Washington, D.C.: L.C. Cataloging Distribution Service, 1988.

Thesaurus for film and video materials. The first national standard for adding moving image genre and form terms to MARC records. Prepared by the National Moving Image Database Standards Committee of the National Center for Film and Video Preservation in Los Angeles and coordinated by the Motion Picture, Broadcasting and Recorded Sound Division of LC. Complements its sister LC volume *Archival Moving Image Materials: A Cataloging Manual*.

White-Hensen, Wendy, comp. *Archival Moving Image Materials: A Cataloging Manual.* Washington, D.C.: Library of Congress, 1984.
(See earlier discussion in this chapter.)

## ARTICLES ON FILM DESCRIPTION, ORGANIZATION, AND ACCESS

Bidd, Donald, Louise de Chevigny, and Margo Marshall. "PRECIS for Subject Access in a National Audiovisual Information System." *Canadian Library Journal* 43 (June 1986): 177-84.
Overview of the PRECIS indexing system used by the National Film Board of Canada in its FORMAT system. Discusses reasons for choosing this system and the problems involved in indexing audiovisual documents.

Clarke, Andrew. "A New Non-Code for Films: *AACR 2* Chapter 7." *Audiovisual Librarian* 6 (1980): 128-29, 132-33.
Critique of *AACR 2*'s chapter on motion pictures and videorecordings. Discusses problems specific to film cataloging and suggests some solutions.

Gorman, Michael. "Cataloging and Classification of Film Study Material." In *Film Study Collections: A Guide to Their Development and Use*, edited by Nancy Allen, 113-23. New York: Frederick Ungar Pub. Co., 1979.
General discussion of cataloging and classification methods for manuscripts, audiovisual materials, stills, photographs, and printed ephemera. Compares *AACR 2* and FIAF system.

Haskell, Gardner. "Cooking Up Film Subject Headings." *Film Library Quarterly* 17 (1984): 30-32.
Describes problems faced by one library when trying to create new headings for films.

Intner, Sheila S. "Cataloging Motion Pictures and Videorecordings Using *AACR2* Chapter 7." In *Policy and Practice in Bibliographic Control of Nonbook Media*, edited by Sheila S. Intner and Richard P. Smiraglia, 128-37. Chicago: American Library Association, 1987.
Focuses on problem areas arising in the cataloging of film and video materials.

O'Connor, Brian. "Access to Moving Image Documents: Background Concepts and Proposals for Surrogates for Film and Video Works." *Journal of Documentation* 41 (December 1985): 209-20.
Examines abstracts designed to serve as surrogates to facilitate user selection of the most appropriate film or video work for a particular use. The surrogate in mind is intended to provide more "booklike" physical and intellectual access. Gives consideration to major differences between a word and a photographic image and object.

# Cataloging of Videorecordings

Cocchini, Marianne. "Cataloguing Video Art: An Approach to Its Philosophy." *Film Library Quarterly* 10, nos. 3-4 (1977): 23-34.

Urbanski, Verna. "Cataloging Locally Produced Videorecording Copies of Motion Pictures." *Online Audio-Visual Cataloger* 2 (June 1982): 17.

_____. "How to Catalog Locally Produced Videorecordings or Motion Pictures." *Online Audio-Visual Cataloger* 2 (March 1982): 12-13.

There have been relatively few articles published on the cataloging of motion pictures and videorecordings. To keep track of current developments in rule interpretations and related issues, the cataloger should read current issues of the *Cataloging Service Bulletin* as well as the *OLAC* [Online Audiovisual Catalogers] *Newsletter*.

Since the medium of film is used in a variety of settings for an even greater variety of purposes, cataloging needs will vary. A school library, a film library or archive, and a news production studio will each have distinctly diverse requirements.

# 5

# *Graphic Materials*

## DECISION AREAS IN
## DESCRIPTIVE CATALOGING

### Scope

### DEFINING CHARACTERISTICS OF A
### DIVERSE CATEGORY

The category of graphic materials in *AACR 2*'s chapter 8 encompasses a wide range of media, all of which are: (1) two dimensional, (2) graphic in representation, and (3) static (in contrast to moving picture images). Formats are varied and include media that are intended for projection, such as slides, filmstrips, and transparencies, as well as opaque media, for example, photographs, art originals and pictures. Some materials in this category are specifically instructional in purpose such as flash cards, transparencies, charts, and technical drawings, while others have an aesthetic purpose, such as original works of art and pictures. While the content is most likely to be pictorial, it can include diagrams (e.g., technical drawings), and even textual material, as in the case of some flash cards.

While microforms and maps may also share some of the characteristics of graphic materials, these media are dealt with in separate chapters in *AACR 2*.

### MEDIA COMBINATIONS

In many instances, a graphic medium may be packaged with a sound component, for example, a filmstrip with sound recording cassette. Rule 1.10B states that if an item has one predominant component, it is to be described in terms of that component, and that the details of the subsidiary component(s) be recorded as accompanying material in the physical description area. In most cases, the visual component is assumed to be more important than the aural one, and in the typical filmstrip-cassette unit, the visual medium is featured. However, the decision as to what constitutes the predominant medium should be made on a case-by-case basis. Rogers suggests using chapter 8 "whenever sound is necessary for, or a complement to, the graphic material," with the assumption that "the intellectual burden is contained in the graphic material with only accompanying information or artistic enhancement presented in the sound accompaniment."[1] Occasionally, as with musical or language-learning items, the sound recording may form the focal point. In other cases, the cataloger may decide that there is no predominant component and that both media contribute equally to the total work; in such instances, the item would be cataloged as a kit.

## ARCHIVAL MATERIALS

While *AACR 2*'s chapter 8 covers graphic materials of all kinds, the description of original, historical, and archival graphic materials is dealt with in detail in a manual issued by LC, *Graphic Materials: Rules for Describing Original Items and Historical Collections* (hereafter referred to as *GM*).[2]

## SPECIALIZED EXPERTISE

For the cataloging of art works, some subject expertise will be useful. It may be necessary to draw upon knowledge of various artists, schools, and movements in art history. The cataloger may also find it necessary to become familiar with the technical aspects of physical formats, such as different types of papers, inks, and printing, and different techniques of creation and reproduction processes. After dealing with the physical or bibliographic aspects, it may be necessary to describe the subject or image represented on the item. In all of these instances, reference sources can serve to supplement subject expertise. And because art is a multicultural medium, and many artistic items appear in different languages, the cataloger may need to be equipped with a number of foreign-language dictionaries and glossaries.

# Sources of Information

The chief source of information for graphic materials is the item itself. Labels or containers may serve as a chief source if they are physically attached to the item or provide the only unifying or collective title for a unit comprised of separate physical parts, such as a collection of pictures or slides. Thus, as with many other kinds of materials, the item itself is preferred as the chief source, but consideration may also be given to additional factors based on a "criterion of persistence" (as in the case of labels that remain with the item) and to sources providing the most complete or comprehensive information (8.0B1).

## CONCEPT OF *CHIEF SOURCE*
## FOR ORIGINAL GRAPHIC MATERIALS

*AACR 2* rules for graphic materials prescribe that the title, statement of responsibility, edition, publication and series area are to be taken from the chief source (8.0B2). For art works, this may pose a problem, since original and unpublished visual media may often lack a text to be transcribed. This problem is addressed by the *GM* manual, which is mindful of differences which need to be drawn between the description of graphic materials and the description of books and other printed or published materials.

> [O]riginal or noncommercial graphic works are generally considered to be unique, though they frequently exist in multiple copies. Even if published, they lack much of the explicit information characterizing books and book-like materials. Furthermore, most collections of graphic items are unique because, as collections, they have never been published. (p. 4)

In its rules for cataloging original and historical graphic materials, *GM* redefines the concepts of *chief source* used in traditional book cataloging, since the kinds of materials covered in *GM* often have little or no text to describe. For example, the *GM* rules for chief source prescribe that when the text is not known to have been provided by the creator or creating body, information from reference sources such as exhibit catalogs can be used (rule 0B1.1, p. 9).

## Title and Statement of Responsibility Area

### SUPPLIED TITLE

*AACR 2* states that a title must be supplied if none is given on the item. However, no particular directives are given, with the exception of collections of graphic materials, for which the cataloger is to supply "a title by which the collection is known or a title indicating the nature of the collection" (8.1B2).

When *GM* gives rules for transcribing the title and statement of responsibility information, it takes into account conditions peculiar to art works. In the case of a "severely abbreviated title, in which it would be cumbersome to bracket interpolated letters or words," *GM* allows the cataloger to spell out the title and enclose it in square brackets (1B1.10, p.19).

Likewise, *GM* allows the statement of responsibility to be inferred from a monogram or device (1.G7, p. 28), while *AACR 2* requires the cataloger to record the statement of responsibility exactly as it appears on the item. *GM*'s rule takes into account the labeling devices unique to art works, and provides a prominent place for important information pertaining to ascription. A reference source useful in this process is Caplan's *Classified Dictionary of Artists Signatures, Symbols, and Monograms*, listed at the end of this chapter.

### PRESENTER'S NAME IN TITLE

In some commercially produced items, such as slides and filmstrips, the title proper may include a statement of responsibility, such as "Walt Disney presents." Such situations are also common in motion pictures and videorecordings. *AACR 2*'s rule 1.1B2 directs the cataloger to include a statement of responsibility in the title proper if the two are grammatically connected. While an LC rule interpretation for motion pictures states that "credits" of this kind should not be regarded as part of the title proper, the same rule interpretation does not apply to graphic materials.[3]

## STATEMENTS OF RESPONSIBILITY
### What to Include?

Although *AACR 2*'s chapter 7 for motion pictures and videorecordings explicitly allows the cataloger to be selective in transcribing statements of responsibility, and to base decisions on criteria such as the importance to the film and the interests of the cataloging agency, no such explicit directives are given in chapter 8. In an LC interpretation that applies to chapter 8 as well as chapter 7, criteria are established for determining overall responsibility for a work, and thus for deciding whether to include certain types of authorship and production functions in the statement of responsibility area or the note area, if at all.

## GENERAL MATERIAL DESIGNATION
### Generic versus Specific

The terms for graphic items in *AACR 2*'s North American list for the GMD are, for the most part, easily identifiable and specific, for example, *flash card, technical drawing, transparency*. The most general and inclusive term is *picture*, which will serve in many instances as the GMD of last resort when no other term appears to apply. In the revised rules, a new GMD, *art reproduction*, has been added for graphic and three-dimensional materials.

For its GMD, *Graphic Materials* has decided to use the more generic term *graphic*, which is the British GMD in *AACR 2* (rule 1.D, p. 23).

# Publication Area

## UNPUBLISHED MATERIALS

*AACR 2* makes a distinction between published and unpublished items, and does not consider it appropriate to include publication data for items that are not issued in "published" form. In the original *AACR 2*, this principle was applied only to graphic media and a few other types of materials, but in revised rules in the general chapter (1.4C8, 1.4D9, 1.4F9), the principle was extended to all media. For unpublished materials such as art originals, the place of publication and name of publisher are not recorded, and the publication data consist of the date only. The date given is that of production (creation, inscription, manufacture) rather than the date of publication or issuance. Likewise, chapter 8 specifies that no place of publication or name of publisher is to be provided for an unpublished collection of graphic items (including those containing published items but not published as a collection) (8.4C2, 8.4D2).

# Physical Description Area

Specific material designations are given for a large number of graphic media, and many of these specific designations are identical to the terms for general material designations; in fact, each of the eight terms for GMDs also serves as a specific designation. If none of the SMDs is suitable, an optional rule allows the cataloger to substitute or add a term more specific than those listed. Given the wide range of materials covered by chapter 8, the cataloger is likely to take frequent advantage of this optional rule.

For certain types of items where extent can be indicated in terms of constituent parts, rule 8.5B2 allows the cataloger to add, in parentheses, a specific indication of extent. For filmslips and filmstrips, the number of frames or double frames is added, and for stereographs, the cataloger can add the number of pairs of frames, for flip charts the number of sheets, and for transparencies the number of overlays, for example, "1 filmstrip (36 fr.)."

A new rule (8.5B6) provides for addition of the term "tactile" to the statement of extent for items in a raised image format; for example, "1 chart (tactile)."

## COUNTING FILMSTRIP FRAMES

Those attempting to apply rule 8.5B2 to filmstrips will note the absence of guidelines for counting filmstrip frames. An LC rule interpretation provides some direction; for example, when counting unnumbered frames, no number should be considered too numerous to count. Specific direction is given for determining what content and noncontent frames should be included in the counting, and separately numbered title frames and test frames are also addressed.[4]

## OTHER PHYSICAL DETAILS FOR ART MATERIALS

In stating the "other physical details" for art originals, the cataloger must give the medium (e.g., oil, chalk) and the base (e.g., canvas, fabric); for art prints, the process must be given (e.g., engraving, lithograph); and for art reproductions and technical drawings, the method of reproduction (e.g., photogravure, collotype, blueprint). This will require some familiarity with technical terms and concepts in this area. For example, rule 8.5C1 for art prints calls for the cataloger to "give the process in general terms (engraving, lithography, etc.) or specific terms (copper engraving, chromolithograph, etc.)." The novice in this field might have trouble with the general terms, not to mention the specific and will need to consult reference books such as those listed at the end of this chapter.

## "INTEGRAL" SOUND

For slides and filmstrips, the rules for other physical details prescribe that sound be indicated only if it is "integral." Some confusion may arise as to what is meant by this term. In this case *integral* does not refer to the intellectual importance of the sound, but to whether or not the sound is physically located on the filmstrip or slide itself. Thus, in the typical instance of a filmstrip with accompanying tape cassette, the sound would not be considered integral, since it is physically separate from the filmstrip.

**DIMENSIONS: Standardization**

*AACR 2* recognizes two standards for dimensions. For slides, the standard dimensions are 2 x 2 inches, and height and width for slides are recorded only if the dimensions vary from this standard. A second standard is implied in that no dimensions are to be given for stereographs, presumably on the assumption that the size and the shape of this medium are uniform. This is an erroneous assumption, however, since there are stereographs that are rectangular in shape and of varying dimensions. A better approach would be to require that dimensions be included whenever they differ from the standard for the medium, as is the rule in the case of slides.

**ARCHIVAL MATERIALS**

*Graphic Materials* allows the cataloger to supply more extensive detail than *AACR 2* in the physical description of an item. Included is provision for: the use of additional SMDs, detailed rules for the listing of photographic materials, greater variety in indicating color and techniques, and detailed rules for indicating the dimension of the item, especially in regard to describing nonrectangular and irregular shapes (rule 3., pp. 42-56).

# Note Area

Notes of particular relevance to graphic materials include those relating to:

the donor, source and previous owner(s) of an art work (8.7B6)

characteristics describing the original of an art reproduction, such as the location and size of the original (8.7B22)

physical details such as the size of an item when framed (8.7B10)

*Graphic Materials* provides many additional suggestions for notes unique to art media. Included are attributions and conjecture as to the creator, and detailed description of the item's physical condition (e.g., tears, creases, and damaged areas), which would be helpful in describing one-of-a-kind originals. Also provided for is an indication of watermarks and trademarks as well as references to published descriptions, biographical notes on the creator or collector, and notes indicating reproduction, copyright, and the location of available reproductions (rule 5., pp. 59-73). Again, in many of these instances, reference works may provide sources for the kinds of information included in the notes area.

# Choice of Access Points

## CONCEPTS OF *AUTHORSHIP*

Chapter 21 of the original *AACR 2* specifically defined artists and photographers as authors of the works they create, and there are specific rules as well for art works in rule 21.16, "Adaptations of Art Works" and in rule 21.17 "Reproductions of Two or More Art Works." These special rules reflect principles prevalent in *AACR 2*'s treatment of authorship.

## SINGLE AUTHORSHIP

The standard concept of the author as the person chiefly responsible for the creation of the intellectual or artistic content of a work is one that has appeared, with slight variations in wording, in established cataloging standards such as *AACR 2* and its predecessors. For certain categories of materials, it is relatively simple to decide which aspect of the work constitutes its principal intellectual or artistic content, and to identify the person chiefly responsible for this creative function. In the category of graphic materials, photographers and artists fall neatly under this straightforward definition of *authorship*.

## MIXED AUTHORSHIP

While it is rare indeed that we would encounter a case of "collaborative authorship" among two or more artists, we do find instances in which the work of one artist has been adapted or reproduced by another artist or individual. Not infrequently, an art work has been adapted from one medium of the graphic arts to another, such as an oil painting to an engraving. Rule 21.16A deals with this authorship situation and prescribes main entry for the person responsible for the adaptation. A name-title added entry is made for the original work. Under the general category of "Works That Are Modifications of Other Works," the general principle is to ascribe authorship, that is, give the main entry under the heading appropriate to the new work, "if the modification has substantially changed the nature and content of the original or if the medium of expression has been changed."

On the other hand, if the art work has merely been reproduced, as in the case of a photograph, or a reproduction of a sculpture, the original artist is still considered primarily responsible for the artistic content of the work, and thus, as "author," receives the main entry (21.16B).

## UNKNOWN AUTHORSHIP

Frequently, authorship is unknown, as in the case where an art work is unsigned and no further information is available. Some reference works may give a clue as to an artist's identity.

# ALTERNATIVE MODES OF ACCESS AND ORGANIZATION

## Item-Level versus Collection-Level Cataloging

The above discussion, and cataloging examples given for this chapter, assume that the items to be cataloged are discrete units and should be described individually. However, it is frequently the case that certain types of graphic items, such as slides, postcards, and photographs, are issued in collections or sets. In many instances, the cataloger may be faced with the decision of whether to treat each item individually or to deal with the set as a unit. The decision will be based on the needs of the library and its users, and the resources available. Those items receiving individual attention should have a particular value that would justify the expense of such treatment. Such items would also be discrete entities, and would have an independent value and meaning, in contrast to those materials that derive their meaning and importance from the collection of which they are a part. For these reasons, *GM* gives equal attention to item-level and collection-level cataloging.

## Self-Indexing Systems

Another option for organization and access is to have the user browse through the items themselves (or their surrogate reproductions) in a "self-indexing" mode. This is more feasible with individual pictorial items than with textual materials, since the content of an image is more directly and succinctly communicated than a textual message. The overall content or "message" of graphic images can be "read" or grasped at a glance, thus enabling the user to look at the image and to ascertain its content in a few moments, in contrast to browsing through the pages of a book. In such instances, the cataloger or indexer need only group the images into broad subject categories, or some other relevant arrangement, provide brief identifying information for each item, and allow the items to "describe" themselves. Still another strategy for dealing with large quantities of individual graphic items is to provide brief cataloging. *Graphic Materials* states in this regard that its rules

> are most significant for the description and identification of graphic materials felt to be of importance and of some permanent value to the institution's holdings. Full cataloging may not be feasible for all pictorial works, especially those that can be efficiently arranged in self-indexing files or shelved by creator, subject, or other category (p. 5)

## Subject Access

Subject access may play a particularly important role in the retrieval of graphic items since a user searching for photographs, pictures, and other pictorial works is not likely to come to the collection with the name of an author or a title. Indeed, for many "unpublished" items that contain no textual information, a traditional citation may not be possible.

In attempting to provide subject access, it often becomes clear that subject heading and classification systems developed for books and print materials may not be appropriate for pictorial works. Wendell Simons points out that "a picture is more analogous to a sentence or a single word than to a book," and "makes a single statement on a single theme," in contrast to a book, which can develop a train of thought or continuity of ideas. "A picture cannot depict the essence of theoretical subjects such as political science, education, religion ... but only some isolated visual phenomenon – an event, a person, a place, a thing."[5] For these reasons, the cataloger may decide that specialized subject access systems designed for graphic materials are more effective for retrieval of pictorial items than are traditional systems which assume a book or textual medium. Some of these specialized subject systems are described later in this chapter.

## Emerging Developments in
## Automated Retrieval

Online technologies provide important new and wholly different enhancements for the retrieval and display of catalog records for graphic materials. First, new technologies will enable users to search by types of access points such as medium, time period, country, culture, and school. Second, videodisc capabilities will enable users to see graphic representations of an item in addition to the bibliographic record.

For graphic items such as pictures, posters, and slides, the viewing of the document or work itself represents the ultimate subject representation. A display of the document gives the viewer a description of the subject far superior to a translation and interpretation into verbal terms. Such complete subject description is possible with static graphic images, such as pictures and maps, because, as noted earlier, the message conveyed by the item is simultaneous and nonlinear, and capable of being grasped and comprehended at once. At present, some projects that employ the medium of videodisc, though largely in the experimental stage, hold promise of offering "complete subject description" for static graphic images.

The idea of graphic representation in a catalog is not new. Irvine outlines the history of graphic card catalogs, and points out that a contact print catalog was developed at Harvard in the 1920s. Graphic card catalogs have been developed to provide access to certain visual media using various methods of photographic reproduction. With the advent of optical disc/videodisc and laser disc storage and retrieval technology, comes the capability of higher quality reproduction in an online, interactive mode.

The value of laser or videodiscs as an information storage and access medium lies in their ability to:

1. store images (both pictorial and textual) and sound;

2. store large quantities of information in a relatively small amount of space, e.g., over 100,000 individual images on a two-sided disc

3. allow random access to individual frames

4. allow instantaneous retrieval and display of images with viewer control via keyboard, hand-held commander, or touch-sensitive screen

5. allow interactive linkage to cataloging data[6]

One experimental program utilizing videodisc technology is the Library of Congress' Optical Disc Pilot Program, designed to provide access to parts of LC's collection. Since June 1984, patrons in the Prints and Photographs Reading Room have been able to browse, through a video monitor, a collection of approximately 49,000 photographs, posters, architectural drawings, and other pictorial items. Items can be displayed automatically at a rate of several per second, or manually, with the user controlling the rate at which the images appear.[7]

Not surprisingly, librarians of visual arts collections have been in the forefront of experimentation with videodisc technology. Markey describes various earlier projects employing computerized information retrieval of images stored on videodisc in university and museum collections.[8] At the Avery Architectural and Fine Arts Library, Columbia University, a project is under way to prepare bibliographic records for 45,000 architectural drawings, enter the records into MARC format in the Research Libraries Information Network (RLIN) using the Visual Materials Format, and store the images on disc. Topical and genre access will be provided through the Art and Architecture Thesaurus subject headings. Users will be able to search for an item using a variety of textual indexes, and see the image on video, or alternatively, to browse through collections of images and then retrieve the corresponding bibliographic records.[9]

## NOTES

[1]JoAnn V. Rogers and Jerry D. Saye, *Nonprint Cataloging for Multimedia Collections: A Guide Based on AACR 2* (Littleton, Colo.: Libraries Unlimited, 1987), 147.

[2]Elisabeth W. Betz, comp., *Graphic Materials: Rules for Describing Original Items and Historical Collections* (Washington, D.C.: Library of Congress, 1982).

[3]*Cataloging Service Bulletin* 13 (Summer 1981): 15. Ben Tucker comments on the application of this rule in the *Music Cataloging Bulletin* 15, no. 6.

[4]*Cataloging Service Bulletin* 33 (Summer 1986): 41.

[5]Wendell W. Simons and Luraine C. Tansey, "A Slide Classification System for the Organization and Automatic Indexing of Interdisciplinary Collections of Slides and Photographs," ED 048 879 (Santa Cruz: University of California, 1970), 2-4.

[6]Carolyn O. Frost, "Nonbook Materials in the Online Public Access Catalog," in *Policy and Practice in Bibliographic Control of Nonbook Media*, ed. Sheila S. Intner and Richard P. Smiraglia (Chicago: American Library Association, 1987), 89-90.

[7]Elisabeth Betz Parker, "The Library of Congress Non-Print Optical Disk Pilot Program," *Information Technology and Libraries* 4 (December 1985): 289-95; "The Library of Congress Optical Disk Pilot Program" (press release, Washington, D.C., June 20, 1984).

[8]Karen Markey, "Visual Arts Resources and Computers," in *Annual Review of Information Science and Technology*, vol. 19, ed. Martha E. Williams (White Plains, N.Y.: Knowledge Industry Publications, 1984), 271-309.

[9]Avery Architectural and Fine Arts Library, "Aviador (Avery Videodisc Index of Architectural Drawings on RLIN)," unpublished typescript, April 15, 1987.

## DESCRIPTIVE CATALOGING EXAMPLES

### Items to Be Cataloged

1. Opaque stereograph

One stereograph (2 identical photographic prints mounted on heavy cardboard), 8¾ x 17¾ centimeters, black and white.

Lower border:

> The descent to Italy - road winding down from the
> Maloja Pass        Engadine, Switzerland

Left corner:

> Underwood & Underwood, Publishers
> New York, London, Toronto

Photograph shows young men and women descending a mountain pass. The attire of the individuals is that of the early 20th century. The photographer's name is not given on the item, but information from the donor identifies the photographer as being William Henry Pleasants, whose dates are 1887-1975.

## 2. Filmstrip

One filmstrip roll, in color, 75 frames, 35 mm. gauge; one sound tape cassette, one teacher's guide, and one script, in container. (Assume that the filmstrip is the dominant medium.)

Title frame:
WHAT YOU SHOULD KNOW ABOUT SUBSTANCE ABUSE
PRODUCED BY THE NATIONAL HEALTH EDUCATION ASSOCIATION

1205 Sixteenth Street, N.W.
Washington, D.C. 20036
Copyright 1983

Informs teenagers about different types of substance abuse, and outlines strategies for avoidance of this problem.

## 3. Poster

One colored poster, mounted on cardbound; 48 centimeters in height; 70 centimeters in width.
A brochure indicates that the exhibit described by the poster took place in 1975.

Text on poster:
FROM THE LANDS
OF THE SCYTHIANS:

ANCIENT TREASURES
FROM THE MUSEUMS
OF THE U.S.S.R.
3000 B.C. - 100 B.C.

A loan exhibition organized in cooperation with the Ministry of Culture of the U.S.S.R.

## 4. Art original

One original oil painting, oil on canvas, colored, metal frame. The painting depicts a young Black brother and sister looking out of the window of their Harlem apartment.
Accompanying printed sheet indicates that the artist's name is Stephen Thomas Fordham, that his date of birth is 1966, and that his forename and middle name have never appeared in full as part of his artistic signature, since he prefers to be known as "S. T."

Size when framed:    40 x 30 centimeters (height x width)
    Unframed:        35 x 25 centimeters

Signature on painting:  S. T. Fordham 1985

Label on painting:     James Jr. and Raquel

# *AACR 2* Records and
# OCLC MARC Tagging

## 1. OPAQUE STEREOGRAPH

### *AACR 2* catalog record

Pleasants, William Henry, 1887-1975.
    The descent to Italy [picture] : road winding down from the
Maloja Pass, Engadine, Switzerland. -- New York : Underwood
& Underwood, [191-?].
    1 stereograph : b&w.

    Photographer's identity provided by donor.
    9 x 18 cm. ; mounted.
    Shows young men and women descending mountain pass. Attire
is early 20th century.

    I. Title.


Record using rules from *Graphic Materials* manual

Pleasants, William Henry, 1887-1975.
    The descent to Italy [graphic] : road winding down from the
Maloja Pass, Engadine, Switzerland. -- New York : Underwood
& Underwood, [191-?].
    1 photoprint on stereo card : stereograph, b&w ; 9 x 18 cm.

    Photographer's identity provided by donor.
    Shows young men and women descending mountain pass. Attire
is early 20th century.

    I. Title.

OCLC MARC Tagging

```
Type: k   Bib lvl: m   Govt pub:      Lang: eng  Source: d  Leng:nnn
          Enc lvl: I   Type mat: i    Ctry: nyu  Dat tp: q  MEBE: 0
Tech: n   Mod rec:         Accomp mat:
Desc: a   Int lvl:     Dates: 1910,1919
```

```
1  040     xxx $ xxx
2  007     k $b h $c $d b $e o $f c
3  100  1  Pleasants, William Henry, $d 1887-1975.
4  245  14 The descent to Italy $h picture : $b road winding down
from the Maloja Pass, Engadine, Switzerland.
5  260     New York : $b Underwood & Underwood, $c [191-?].
6  300     1 stereograph : $b b&w.
7  500     Photographer's identity provided by donor.
8  500     9 x 18 cm.; mounted.
9  520     Shows young men and women descending mountain pass.
Attire is early 20th century.
```

### *AACR 2* applicable rules

**8.0B1:** Chief source is item itself.

### Area 1

**8.1B1:** Title proper as in 1.1B.

**8.1C1:** GMD as in 1.1C1. GMD is *picture.* "Slide" was not used, since the glossary defines a slide as "transparent material on which there is a two-dimensional image, usually held in a mount, and designed for use in a projector or viewer." This item is opaque rather than transparent.

**1.1E1:** Record other title information.

**1.1F2:** If no statement of responsibility appears prominently on the item, do not construct one.

### Area 4

**8.4C1:** [new] Record place of publication of a published graphic item as instructed in 1.4C.

**1.4C5:** If publisher has offices in more than one place and these are named in the item, give the first named place.

**8.4D1:** [new] Record name of publisher of a published graphic item as in 1.4D.

**1.4D2:** Give publisher's name in shortest form by which it can be understood and identified.

**8.4F1:** [new] Record date of publication of a published graphic item as in 1.4F.

**1.4F7:** If no date of publication can be assigned to an item, give an approximate date of publication.

Example: " , [197-?] Probable decade."

**Area 5**

**8.5B1:** Give number of physical units and SMD.

**8.5B2:** *AACR 2* clearly has in mind the modern stereograph reel (e.g., "Viewmaster") intended for projection. For this reason rule 8.5B2, calling for the number of double frames in a stereograph reel, is not appropriate.

**8.5C2:** Indicate if color or black and white.

**8.5D3:** No dimensions given for stereographs. Once again, the *AACR 2* rule was designed with the standard size of the "Viewmaster" stereographs in mind. This does not take into account the earlier opaque stereograph, which had its own standard dimensions.

**Area 7**

**8.7B6:** Statement of responsibility note.

**8.7B10:** Physical details affecting use.

**8.7B17:** Summary of content.

**Choice of access points**

**21.4A:** Enter work of single personal authorship under the heading for the person whether named in the work or not.

**21.30J:** Added entry under title for work entered under personal author.

Applicable *Graphic Materials* manual rules

**1D:** *graphic* is GMD used.

**3B6.4:** Secondary support (optional). An image with secondary support may be noted if the mount or mat is of historical, informational, aesthetic, or archival importance.

1 photoprint mounted on cardboard

39 photoprints on stereo cards

**3C2.4:** Other physical details.

1 photoprint on stereo card : stereograph

(i.e., a full stereograph)

**3D3.4:** For photoprints affixed to standard mounts, ... record only the dimensions of the mount.

1 photoprint on stereo card : stereograph ; 9 x 18 cm.

## 2. FILMSTRIP

### *AACR 2* catalog record

What you should know about substance abuse [filmstrip] / produced by the National Health Education Association. -- Washington, D.C. : NHEA, c1983.
1 filmstrip (75 fr.) : col. ; 35 mm. + 1 sound cassette + 1 teacher's guide + 1 script.

Informs teenagers about different types of substance abuse, and outlines strategies for avoidance of this problem.

I. National Health Education Association.

```
OCLC MARC Tagging

Type: g  Bib lvl: m  Govt pub:       Lang: eng  Source: d  Leng: nnn
          Enc lvl: I  Type mat: f    Ctry: dcu  Dat type: s  MEBE: 0
Tech: n  Mod rec:          Accomp mat: r
Desc: a  Int lvl: d  Dates: 1983,

1  040     xxx $ xxx
2  007     g $b o $c  $d c $e j $f b  $g f $h f $i
3  245 00  What you should know about substance abuse $h filmstrip
/ $c produced by the National Health Education Association.
4  260     Washington, D.C. : $b NHEA, $c c1983.
5  300     1 filmstrip (75 fr.) : $b col. ; $c 35 mm. + $e 1 sound
cassette + 1 teacher's guide + 1 script.
6  520     Informs teenagers about different kinds of substance
abuse, and outlines strategies for avoidance of this problem.
7  710 21  National Health Education Association.
```

## *AACR 2* applicable rules

**8.0B1:**   Chief source is item itself (i.e., the title frames).

**Area 1**

**8.1B1:**   Title proper.

**8.1C1:**   GMD.

**8.1F1:**   Record statements of responsibility as in 1.1F. "Produced by" is being considered here as a statement of responsibility as well as a publishing statement; an alternative interpretation would place this statement solely in the publication area.

**Area 4**

**8.4C1:**   Place.

**8.4D1:**   Name of publisher.

**1.4D4:**   Publisher's name is shortened since it has already been given in full in the statement of responsibility area.

**8.4F1:**   Date.

**1.4F6:**   Copyright date given in absence of publication date.

**Area 5**

**8.5B1:**   Number of physical units and SMD.

**8.5B2:**   Add number of frames of filmstrip.

**8.5C2:**   For filmstrips, indicate if color. Since the "sound" (i.e., cassette) is physically separate, and thus not "integral," the term *sd.* is not given.

**8.5D2:**   For filmstrips, give dimensions in terms of the gauge, in millimeters.

**8.5E1:**   Give name of accompanying material components. Detailed physical description is optional, and not given here.

**1.5E1:**   Four options are possible for recording accompanying material. Option "d" (to record at end of physical description area) seems most appropriate in this case. LC rule interpretations give guidelines.

**Area 7**

**8.7B17:**   Summary.

## Choice of access points

**21.1C1:**   Main entry under title since item does not fit any of the corporate body main entry categories in 21.1B2 and is not of personal authorship.

**21.30E:** Added entry under a prominently named publisher whose responsibility extends beyond publishing.

## 3. POSTER

### *AACR 2* catalog record

From the lands of the Scythians [picture] : ancient treasures from the museums of the U.S.S.R., 3,000 B.C.-100 B.C. -- [United States? : s.n., 1975?]
1 poster : col. ; 48 x 70 cm.

"A loan exhibition organized in cooperation with the Ministry of Culture of the U.S.S.R."
Mounted on cardboard.

OCLC MARC Tagging

Type: k Bib lvl: m Govt pub:     Lang: eng Source: d Leng: nnn
        Enc lvl: I Type mat: i Ctry: us  Dat tp: s MEBE: 0
Tech: n Mod rec:           Accomp mat:
Desc: a Int lvl:   Dates: 1975,

```
1  040      xxx $ xxx
2  007      k $b f $c $d c $e o $f c
3  245 00   From the lands of the Scythians $h picture : $b ancient
treasures from the museums of the U.S.S.R., 3,000 B.C.-100 B.C.
4  260 0    [United States? : $b s.n., $c 1975?].
5  300      1 poster : $b col. ; $c 48 x 70 cm.
6  500      "A loan exhibition organized in cooperation with the
Ministry of Culture of the U.S.S.R."
7  500      Mounted on cardboard.
```

### *AACR 2* applicable rules

**Chief source of information**
**8.0B1:** Chief source is item itself.

**Area 1**
**8.1B1:** Title proper.

**8.1C1:** GMD.

**8.1E1:** Other title information.

**Area 4**

Since the item has been issued in multiple copies, publication information is appropriate.

**8.4C1:**   Place of publication.

**1.4C6:**   Since the city of publication is not given on the item or accompanying materials and cannot be conjectured, a probable place of publication can be given in terms of the country; a question mark indicates that some uncertainty exists. Another option would be to give the indication "S.l." to indicate no probable place, but it can be argued that a probable place is better than none, and the question mark indicates that the information is not definite.

**8.4D1:**   Name of publisher.

**1.4D7:**   Give abbreviation *s.n.* if publisher is unknown.

**8.4F1:**   Date.

**1.4F7:**   Give probable date (indicated by question mark, since no date appears on item or accompanying material). Date on brochure is being used as basis for probable date of publication.

**1.0C:**   One set of brackets is used for information taken from outside elements, since all information within the brackets applies to one area.

**Area 5**

**8.5B1:**   Number of items and SMD.

**8.5C2:**   For posters, indicate color.

**8.5D1:**   Indicate dimensions in terms of height and width in centimeters.

**Area 7**

**8.7B6:**   Statements of responsibility.

**8.7B10:**   Physical details.

**Choice of access points**

**21.1C:**   Entry under title for works of unknown authorship.

## 4. ART ORIGINAL

### *AACR 2* catalog record

Fordham, S. T. (Stephen Thomas), 1966-
   James Jr. and Raquel [art original] / S. T. Fordham. --
1985.
   1 art original : oil on canvas ; 35 x 25 cm.

   Title from label.
   Size when framed: 40 x 30 cm.
   Depicts a young Black brother and sister looking out of the
window of their Harlem apartment.

   I. Title.

```
OCLC MARC Tagging

Type: k  Bib lvl: m  Govt pub:      Lang: eng  Source: d  Leng: nnn
         Enc lvl: I  Type mat: a   Ctry: xx   Dat tp: s  MEBE: 1
Tech: n  Mod rec:        Accomp mat:
Desc: a  Int lvl:    Dates: 1985,

1 040     xxx $ xxx
2 007     k $b e $c  $d c $e a $f h
3 100 1   Fordham, S. T. $q (Stephen Thomas), $d 1966–
4 245 10  James Jr. and Raquel $h art original / $c S.T. Fordham
5 260     $c 1985.
6 300     1 art original : $b oil on canvas ; $c 35 x 25 cm.
7 500     Title from label.
8 500     Size when framed: 40 x 30 cm.
9 520     Depicts a young Black brother and sister looking out of
the window of their Harlem apartment.
```

### *AACR 2* applicable rules

**8.0B1:**    Chief source of information is item itself, including permanently affixed labels.

**Area 1**

**1.1B1:**    Title proper.

**8.1C1:**    GMD.

**1.1F1:**    Record statement of responsibility in form in which it appears on item.

**Area 4**

**1.4C8:**    [new] Do not record a place of publication for unpublished items (e.g., art originals). Do not record *s.l.*

**8.4D2:** [new] Do not record the name of a publisher for an unpublished graphic item.

**1.4F9:** [new] For unpublished items (e.g., art originals), record the date of creation, inscription, etc.

**Area 5**

**8.5B1:** Number of physical units and SMD.

**8.5C1:** Give the medium and the base of an art original.

**8.5D4:** Give the height and and width of an art original, excluding the frame.

**Area 7**

**8.7B3:** Source of title proper. This note is not essential, since the label is considered a chief source; however, the cataloger may wish to indicate that the title is not from the painting itself.

**8.7B10:** Physical details.

**8.7B17:** Summary.

**Choice of access points**

**21.1A1:** Artists are the authors of the works they create.

**21.4A:** Work of single personal authorship.

**21.30J:** Added entry under title for work of personal author.

**Form of heading**

**22.3A:** Choose form of name most commonly found (thus, initials rather than full forenames in this case).

**22.18A:** Add spelled out form of name in parentheses if part of name is represented by initials and full form is known. (Optional, if not needed to distinguish between identical names.)

**22.17A:** Add dates. (Optional, if not needed to distinguish between identical names.)

# REFERENCE SOURCES

## Encyclopedias and General Reference Sources

Ehresmann, Donald L. *Fine Arts: A Bibliographic Guide to Basic Reference Works, Histories, and Handbooks.* 2d ed. Littleton, Colo.: Libraries Unlimited, 1979.

Annotates more than 1,675 reference works covering architecture, sculpture, and painting.

*Encyclopedia of World Art.* New York: McGraw-Hill, 1959-83. 16v.

Comprehensive encyclopedia for the history of art. Includes architecture, sculpture, painting and any other man-made object that may be considered as art. Covers cultures and civilizations from prehistoric times to the present. Includes styles, movements, schools, techniques, and individual works of art and architecture. Lengthy entries, separate index volume.

Myers, Bernard S., ed. *McGraw-Hill Dictionary of Art.* New York: McGraw-Hill, 1983. 5v.

Includes articles on artists, artistic styles, periods, and art terms.

Osborne, Harold, ed. *The Oxford Companion to Art.* Oxford: Clarendon Press, 1970.

Authoritative fine arts dictionary designed for the nonspecialist. Covers painting, sculpture, printing, architecture, and drawing from ancient times to the present. Also includes artists, movements, styles, terminology, processes and materials. Extensive bibliography.

*A Visual Dictionary of Art.* Greenwich, Conn.: New York Graphic Society, 1974.

Contains thirty essays on painting and sculpture of various periods and cultures. Information on the date of creation, present location, and dimensions of original works. Biographies, color and black and white illustrations, cross-references and bibliographies.

## Biographical Dictionaries and Sources

Caplan, H. H. *The Classified Directory of Artists Signatures, Symbols and Monograms.* Detroit: Gale, 1982.

An alphabetical list of artists, mainly painters, with artist's signature or identifying symbol. Contains a separate listing reproducing monograms, known signatures and corresponding artists, illegible or misleading signatures, symbols and "unclassified signatures." Majority of the signatures belong to well-known artists. All entries give date and place of birth, and indicate the type of artist. International in scope.

*Contemporary Artists.* 2d ed. New York: St. Martin's Press, 1983.

Contains names of about 960 contemporary artists whose work is represented in permanent collections in major museums throughout the world. Biographical sketches in great detail. Bibliography includes books both by and about the entrants.

*Larousse Dictionary of Painters.* New York: Larousse and Co., 1981.

Short biographies of well-known painters. Excludes Oriental art. Color reproductions of significant works. Contains dates, country of origin, alternate or full names. Signed entries, some quite lengthy. Selected bibliography. The cataloger can benefit from information such as that included for the differences in Brueghel's names and dates: Larousse explains that Pieter Bruegel the Elder, also spelled "Brueghel," is shown to have been born in Brueggek or Breda, in the year 1525 or 1530.

*Who's Who in American Art.* 1936/37- . New York: Bowker, 1935- .

Contains entries on contributors to the visual arts field: artists, historians, art librarians, art critics, art teachers, collectors and dealers, designers, curators, sculptors and ceramists. Entries include where the artist studied and with whom, where the person worked and exhibited, the name of the dealer and a mailing address. Updated regularly and includes artists in the U.S., Canada, and Mexico, and to a lesser degree, artists in thirteen different foreign countries.

# Directories

Cashman, Norine D., ed. *Slide Buyers Guide: An International Directory of Slide Sources for Art and Architecture.* 5th ed. Littleton, Colo.: Libraries Unlimited, 1985.

An international directory of slide producers and distributors. Lists commercial vendors, museums, and other institutions. Gives addresses and contact names, evaluates technical qualities of the films used in reproduction, and price and ordering information. Name and subject index.

*Directory of Art Libraries and Visual Resources Collections in North America.* New York: Neal-Schumann, 1978.

Lists 1,300 libraries, museums, galleries, and art schools both private and in colleges and universities. Excludes film libraries and historical societies. Entries are arranged by state, and specify type of reference services offered, reprographic services, publications, holdings, and special collections.

Hudson, Kenneth, and Ann Nicholls, eds. *The Directory of World Museums.* 2d ed. New York: Facts on File, Inc., 1981.

A list of world museums and people professionally engaged in any type of museum work. Gives addresses and phone numbers, and indicates the subject areas collected by the museums. Arranged alphabetically by country and city.

*The Official Museum Directory.* New York: American Association of Museums and Crowell-Collier Educational Corp., 1971- . Annual.

Includes museums throughout the United States and Canada. Gives addresses, telephone numbers, governing authority, type of collection, description of facilities and hours. Arranged by state, then city. Includes name and institution indexes.

## Photography

*Focal Encyclopedia of Photography.* London: Focal Press, 1965.

A two-volume set that concisely defines the materials, processes, and terminology of photography. Also includes brief biographies of prominent photographers. Illustrated with color plates.

*International Center of Photography Encyclopedia of Photography.* New York: Crown Publishers, 1984.

Approximately 1,300 entries describe current techniques, applications, history, collecting practices, and the compilation of photographic collections. Includes biographies of significant photographers, definitions of materials, processes, and techniques used from the beginning of photography to the present. Provides 250 biographical entries of photographers whose work has shaped or redefined an aspect of the medium.

Keefe, Laurence E., and Dennis Inch. *The Life of a Photograph: Archival Processing, Matting, Framing and Storage.* Boston: Focal Press, 1984.

Discusses techniques, tools, chemicals, and processes used in the preservation of photographs, slides, and prints. Gives detailed analysis of the physical properties of films.

## Dictionaries and Glossaries

Allen, Edward M. *Harper's Dictionary of the Graphic Arts.* New York: Harper & Row, 1963.

Defines briefly the processes, materials, and machines used in the graphic arts. Includes 6,500 basic terms.

Haggar, Reginald G. *A Dictionary of Art Terms.* New York: Hawthorn Books, 1975.

Briefly defines the terminology of painting, sculpture, architecture, engraving, etching, lithography, and other art processes. Excludes photography.

Hall, James. *Dictionary of Subjects and Symbols in Art.* New York: Harper & Row, 1974.

Standard reference source for background information on subjects, themes, and iconographic meaning. Emphasizes Christian and Classical themes found in Western art. Lists concepts by word or phrase in alphabetical order, and makes references to literature where the subject is discussed. Includes bibliography and index. Covers recurring themes in works of artists from different time periods and different geographic areas.

Mayer, Ralph. *Dictionary of Art Terms and Techniques.* New York: Thomas Y. Crowell, 1969, reprinted 1981 by Barnes & Noble.
   Definitions of materials and methods of painting, drawing, sculpture, print-making, ceramics, and art conservation. Emphasis is on the schools, styles of art, technical processes, and materials. Black and white and color illustrations, cross-references, and bibliographies.

Mintz, Patricia Barnes. *Dictionary of Graphic Arts Terms: A Communication Tool for People Who Buy Type and Printing.* New York: Van Nostrand Reinhold Company, 1981.
   Defines commonly used terminology of printing, typography, binding, publishing, and design.

## Sources on Techniques and Processes

Field, Janet N. *Graphic Arts Manual.* New York: Mursarts Publishing Corp., 1980.
   Comprehensive guide to creating, producing and purchasing printed materials. Gives detailed information on graphic arts technology and processes, and has articles on color, composition, inks, binding, plates, prints, and the technologies, tools, and processes used in graphic arts. Discusses physical properties of films used for slides and photographs. Illustrated, with an index.

Herberts, Kurt. *The Complete Book of Artists Techniques.* New York: Frederick A. Praeger, 1958.
   Discusses materials used and method of application for various techniques. Chapters are divided according to techniques dependent on the support or ground, techniques dependent on materials, and those dependent on tools. Includes color plates and a bibliography.

Wehlte, Kurt. *The Materials and Techniques of Painting.* New York: Van Nostrand Reinhold Co., 1975.
   Outlines techniques, methods and processes used in wall and easel painting. Discusses properties of paint and painting surfaces.

## Subject Access
### Thesauri, Classification Systems, and Tools

Barnett, Pat, and Toni Peterson. "Extending MARC to Accommodate Faceted Thesauri: The AAT Model." *Library Resources and Technical Services.* In press.

Bonnifield, Lizette, and Alan Boyd, comps. *Oberlin AACR2 Art Names with LC Classifications.* Tucson, Ariz.: ARLIS/NA (Art Libraries Society of North America).
   Begun in 1982 as a name authority and classification tool recording the LC classification numbers of individual artists. Scope of the list was later expanded to include all name headings added to the Oberlin College Art Library in their *AACR 2* form. Contains nearly 5,000 names and 2,500 LC class numbers.

Chenhall, Robert G. *Nomenclature for Museum Cataloging: A System for Classifying Man-Made Objects.* Nashville: American Association for State and Local History, 1978.
(See discussion in chapter 7.)

Dane, William J. *The Picture Collection Subject Headings.* 6th ed. New York: Shoe String Press, 1968.

Glass, Elizabeth, comp. *A Subject Index for the Visual Arts.* London: Her Majesty's Stationery Office, 1969. 2v.

Green, Stanford J. *The Classification of Pictures and Slides.* Denver, Colo.: Little Books, 1984.
Guidelines for the classification and retrieval of photographic material in a wide variety of subject areas including the arts and humanities, nature, travel, technology, medicine, and science.

Parker, Elisabeth Betz. *LC Thesaurus for Graphic Materials: Topical Terms for Subject Access.* Washington, D.C.: Library of Congress Cataloging Distribution Service, 1987.
Alphabetical list of topical terms for cataloging and indexing the subject content of graphic materials. Applicable to a broad range of picture formats (e.g., original prints, photographs, drawings). More than 6,000 headings with cross-references; uses ANSI standards for thesaurus structure and syntax—for example, Broader Term (BT), Narrower Term (NT). Includes examples and extensive scope notes for definition and application.

Simmons, Wendell W., and Luraine C. Tansey. "A Slide Classification System for the Organization and Automatic Indexing of Interdisciplinary Collections of Slides and Photographs." ED 048 879. Santa Cruz: University of California, 1970.
A classification scheme intended for the organization of general collections, rather than those devoted to a single subject field, such as art.

Waal, Henri van de. *Iconclass: An Iconographic Classification System.* Amsterdam: North-Holland Publishing, 1973- .

Zinkham, Helena, and Elisabeth Betz Parker. *Descriptive Terms for Graphic Materials: Genre and Physical Characteristic Headings.* Washington, D.C.: Library of Congress, 1986.
An indexing vocabulary designed to improve access to original and historical graphic materials in library collections. The list can be used in a wide variety of cataloging systems. The 513 authorized terms and 290 cross-references are accompanied by numerous scope notes. Among the genre terms provided are *advertisements, censored works,* and *competition drawings.* Physical characteristic terms include *etchings, albumen photoprints,* and *computer-aided designs.* Includes a classed display of the terms, and a hierarchical display of print and photograph terms.
Cataloging applications are explained in the introduction. Includes special field designations for users of the MARC format: terms use field 655 for object category (genre) and field 755 for object type (physical characteristic).

# Sources of Reproductions

*Arts & Humanities Citation Index*. 1976- . Philadelphia: Institute for Scientific Information, 1978- .

Can aid art historians, scholars, and librarians searching for reproductions of specific works of art. Treats reproductions of paintings, illustrations, or various works of art appearing in art journals as implicit references. Cited references appear under artists' names, and titles of cited works are followed by the designation "ILL."

UNESCO. *Catalogue of Colour Reproductions of Paintings: 1860 to 1961* (Vol. 1) and *1961 to 1974* (Vol. 2). New York: International Documents Service, Columbia University Press, 1974.

Alphabetical by artist. Small black and white reproductions accompany each entry. Titles for the works are given in French, English, and Spanish. Also gives medium used, size and location of original, method of reproduction (offset, lithography, etc.), and address of reproductionists. Useful for locating companies that offer reproductions of well-known works of art.

(Catalogs such as those listed by G. K. Hall, the Metropolitan Museum of Art, and the Freer Gallery of the Smithsonian also provide location information.)

# Cataloging

Betz, Elisabeth W., comp. *Graphic Materials: Rules for Describing Original Items and Historical Collections*. Washington, D.C.: Library of Congress, 1982.

Created as a supplement to *AACR 2*'s chapter 8, *Graphic Materials* is to be used specifically for the descriptive cataloging of original and historical items collections. Its rules apply to two-dimensional graphic materials (such as prints, drawings, photographs, and posters) both as individual items and as groups.

The scope is described as "single two-dimensional pictorial works that are original. Typical examples are prints, posters, drawings, paintings, photoprints, photonegatives, transparencies, slides, etc. (Single photographic copies and photomechanical reproductions of such works are included as well.)" "The rules assume the copy or reproduction is somehow significant, either because it is the only existing representation of a now destroyed or unavailable image, or the creator of the copy is important." "Single items may be unpublished (though they may exist in multiple copies) or published."

As its introduction explains, *AACR 2*'s rules were not designed with the needs of specialist and archival libraries in mind. Instead, it is recommended that "such libraries use the rules as the basis of their cataloguing and augment their provisions as necessary," and this is precisely what *Graphic Materials* has done, by providing rules that augment those in *AACR 2*'s chapter 8, and are consistent with the general structure and theory of *AACR 2*, but depart from this base when necessary to meet requirements for describing original and historical graphic materials.

Since its focus is both on methods of cataloging used in libraries and on principles of archives and museum documentation, *Graphic Materials* draws upon two sources: *AACR 2* and *Bibliographic Description of Rare Books* (1981) as a foundation for its rules. It thus incorporates many archives and museum documentation practices in a national library cataloging standard.

The cataloger would use *Graphic Materials* for original and historical items. *AACR 2*'s chapter 8 would still be used for commercially available audiovisual materials such as filmstrips and slide sets, for commercially produced art works such as published and/or documented artists' prints and photographs, portfolios, and for reproductions accompanied by printed information, and postcards. In using *Graphic Materials*, the cataloger would still need to consult *AACR 2* for rules concerning choice and form of access points, and for the basic rules.

Giral, Angela. "Architectural Drawings." *Art Documentation* 5 (Spring 1986): 11-13.

Hennessey, Christine. "The Status of Name Authority Control in the Cataloging of Original Art Objects." *Art Documentation* 5 (Spring 1986): 3-10.

Library of Congress catalog records for filmstrips, and transparency and slide sets can be found in the following catalogs:

Library of Congress. *Audiovisual Materials*. 1983- . Microform.

_____. *Audiovisual Materials*. 1979-1982.

_____. *Films and Other Materials for Projection*. 1973-1978.

Earlier LC catalogs (1953-1972, and 1951-1952) cover filmstrips.

Petersen, Toni. "The AAT [Art and Architecture Thesaurus]: A Model for the Restructuring of LCSH." *The Journal of Academic Librarianship* 9 (September 1983): 207-10.

Discusses efforts undertaken by the art community to improve the state of art indexing through the production of a comprehensive thesaurus. The Art and Architecture Thesaurus is based on headings in *LCSH* and other art subject heading lists. *LCSH* is modified to follow ANSI standards for thesaurus construction, and NLM's MeSH is used as a model.

Shatford, Sara. "Describing a Picture: A Thousand Words Are Seldom Cost Effective." *Cataloging & Classification Quarterly* 4 (Summer 1984): 13-30.

Points out that different users require different kinds of information from pictures. One user may be interested solely in the subject portrayed, for example, a portrait of Lincoln, while another may be interested in how a particular artist portrays the subject. Some users may be satisfied with a reproduction of the work, while others may have the original as a focus. Shatford advocates describing both the reproduction and the original, and the relationship between the two.

Shaw, Renata V. "Picture Organization: Practice and Procedures." *Special Libraries* 63, part 1 (October 1972): 448-56; part 2 (November 1972): 502-6.

Although pre-*AACR 2*, these two articles are useful for their overview of principles underlying picture organization. Covers self-indexing files, and individual versus group cataloging.

## Graphic Materials Librarianship

Harrison, Helen, ed. *Picture Librarianship*. Phoenix, Ariz.: Oryx Press, 1981.

Articles cover sources, acquisitions, processing, storing and conservation, arrangement, indexing, cataloging, copyright, and administration.

Hill, Donna. *The Picture File: A Manual and Curriculum-Related Subject Heading List*. 2d ed., rev. and enl. Syracuse, N.Y.: Gaylord Professional Publications, 1978.

Describes how to create and maintain a curriculum-related picture file for use in the library or classroom. Covers organization and use of the subject heading list.

Irvine, Betty Jo, and P. Eileen Fry. *Slide Libraries: A Guide for Academic Institutions, Museums, and Special Collections*. 2d ed. Littleton, Colo.: Libraries Unlimited, 1979.

Deals with the management of slide libraries, including administration and staffing, acquisitions and projection systems. Detailed coverage of cataloging and classification. Directories of manufacturers and distributors, and of slide sources. Bibliography.

Jones, Lois Swan, and Sarah Scott Gibson. *Art Libraries and Information Services: Development, Organization, and Management*. Orlando, Fla.: Academic Press, 1986.

Part 2 deals with the collection, evaluation, analysis, and standards. Reference tools are discussed along with special formats, and exhibition and auction catalogs. Part 4 covers administrative and managerial issues, from cataloging to budgets. The appendixes of Part 5 include lists of acronyms, database vendors, and professional groups.

Miller, Shirley. *The Vertical File and Its Satellites: A Handbook of Acquisitions, Processing, and Organization*. 2d ed. Littleton, Colo.: Libraries Unlimited, 1979.

Covers vertical files for pamphlets, clippings, and such "satellite" collections as pictures and maps.

## Online Access Systems

Brooks, Diane. "System-System Interaction in Computerized Indexing of Visual Materials: A Selected Review." *Information Technology and Libraries* 7 (June 1988): 111-23.

Discusses conventional retrieval systems for visual materials, e.g., the Universal Slide Classification System, PRECIS, and Iconclass. Considers videotex, videodisc, and digital storage as options for the reproduction, storage and display of images.

Logan, Anne Marie. "Online Subject Access in the Photographic Archives at the Yale Center for British Art." In *Information Interaction: Proceedings of the American Society for Information Science.* Edited by Anthony E. Petrarca, Celianna I. Taylor, and Robert S. Kohn, 169-72. White Plains, N.Y.: Knowledge Industry Publications, 1982.

Markey, Karen. *Subject Access to Visual Resources Collections: A Model for Computer Construction of Thematic Catalogs.* New York: Greenwood Press, 1986.
Presents a system for describing subject content in visual images. Designed to help users find images of interest by "[translating] their search inquiry into the terminology of the specialized collection," and thus does not require that users have specialized knowledge required to search visual resources collections effectively. Designed for a wide variety of materials, such as slide collections, picture postcards, photographs, postage stamps, and original artefacts. Also applies to a diverse set of institutional settings which might have collections of visual resources, such as the vertical file of a public library, museums and art galleries, universities, magazine and newspaper morgues, and even personal collections.

Parker, Elisabeth Betz. "The Library of Congress Non-Print Optical Disk Pilot Program." *Information Technology and Libraries* 4 (December 1985): 289-95.
Describes LC project to record a variety of visual media from the pictorial collections of the Prints and Photographs Division on analog laser videodiscs and to link still image disks to a microcomputer database. Discusses implications for improved access to visual images and its application to picture research.

Sarasan, Lenore. "Visual Content Access: An Approach to the Automatic Retrieval of Visual Information." In *Papers: Automatic Processing of Art History Data and Documents*, edited by Laura Corti, 1:387-406. Los Angeles: J. Paul Getty Trust, 1984.

# 6

θθθθθθθθθθθθθθθθθθθθθθθθθθθθθθθθθθθθθθθθθθθθθθθθθθθθθθθθθθθθθθθθθθθθθθθθθθθθθθθθθθθθθθθθθθθθθθθθ

# Computer Files

θθθθθθθθθθθθθθθθθθθθθθθθθθθθθθθθθθθθθθθθθθθθθθθθθθθθθθθθθθθθθθθθθθθθθθθθθθθθθθθθθθθθθθθθθθθθθθθθ

## TRENDS AND ISSUES IN THE
## DEVELOPMENT OF BIBLIOGRAPHIC STANDARDS

Rules for computer files have been the subject of considerable controversy and subsequent revisions since the publication of the original *AACR 2*. Therefore, the present rules must be placed in the context of the earlier *AACR 2* standards.

## *AACR 2* Standards

### INTRODUCTION

The development of bibliographic standards for computer files is a classic example of an attempt to codify standards for an evolving and dynamic medium. At the time that *AACR 2* rules for "machine-readable data files" were being developed in the 1970s, the prevailing type of medium in this category was radically different from the medium that would become prevalent soon after the implementation of the rules in 1981. The original version of chapter 9 was designed primarily to deal with machine-readable files to be run on large mainframe computers. Characteristics of these computers shaped the rationale for the resulting rules. The programs created for operation, and for input and storage of data on large mainframes were chiefly intended for the use of the organization that owned the files. Thus, such files typically were not distributed for public or commercial use. Unpublished materials of all kinds are less likely to present bibliographic information in a standardized way, and this was reflected in the rules for sources of information.

The most important difference, however, was shown in the rules (or lack thereof!) for physical description. Replacing the physical description area was the "file description," which was used to describe the content of the file (namely the number of files and the number of records within them) rather than physical characteristics. These rules were designed for a type of medium whose physical characteristics were subject to change in the course of use; accordingly, the code framers felt it more important to describe the intellectual content of the software than its physical format.

## INADEQUACIES

Soon after the publication of *AACR 2*, at just about the time of its implementation, however, dramatic changes occurred in the computer industry. Although large mainframe computers still remained in use, many structural changes and modifications were taking place which revolutionized the technology. Today many of the formats prevalent in the earlier stages of computer development, such as punched cards, aperture cards, and paper tape are no longer dominant, if not virtually obsolete, thus rendering many of the terms and concepts in the original chapter 9 archaic. In addition, the advent of microchip technology has resulted in a proliferation of smaller systems, both minicomputer and microcomputer. These systems greatly expanded the use of computers and resulted in software that was developed and distributed commercially. Thus, the original chapter 9, written for mainframe computer software, was largely inappropriate for cataloging commercial microcomputer software, which differs radically from earlier computer media both in terms of physical characteristics and in mode of production. Although *AACR 2*'s introduction claims that its rules can be used as a basis for cataloging "library materials yet unknown," the developments in computer technology demonstrated that such an extension of the existing rules is not always so easily accomplished.

In many aspects, a parallel can be drawn between *AACR 1*'s inability to provide adequate standards for emerging audiovisual media shortly after its publication in the late 1960s, and the need for guidelines for cataloging microcomputer software after the publication of *AACR 2*. In both cases, there was recognition of an acute need to revise the existing rules, and efforts were made to develop new standards. For computer files, this resulted in the creation of an ALA Task Force appointed by the Resources and Technical Service Division's Committee on Cataloging: Description and Access (CCDA). Specialized guidelines for cataloging microcomputer software were developed over a period of two years and published in 1984 by ALA as a document entitled *Guidelines for Using AACR2 Chapter 9 for Cataloging Microcomputer Software* (hereafter referred to as the *1984 Guidelines*).[1]

# 1984 Guidelines

The *1984 Guidelines* for cataloging microcomputer software were not intended to replace *AACR 2*'s chapter 9 but instead were to be used as an "interpretation." Their scope was also more limited than chapter 9, in that they concentrated on a few areas recognized as posing "special problems," and referred the reader to chapter 9 for all remaining areas. As an "interpretation" rather than rules, the *1984 Guidelines* were intended to be optional. Nevertheless, after their completion, the major bibliographic utilities considered the guidelines to be sufficiently authoritative to warrant the creation of Machine Readable Data File MARC formats and to allow input of these materials into the bibliographic databases.

The major areas addressed in the *1984 Guidelines* are scope, source of information, title and statement of responsibility, edition, and file description. Individual programs in a collection are briefly discussed and an extensive glossary comprises the latter half of the work.

Since the *1984 Guidelines* were intended as a provisional measure, CCDA's involvement continued as work was begun on the formal revision of chapter 9. Meanwhile, attention on the international level was also being focused on the preparation of revised rules for computer software. In late 1984, a British proposal for revision of chapter 9 was submitted to the Joint Steering Commmittee for the Revision of AACR (JSC). In 1985 Michael Gorman, one of the editors of *AACR 2*, was appointed by JSC to prepare a draft revision of chapter 9. The ensuing drafts received the attention of cataloging committees in the United States, Canada, the United Kingdom, and Australia. Gorman's proposed revision was published in the spring of 1987, and forms the basis of chapter 9 in *AACR 2*, 1988 rev.[2] Thus, of all the chapters in *AACR 2*, chapter 9 has undergone the most wide-ranging revision. The significance of these new rules is far-reaching: There is now a single, internationally recognized standard for the bibliographic description of computer files. Catalogers, for the present at least, will no longer have to attempt to mesh two sets of rules with different levels of coverage, or try to fit emerging formats into rules for an outdated medium.

The revised chapter 9 now supersedes previous standards for the cataloging of computer files.[3] However, the following narrative will include a detailed discussion of the original chapter 9 in *AACR 2*, and the *1984 Guidelines*, since it is essential to gain an understanding of previous standards used to formulate large numbers of records still found in databases and sources of cataloging copy.

## DECISION AREAS IN DESCRIPTIVE CATALOGING

### Scope

**REVISED CHAPTER 9**

Broadly defined, chapter 9 covers "files that are encoded for manipulation by computer." As in the earlier rules, the scope includes both data files and program files. A key difference from the earlier rules is that the scope of the new rules has been expanded to include files stored on, or contained in, carriers available only by remote access as well as those directly available.

Electronic devices such as calculators fall outside the scope of this chapter and are to be cataloged using the chapter for three-dimensional materials (chapter 10). Programs that reside in the permanent memory of a computer (ROM) or firmware (e.g, a computer program that is built into a microchip) are considered as part of the device and are described in conjunction with the device.

## ORIGINAL CHAPTER 9

The original chapter 9 was entitled "machine-readable data files," and defined as "a body of information coded by methods that require the use of a machine (typically a computer) for processing." In addition, the rules covered accompanying documentation as well as the machine-readable data files themselves.

The examples given in the chapter reflected the types of storage media in use at the time the rules were framed: files stored on magnetic tape, punched cards, aperture cards, punched paper tapes, disk packs, mark sensed cards, and optical character recognition font documents.

## 1984 GUIDELINES

The *1984 Guidelines* made a crucial distinction between commercially marketed files produced in multiple copies and noncommercial files. Only the commercially marketed files were covered by the *1984 Guidelines*, and the cataloger was referred to the original chapter 9 for noncommercial items.

This created a dichotomy within the *1984 Guidelines* based on whether the software was commercially marketed; and applied a distinction based on mode of publication. As a result, the *1984 Guidelines* often excluded data that are closely related, if not identical, to commercially produced data in terms of physical format and intellectual content; for example, a blank disk used to create a file as part of a program, or a blank disk used as a back-up to copy data. Thus, relatively identical software could have very different catalog records.

# Sources of Information

## REVISED CHAPTER 9

### THE PROBLEM OF AVAILABILITY

As is true for many other nonbook materials, the cataloging of microcomputer software is dependent upon machinery for procurement of information. If an internal label is to be considered as a chief source of information, a cataloger must have a means of gaining access to the label. This requires that a cataloging agency own or have access to the necessary hardware as well as the expertise to operate it. The flexibility provided by the new rules to use information from external sources alleviates some of this problem. Occasionally however, there may be problems with the availability of external labels and in the comprehensiveness of the information they provide.

The cataloger may encounter additional difficulties when documentation issued by the producer or distributor of the software is used as a source of information, since existing documentation may be incomplete.

### INTERNAL SOURCES: When Is the Cataloger Required to Use Them?

As with other media in *AACR 2*, information from the item itself is preferred, and the chief source of information for computer files is the title screen. In the absence of a title screen, the cataloger can take the information from other internal sources such as main menus and program statements (9.0B1).

While an internal source (i.e., the item itself) is preferred as a chief source, a key difficulty in obtaining the necessary bibliographic information may lie in the lack of availability of computer equipment needed to read the file to be cataloged. The revised rules recognize this limitation, and provide that, if the information required is not "available" from any of the above-named sources, it can be taken from other published descriptions of the file, or from "other sources." The term *not available* applies to situations in which the cataloger lacks access to equipment needed to mount or read the file. (This is in contrast to the definition of *not available* in other chapters, where the term refers to the fact that the desired information simply does not exist.)

Since the crucial factor of *availability* has been introduced to the rules for sources of information, the cataloger has an alternative in situations in which equipment is not readily at hand to mount or read the file. The concept of *availability* is still relative, however. Who is to decide what effort is too great, or what distance too far, to secure the necessary information? Convenience and expense will no doubt play a role in such decisions. Gorman would prefer a wider interpretation of the chief source. In his opinion, *AACR 2*'s rule will not be adhered to and catalogers will use the sources most readily available to them.[4]

There is another instance in which information from external sources is allowed: a container or permanent label can serve as the chief source if it alone provides a collective title for two or more separate physical parts. The same situation occurs in rules for sound recordings and graphic materials.

## ORIGINAL CHAPTER 9

The chief source for data files was an internal user label, defined as "a machine-readable identifier containing alphabetic and/or numeric characters providing information about the file." If not available from the chief source, the information could be taken from (1) the documentation issued by the creator, (2) other published descriptions of the file, or (3) other sources, including the container and labels.

The original chapter 9 was developed for an environment in which "unpublished," or noncommercial computer programs prevailed. Unlike today's computer programs, the early programs had little standardization in the provision of bibliographic data, and little consistency in the placement of this data in a predictable place, such as in a title frame.

## 1984 GUIDELINES

The *1984 Guidelines* also preferred internal sources of information, but did not identify the title screen as the explicit first choice of chief source.

As with the present rules, a recognition was made of the difficulty of gaining access to necessary equipment. Alternative sources were to be used if adequate bibliographic information was not available internally on the item, or if the cataloger did not have access to a microcomputer that could display the data.

The *1984 Guidelines* differed from the original chapter 9 in that the external labels were given greater priority as an alternative chief source. The original rules gave preference to documentation and published descriptions.

An LC pilot program has been implemented to provide Cataloging in Publication (CIP) for software on the verso of the title page of the documentation. The CIP data for computer files will be more complete than information that has been typically provided for books, and will include the physical description area and complete systems requirement notes.[5]

## Title and Statement of Responsibility Area

**REVISED CHAPTER 9**

*TITLE PROPER: Source*

An important change in the revised rules is that the source of the title proper is recorded in a note, even if the title proper comes from the chief source (9.1B2).

*STATEMENT OF RESPONSIBILITY: Defining Intellectual Contributions*

A distinction is made between "persons or bodies responsible for the content of the file," and "sponsors, etc., or persons or bodies who have prepared or contributed to the the production of the file." Statements relating to the first category are recorded in the statement of responsibility area, while the second category is recorded in a note (9.1F1). The distinction made between content and production points out the primacy accorded to roles involving intellectual responsibility.

With the advent of microcomputer technology, it is now more likely that a single individual can bear primary responsibility not only for the intellectual content of the work, but also for its technical production. In the past, such productions would have required expensive, complex equipment and highly skilled technicians. Analogous situations can be found in the development of audio, motion picture, and video technology formats.

*ITEMS WITHOUT A COLLECTIVE TITLE: File Names versus Titles*

Items that contain separately titled files without a collective title are a common occurrence in computer software. Rule 9.1G deals with items without a collective title, but contains no rules specific for this chapter. Instead, the cataloger is referred to rule 1.1G in the general chapter. Since there is often no intellectual relationship among the files, the argument can be made that individual records under each title would provide better access for the user. In the original *AACR 2*, this option was provided only for sound recordings, maps, and motion pictures and videorecordings. In the revised rule 1.1G2, the option is included in the general rules applicable to all materials. The *1984 Guidelines* added a section on cataloging individual files within a collection, and gave instruction on formulating records for an individual file, but this applied only to works with a collective title.

In a related situation, an item might contain the name of a file or of a data set. These names should not be recorded as the title proper unless they are the *only* names given in the chief source (9.1B3).

## ORIGINAL CHAPTER 9

In the original chapter 9, the source of the title was recorded in the note area only if the title had been taken from outside the file itself.

## *1984 GUIDELINES*

The *1984 Guidelines* include no rules for recording the title or the statement of responsibility. The reader would refer instead to the original chapter 9.

## GENERAL MATERIAL DESIGNATION: Finding a
## Name for an Emerging Medium

### *REVISED CHAPTER 9*

A major change in the revised chapter 9 is the introduction of a new GMD, "computer file" (9.1C1).

### *ORIGINAL CHAPTER 9 AND 1984 GUIDELINES*

In the original chapter 9, the term given on both the North American and British lists was *machine-readable data file*. The *1984 Guidelines* recognized the "widespread agreement that a general material designation ... for describing microcomputer files would be useful," and that "some dissatisfaction exists with the GMD as specified in AACR2, [i.e., original chapter 9]," but could identify no widely agreed-upon alternative. Although other terms were considered, such as *microcomputer software, computer software, software,* and *machine readable files*, none of the alternatives met with universal acceptance, and the *1984 Guidelines* retained the original GMD.

A major objection was that use of the term *machine-readable data file* could be misleading. As Intner explains, "the word 'data' means information to librarians, but to computer people, data files are only one kind of computer-readable item, containing nothing but pieces of information, without the addition of instructions for the computer to use when working on them, called 'program files' or simply 'programs.' "[6] Thus, the GMD appeared to be limited to certain types of files, and the differentiation between data and program files was not made until much later in the catalog record.

While some objected that the term *machine-readable data files* was too limiting, others felt the term to be too comprehensive, since any item requiring a machine to be "read" might fit in this category, as, for example, a microform. Still another faction argued that the basic objective of the GMD should be to indicate the format of the item being represented, and that the term *data files* appeared to convey the idea of subject content rather than physical form.

## Edition Area

**REVISED CHAPTER 9**

### CONCEPT OF EDITION FOR COMPUTER FILES

The rules specify that an edition statement is given for a named reissue of a computer file, or for an edition of the file that contains differences from other editions (9.2B1). In case of doubt about what to regard as an edition statement, words such as *edition, issue, version, release, level, update* should be regarded as evidence of an edition statement (9.2B2).

Gorman argues that the new rules have diluted the concept of *edition*. He feels that a distinction should be made between "something recorded as an edition because it says it is, and manifestations which contain substantial changes from a previous edition." He gives the example of "Apple edition" — in which a file prepared physically to be used on an Apple computer becomes recorded as an edition statement (though the files themselves do not differ in content).[7]

### WHEN TO SUPPLY AN EDITION STATEMENT?

If the file lacks an edition statement but is known to contain significant changes from other editions, the cataloger has the option of supplying an edition statement and enclosing it in square brackets. Essentially, the decision should be based on whether the changes are substantive or minor in nature. Substantive changes would include:

- changes in the data involving content

- changes in the program statements, programming language, and programming routines and operations

- the addition of sound or graphics (9.2B3)

On the other hand, there are certain types of changes that are minor in nature and should not be regarded as constituting a new edition. Examples of minor changes include corrections of misspellings of data, changes in the arrangement of the contents, changes in the output format or the display medium, and changes in the physical characteristics (blocking factors, recording density, etc.). These changes can be given in the edition and history note (9.2B4).

## DIFFERENTIATING EDITIONS

It is often very difficult to tell if the contents of the software have actually been modified or if the software has merely been copied. Since microcomputer software is easily copied, taking edition information from accompanying documentation may be misleading because the edition statement on the software and the title page of the documentation may not be in agreement.

The decimal numbers used with the edition statements of software indicate the number of times the program has been revised or debugged. The number to the left of the decimal point signifies major revisions (e.g., Release 1.0, 2.0, etc.); the number to the right indicates less radical changes or minor additions (e.g, Release 1.2, 1.3, etc.).[8]

Olson cautions that it is important to differentiate between a new version of the software and the version of the operating system needed to run it. She explains "both are usually expressed as 'version 3.3' or some other decimal number. The term that refers to the operating system generally will be prefaced by the letters 'DOS' or 'CP/M' or some combination of numbers and letters, frequently including the letters 'os' for operating system. A statement referring to the version of the software is recorded as an edition statement; the statement referring to the version of the operating system needed to run that software is included in the System requirement note."[9]

## 1984 GUIDELINES

The *1984 Guidelines* established a criterion that differentiated between substantive changes from previous editions, as opposed to statements from the publisher regarding edition. In its discussion of what constitutes a new edition, the *1984 Guidelines* called attention to new material which is intended to supplement an existing issue. In situations of this kind, a statement of numbers and/or generic words such as edition, version, level, and so on, is *not* to be considered as an edition statement. Instead, "the item may be described separately or as an accompanying part of the existing content described on the record for the original."

The *1984 Guidelines* strongly cautioned against creating "ghost" editions, and advised against the optional rule that allows catalogers to create an edition statement if changes are known to have been made.

# File Characteristics Area

## REVISED CHAPTER 9

### *A PLACE FOR UNIQUE CHARACTERISTICS*

*AACR 2*'s area 3, awkwardly titled the "Material (or Type of Publication) Specific Details Area," is designed "for details that are special to a particular class of material or type of publication." This area is an innovation of the ISBD(G) and recognizes that some types of materials have essential characteristics which are unique and cannot be described using the overall framework for description. In the original *AACR 2,* area 3 was used in only two chapters: in chapter 3 to describe the mathematical data area for cartographic materials, and in chapter 12 to describe numeric, alphabetic, and chronological designations for serials. In the revised *AACR 2,* an area 3 has been assigned to computer software, to allow provision for recording the file characteristics.

### *CONTENT OF THE FILE CHARACTERISTICS AREA*

The file characteristics area gives important information in an early part of the sequence of a bibliographic record. It states whether a file consists of data and/or programs, and gives the number of files.

Elements of information in this area indicate the type of file, for example, computer data, computer program(s), and the number of files that make up the content. These elements are recorded if the information is readily available. Further details can be given recording the number of records, bytes, or statements.

Area 3 will not be used by LC "for the most part," but will be applied "when cataloging remote access files for which no physical description can be provided."[10]

### *THE ACCESSIBILITY PROBLEM AGAIN*

It may be difficult to ascertain information needed for this area. The cataloger must first have access to the appropriate equipment, second, the skills necessary to mount the file, and third, the skills to determine information that may not be explicitly stated in terms needed for the catalog description. While most individuals would recognize a title screen, specialized skills are needed to ascertain the type or number of files present. A file directory may assist in this regard, but not all items will have a directory available to the user.

Information such as the number of files, records, bytes, and statements may not always be accessible, since files in commercially produced items are often protected and secured specifically so they cannot be examined. Programming language may not be noted in the sources of information, but implied by the operating system or the make or model of machine on which the software runs.[11] The revised rules take these difficulties into account by allowing certain types of information to be omitted if they are not readily available. Reference sources may assist in this task, especially when the cataloger lacks familiarity with computer concepts and terminology.

## ORIGINAL CHAPTER 9

In the original chapter 9, information relating to file characteristics was recorded in the file description area. This was a substitution for the physical description area, and was located in the place of the catalog record where physical characteristics would normally be recorded. (No rules were given for physical description, with the exception of rules for describing accompanying material.) The area called for a word phrase stating the number of data files along with terms to describe the number of logical records, programming language, and machine compatibility. For a data file, the cataloger was instructed to add in parentheses the number of logical records; for a program file, the number of statements and name of the programming language; and for an object program, the name of the machine on which it ran.

## *1984 GUIDELINES*

The *1984 Guidelines* retained the file description area, but did extend the scope of this area to include physical characteristics as well. (For additional discussion of this area, see the section in this chapter on the physical description area.)

# Publication Area

## REVISED CHAPTER 9

Revised rules, applicable to materials in general, also accommodate unpublished computer files. No place of publication and no name of publisher are given for an unpublished file (9.4C2, 9.4D2). However, the publication area for unpublished files will still include a date (9.4F3).

## PREVIOUS RULES

In the original *AACR 2*, no provisions were made for unpublished computer software. The *1984 Guidelines* did not contain rules for the publication area.

# Physical Description Area

## REVISED CHAPTER 9

The rules introduce a provision for computer files that are not directly available. For carriers that are available only by remote access, the physical description is omitted. This is the only instance in *AACR 2* in which physical description is not required.

Although four SMDs are given—"computer cartridge," "computer cassette," "computer disk," and "computer reel"—the rules recognize that new physical carriers will be developed, and that none of the present SMDs may be appropriate for these new formats. In such instances, the cataloger can give the specific name of the new format as concisely as possible, preferably qualified by the word *computer*. Such flexibility is imperative in a medium that is in a dynamic state of development.

The cataloger can give information on the physical characteristics of disks, such as the number of sides used, and recording density (e.g., single, double sectoring). This is optional and is indicated if the information is readily available and considered important (9.5C2). Such information is often explicitly stated on the item, but is not always considered important. In deciding on the relative significance of this information, the cataloger should give thought to whether these characteristics differ from the norm expected by the user, and would thus affect its use.

Dimensions are given as appropriate for the type of carrier. Gorman points out that, owing to the present lack of stability of computer development, there are no standard dimensions for computer carriers.[12]

## ORIGINAL CHAPTER 9

Unlike chapters for other types of materials in *AACR 2*, the original chapter 9 had no section called the physical description area. In its place was the file description area, reflecting the chapter's emphasis on the content of the files rather than the physical form. Instead of using this area to describe the physical characteristics of computer files, chapter 9 asked the cataloger to describe the characteristics of the intellectual item or the "extent of file."

This situation reflected the kinds of data storage employed by large mainframe computers at the time that chapter 9's rules were drafted. The physical carriers which were used to store data in these computers were subject to change in the course of storage and use: A file might begin as a magnetic tape, punched paper cards, or paper tapes. Data on the tapes or cards might then be transferred to another medium, for example, a plastic disk or magnetic tape, as the data are "read" into the computer. The data might next be transferred again to still another form of storage. With this instability of the physical storage medium in mind, the *AACR 2* rule drafters developed a set of rules designed to accommodate the constantly changing physical entity.

The physical manifestation of an item was deemed to be of limited value in the catalog description. The physical attributes of computer materials, it was felt, would be of minimum interest to the user, as well as difficult to describe, in all of its transient forms.

Instead of requiring that physical attributes of computer materials be recorded, the original chapter 9 provided rules to describe the files housed in the physical entity. This description was given in terms of the logical records (i.e., data units or program statements) contained in the files. This requirement would be comparable to describing books not in terms of the number of pages, but instead the number of chapters, with the number of words in parentheses.[13]

Since the basic rationale for this approach assumed an environment in which instable physical formats were used in large mainframes, the rules proved to be largely unsuitable for the more stable physical formats of commercially produced microcomputer software.

## *1984 GUIDELINES*

The *1984 Guidelines* revised and expanded chapter 9's rules for file description, and allowed the cataloger to add information considered necessary for the physical description of the item.

The file description area grouped information on both file and physical characteristics in one place. The first category was used to record the type of file (data or program), number of files, and number of records or statements. The second category gave information on the physical medium (e.g., computer disk, computer cartridge, or computer cassette). Optionally, one could add the programming language if it was specifically indicated in the sources of information. Information on disk characteristics was given in a note.

Whereas the revised rules prescribe that the trade name be given only in a note, the *1984 Guidelines* allowed the cataloger to add the name, model, and number of the computer for which the software was developed if it had been designed to run on a specific kind and model of computer.

Rule 9.5D of the *1984 Guidelines* went into detail to clarify what was to be considered as subordinate (i.e., "accompanying") material, if an item consisted of both data and program files. In addition, the *1984 Guidelines* gave directives on when subordinate material was to be recorded as accompanying material and when it was to be recorded as a note.

# Note Area

## REVISED CHAPTER 9

Presumably most users will be seeking programs that can be run on the particular type of computer to which they have access. Most software programs are "machine specific," that is, designed to run on a particular make and model computer, with sufficient memory and operating efficiency. Information on system requirements is thus of particular importance to users, and the location of this note in the catalog record has been a topic of concern. Gorman points out that in *AACR 2*, 1988 rev., the first note embodies a concept found throughout the entire edition—that each medium should be provided with the opportunity to have a relevant note given first, as opposed to the idea of a fixed and inflexible sequence to be applied to all media (rule 1.7B).[14]

Because use of a computer file is contingent upon securing the necessary hardware, and because there is a wide range of hardware configurations available, it is easy to see why the rules require a mandatory note on the system requirements of the file if the information is readily available. This note includes information such as the make and model of the computer(s) on which the file is designed to run, the amount of memory required, the name of the operating system (e.g. "DOS 3.3"), the software requirements, and peripherals needed (9.7B1b).

A second mandatory note, if applicable, is the note indicating that a file is available only by remote access, and specifying the mode of access. This note is similar in purpose to the systems requirement note and contains information essential to the use of the item (9.7B1c).

Additional information about remote files is contained in the physical description note. This note is the only place in which the cataloger can describe physical characteristics for such files, since the rules prescribe that no physical description area can be given for these materials. The note for remote files can include any physical details (e.g., color, sound) that are readily available and considered important (9.7B10).

A third mandatory note is the source of the title proper. Unlike its use in chapters for other media, this note is given even if the title has been taken from the chief source, that is, the title screen (9.7B3).

Rule 9.7B2 clarifies an ambiguity that existed in previous rules. The revised rules point out that the note for language refers to the spoken or written content of a file, and not to the programming language; the latter information is indicated in the note given for system requirements (9.7B1).


## ORIGINAL CHAPTER 9

### *SOME MAJOR DEFICIENCIES*

The original chapter 9 paid scant attention to the physical characteristics of computer programs. The note area was likewise notable for its absence of directives for recording information relating to hardware and equipment needed to run the program. In contrast, other chapters in the original *AACR 2* did provide rules for the description of equipment needed to use motion pictures and videorecordings, microforms, and certain types of graphic materials. With computer programs, the assumption was made that individuals who wanted to use the software would be familiar with its hardware requirements.


### *ADDITIONS AND RELOCATIONS*

The note on the source of the title proper was given only if the title proper had been taken from somewhere other than the data file itself.

The "program" note described the program version and/or level. This information is now given in the edition area.

The "file description and physical description" note allowed the cataloger to record physical characteristics if the size of the file could not be ascertained, or if the file consisted of "physical exemplars retained for their physical characteristics" (e.g., "75 plastic credit cards with magnetic strip on back").

*1984 GUIDELINES*

*A STEP IN THE RIGHT DIRECTION*

In the *1984 Guidelines*, three notes relating to equipment were added. These provided a means of indicating systems requirements, other systems on which the software could run, and the physical characteristics of the carrier itself.

While the original chapter 9 had no note to describe system requirements, the *1984 Guidelines* expanded original chapter 9's "mode of use" note to become "Systems Requirements and Disks Characteristics." (Unlike the present rules, however, the *1984 Guidelines* did not combine the systems requirements note with the "nature and scope" note.) The cataloger was instructed to give all pertinent information that would identify the type of equipment needed to use the software, such as the make and model of computer, memory, and so on.

Disk characteristics, such as the number of sides and recording density were also given here, in contrast to the present rules, which prescribe that this information be recorded in the physical description area.

## Standard Number

R. R. Bowker Co., administrator of the U.S. ISBN agency, began assigning International Standard Book Numbers to microcomputer software in 1983.[15] In 1984, microcomputer software numbering was included within the scope of the worldwide ISBN system; at that point more than 5,000 software publishers and producers had been issued ISBN numbers.[16]

## Choice of Access Points

### THE COMPUTER AS ACCESS POINT?

Discussions on access points for computer software have considered traditional access by title, author, producer, and subject, as well as access by features unique to the medium, such as programming language, operating system, and model or family of microcomputer. Many have felt that access points should be provided under the make and model of a computer needed to run the program. It has been suggested that an added entry be made under rule 21.29D, which allows for added entries to be given other than the ones prescribed in the specific rules. (See also the discussion under subject analysis in this chapter.) There is little precedent however for such an added entry in *AACR 2*'s rules for choice of access points. There is also no provision in the chapters for form of heading that would prescribe how to formulate the name of a machine.

An alternative suggestion is to provide access to the microcomputer make and model through subject headings such as the following:

IBM Personal computer--Computer programs--Specimens

Apple (Computer)--Computer programs

Bibliographic utilities have already taken steps to provide access through microcomputer make and model. OCLC and UTLAS make this type of access possible through field 753 in the MARC format, which will provide an added entry for make and model of machine, programming language, and operating system.

# SUBJECT ACCESS
# AND ORGANIZATION

## Guidelines from ALA

The Subject Analysis Committee of ALA's Resources and Technical Services Division formed an ad hoc Subcommittee on Subject Access to Microcomputer Software to propose guidelines on subject analysis and classification of microcomputer software.[17]

The committee produced a document entitled *Guidelines on Subject Access to Microcomputer Software*, published in 1986.[18] The subject guidelines address three major areas: (1) the incorporation of the machine or operating system in the subject analysis, (2) primary versus secondary components in subject heading access, and (3) primary versus secondary components in classification access. Some of the major points are summarized in the discussion below.

### ACCESS POINTS UNDER NAME OF
### MACHINE OR OPERATING SYSTEM

Information derived from the system requirements note can be used as added entry headings in the 753 field. The contents of this field can be standardized by using the form of the heading for the machine, operating system, and programming language found in *LCSH*. If no heading exists, one should be developed using similar *LCSH* headings as models. By repeating the 753 field, the cataloger can provide access in an added entry to any of these details. Whereas the description of the system requirements is a mandatory field, the creation of any or all of the added entry headings in the 753 field is local option.

### SUBJECT HEADINGS AND CLASSIFICATION

The subject content of microcomputer software should be viewed no differently from that of other materials. Subject headings and classification should be applied according to the same criteria as other materials in the collection.

Classification policy should allow software to be mainstreamed according to the subject instead of developing accession number schemes or grouping together all software in the computer science area.

While a form subdivision may be added to indicate the medium of microcomputer software, the main subject heading should indicate the topic or genre of the material. Likewise, in the use of the Dewey Decimal Classification, a standard subdivision may be added to the class number to indicate the form, but the main class number should be determined according to the subject of software rather than the fact that it is software.

Headings should *not* be assigned for the name of the program, the name of the computer, the computer language, the operating system, or any other information described in the systems requirements note. Access to this information can be provided in the 753 field.

There may be a need to provide access to the genre of the software (e.g., *Adventure games* would be an appropriate subject heading for a specific adventure game). While this is not current LC practice, users have expressed the need for such access.

The only heading now in *LCSH* that is appropriate as a form subdivision for microcomputer software is the free-floating subdivision *Computer programs*. Applying this subdivision to microcomputer software blurs the distinction between books containing listings of programs and the software itself. The Subject Analysis Committee recommends the use of *Software* as the form subdivision for the actual software.

## SUBDIVISIONS FOR HARDWARE?

The addition of a second subdivision in the subject heading for the machine or operating system used by the microcomputer software should be considered as local option (e.g., Topic-Form subdivision-Computer model or Operating system). Separate subject entries should not be given for the machine model, operating system, or programming language. Separate headings should also not be given under *Computer software* or *Computer programs*. This would result in files too large to be of use in the physical card catalog, and possibly too ambiguous to be of use in the online catalog.

Weihs disagrees with the idea of a subdivision for a computer model or an operating system. She argues that this information is duplicated by other elements in the bibliographic description, and in the MARC record. In addition, she suggests that, as software becomes less machine-specific in the future, there will no longer be a need for this information.[19]

The ALA subject guidelines include an appendix of selected subject headings for computer topics and equipment compiled from *LCSH* and the Hennepin County Library Authority List. Also given are reference books which can serve as sources for new subject headings.

# NOTES

[1]American Library Association. Committee on Cataloging: Description and Access, *Guidelines for Using AACR2 Chapter 9 for Cataloging Microcomputer Software* (Chicago: American Library Association, 1984).

[2]Nancy B. Olson, "Cataloging Microcomputer Software: Using the Newly Revised AACR2 Chapter 9," in *Policy and Practice in Bibliographic Control of Nonbook Media*, ed. Sheila S. Intner and Richard P. Smiraglia (Chicago: American Library Association, 1987), 157.

[3]*Anglo-American Cataloguing Rules. Second Edition. Chapter 9, Computer Files*, draft revision, ed. Michael Gorman for the Joint Steering Committee for Revision of AACR (Chicago: American Library Association, 1987).

[4]Michael Gorman, Presentation at program sponsored by Online Audiovisual Catalogers (OLAC), San Francisco, June 1987.

[5]Richard Thaxter, Presentation at American Library Association Annual Conference, San Francisco, June 1987.

[6]Sheila S. Intner, "Problems and Solutions in Descriptive Cataloging of Microcomputer Software," *Cataloging & Classification Quarterly* 5 (Spring 1985): 51, 52.

[7]Gorman, OLAC presentation.

[8]Calvin Covert, "The Impatient Writer's Dream," *Detroit Free Press*, 19 November 1985, 3C.

[9]Nancy B. Olson, *Cataloging of Audiovisual Materials: A Manual Based on AACR 2*, 2d ed., ed. Edward Swanson and Sheila S. Intner (Mankato, Minn.: Minnesota Scholarly Press, 1985).

[10]Verna Urbanski, "Questions and Answers," *OLAC Newsletter* 8 (June 1988): 20.

[11]Sue A. Dodd, "Changing AACR2 to Accommodate the Cataloging of Microcomputer Software," *Library Resources & Technical Services* 29 (January/March 1985): 58.

[12]Gorman, OLAC presentation.

[13]Intner, "Problems and Solutions in Descriptive Cataloging of Microcomputer Software," 52.

[14]Gorman, OLAC presentation.

[15]"Bowker Assigning ISBN's to Software," *Wilson Library Bulletin* (September 1983): 10.

[16]"ISBN Numbers for Micro Software Affirmed by International Body," *Library Journal* (1 September 1984): 1591.

[17]American Library Association, Ad Hoc Subcommittee on Subject Access to Microcomputer Software, *Guidelines on Subject Access to Microcomputer Software* (Chicago: American Library Association, 1986), 1.

[18]*Guidelines on Subject Access to Microcomputer Software.*

[19]Jean Weihs, "Access to Nonbook Materials: The Role of Subject Headings and Classification Numbers for Nonbook Materials," in *Policy and Practice in Bibliographic Control of Nonbook Media*, ed. Sheila S. Intner and Richard P. Smiraglia (Chicago: American Library Association, 1987), 56.

# DESCRIPTIVE CATALOGING EXAMPLES

## Items to Be Cataloged

1. Computer program and data

> 2 computer disks, 5¼ inches, one user manual (44 pages), in jacket/folder.

Title screen:

> Creative Cookbook System
> Version 1.1          IBM PC #8373
>
> (c) Copyright 1985
> CCJ Associates, Inc.
>   P.O. Box 9845 Washington, DC 20002

Disk label:

> Program Disk 128 K, Two Sided IBM-PC
> Creative Cookbook System
> (c) 1985 CCJ Associates, Inc.
> P.O. Box 9845 Washington, DC 20002
> v1.1          No. 8373

Disk label:

> Data disk 128K, Two Sided IBM-PC
> Creative Cookbook System
> (c) 1985 CCJ Associates, Inc.
> P.O. Box 9845 Washington, DC 20002
> v.1.1          No. 8373

Jacket:

> Requires: 128K
>
> Runs on IBM PC or 100% compatible
>
> This program allows you to create and maintain your own personalized file of recipes. You may record and search recipes by major ingredient, cooking time, holiday theme, ethnic origin, keywords.
>
> You may make and distribute as many copies as you wish. This "Shareware" distribution system depends on your honesty. If you make use of the program please remit $35.00, payable to CCJ Associates, for each installation.

2. Video game

One computer disk, 5¼ inches, sound, color; one instruction card.

Title screen:

Haunted House
by Miriam Rogers
copyright 1983
Challenge Software

Disk label:

HAUNTED HOUSE
by Miriam Rogers

CHALLENGE SOFTWARE
1948 Sixth St., Englewood, Calif.

Container:

> You'll move your good ghost through a haunted house beset by evil spirits.
>
> An arcade style game designed and coded by Miriam Rogers. Requires 48K Apple II, DOS 3.3, and is joystick or keyboard controlled.

CHALLENGE SOFTWARE          c1983.

3. Instructional game

One computer disk, 5¼ inches, 1 manual, 1 pad of budget sheets, 1 packet of play money, in container.

Title screen:

Family Finance
Budget Analysis Package
by Ruth Brett
copyright 1986

Disk label:

FAMILY FINANCE
Budget Analysis Package
c1986 Falcon Software, Inc.
Austin Texas

Menu display:

   1.  Daily expenses.

   2.  Monthly expenses.

   3.  Savings/investments.

   4.  Income.

   5.  Monthly budget status.

Container:

Commodore 64          Disk drive, color monitor required.

Revised 1986 edition.

     Have fun with finance! For six players. An easy and entertaining way to learn family budgeting. Includes 8 scenarios in which budgeting decisions must be made. Players decide how to allocate family resources.

     Contents: 1. Daily expenses. 2. Monthly expenses. 3. Savings/ investments. 4. Income. 5. Monthly budget status.

4. Video game without collective title

One computer disk, 3½ inches, sound, color, in container. No title screen.

Disk label:

LORD OF THE LIONS
THE CREATURES IN THE CAVERN

Commodore 128

Lord of the Lions and Creatures in the Cavern program and game concept     c1984 William Chapman

Computerscape, Inc.

Container:

Lord of the Lions

The Creatures in the Cavern

Commodore 128     Disk drive, joystick required

Lord of the Lions
(joystick required)

Your quest: find the Lord of the Lions and learn the words which will help you find your way through the Jungle of Saturn and flee the fierce animals lurking in every bush.

The Creatures in the Cavern
(joystick required)

The Monster of the Universe awaits you in the Dark Cavern. You, and your brave and faithful companion, Merdolf, must master the words to get through the 28 caverns to a final confrontation with the Cavern Creatures.

Vocabulary Learning Series.
Ages 8-10.

Computerscape, Inc.
380 Hill St.
Elmhurst, IL 60062

## *AACR 2* Records and OCLC MARC Tagging

### 1. COMPUTER PROGRAM AND DATA

Creative cookbook system [computer file]. -- Version 1.1. --
Computer data (1 file) and program (1 file). -- Washington, D.C. : CCJ Associates, c1985.
2 computer disks ; 5¼ in. + 1 user manual.
System requirements: IBM or IBM PC compatible ; 128K.

Title from title screen.
User may make and distribute as many copies as desired, if $35.00 remittance is made with each use to CCJ Associates.
Allows the user to create and maintain file of recipes.
No. 8373.

I. CCJ Associates.

OCLC MARC Tagging

Note: These examples reflect changes resulting from the Draft
Revision of Chapter 9.

```
Type: m  Bib lvl: m  Govt pub:      Lang: N/A  Source: d  Frequn: n
File: b  Enc lvl: I  Machine: a    Ctry: dcu  Dat tp: s  Regulr:
Desc: a  Mod rec:    Dates: 1985,
```

```
1    040     xxx $c xxx
2    245 00  Creative cookbook system $h computer file
3    250     Version 1.1.
4    256     Computer data (1 file) and program (1 file).
5    260     Washington, D.C. : $b CCJ Associates, $c c1985.
6    300     2 computer disks ; $c 5 1/4 in. + $e 1 user manual.
7    538     System requirements: IBM or IBM PC compatible ; 128K.
8    500     Title from title screen.
9    500     User may make and distribute as many copies as desired,
if $35.00 remittance is made with each use to CCJ Associates.
10   520     Allows the user to create and maintain file of recipes.
11   500     No. 8373.
12   710 20  CCJ Associates.
13   753     IBM PC.
```

## *AACR 2* applicable rules

**9.0B1:**    Chief source of information is title screen.

**Area 1**

**9.1B1:**    Record title as in 1.1B.

**9.1C1:**    GMD as in 1.1C1, following title proper, in brackets. Term *computer file* replaces former GMD *machine-readable data file.*

**Area 2**

**9.2B1:**    Record statements relating to a named reissue, or to an edition that contains differences from other editions.

**9.2B2:**    In case of doubt, take presence of words such as *edition, version,* as evidence of an edition statement.

**Area 3**

**9.3B1:**    Indicate type of file, if information is readily available. Use term *computer data and program(s).*

**9.3B2:**    Record number of files, if information is readily available.

**9.3A1:**    Enclose statement in parentheses.
The number of records, bytes, and statements would be given, if known.

**Area 4**

**9.4C1, 9.4D1, 9.4F1:**
Record place, name, and date for published computer files as in 1.4.

**1.4F6:**     Copyright date in absence of publication date.

**9.0B2:**     Prescribed sources of information for publication area include carrier label.

**Area 5**

**9.5B1:**     Record number of physical units and SMD "computer disk."

**9.5D1:**     Give diameter of disk in inches, to next ¼ inch up.

**9.5E1:**     Record details of accompanying materials as in 1.5E.

**Area 7**

**9.7B1b:**   Always make note on system requirements, if information is readily available. Give characteristics in following order: make and model of computer, amount of memory required. Statements are preceded by semicolon.

**9.7B3:**     Source of title proper given even if title proper comes from chief source.

**9.7B9:**     Additional publication details.

**9.7B17:**   Summary.

**9.7B19:**   Important numbers other than ISBNs and ISSNs.

**Choice of access points**

**21.1C:**     Work emanates from corporate body but does not fit categories in 21.1B2 and is not of personal authorship.

**21.30E:**   Added entry for publisher whose responsibility extends beyond publishing.

## 2. VIDEO GAME

> Rogers, Miriam.
> Haunted house [computer file] / by Miriam Rogers. -- Computer program (1 file). -- Englewood, Calif. : Challenge Software, c1983.
> 1 computer disk : sd., col. ; 5¼ in. + 1 instruction card.
>
> System requirements: Apple II; 48K; DOS 3.3; color monitor; joysticks optional.
> Title from title screen.
> Designed and coded by Miriam Rogers.
> Player moves good ghosts through haunted house beset by evil spirits.
>
> I. Challenge Software.   II. Title.

OCLC MARC Tagging

```
Type: m  Bib lvl: m  Govt pub:     Lang: N/A  Source: d  Frequn: n
File: b  Enc lvl: I  Machine: a    Ctry: cau  Dat tp: s  Regulr:
Desc: a  Mod rec:    Dates: 1983,

1    040     xxx $c xxx
2    100 1   Rogers, Miriam.
3    245 10  Haunted house $h computer file / $c by Miriam Rogers.
4    256     Computer program (1 file).
5    260     Englewood, Calif. : $b Challenge Software, $c c1983.
6    300     1 computer disk : $b sd., col. ; $c 5 1/4 in. + $e 1
instruction card.
7    538     System requirements: Apple II; 48K; DOS 3.3; color
monitor; joysticks optional.
8    500     Title from title screen.
9    500     Designed and coded by Miriam Rogers.
10   520     Player moves good ghosts through haunted house beset by
evil spirits.
11   710 20  Challenge Software.
12   753     Apple II $c DOS 3.3.
```

### *AACR 2* applicable rules

**9.0B1:**   Chief source is title screen.

**Area 1**

**9.1B1:**   Title proper.

**9.1C1:**   GMD.

**9.1F1:**   Record statement of responsibility as in 1.1F.

**Area 3**

**9.3B1:** Indicate type of file; i.e., "computer program."

**9.3B2:** Record number of files.

**Area 4**

**9.4C1, 9.4D1, 9.4F1:**
Place, name, date.

**9.0B2:** Carrier label is prescribed source.

**Area 5**

**9.5B1:** Number of units and SMD.

**9.5C1:** Indicate if file produces sound and displays color.

**9.5D1:** Diameter of disk.

**9.5E1:** Accompanying materials.

**Area 7**

**9.7B1b:** System requirements: make and model of computer, memory, name of operating system, kind and characteristics of any required or recommended peripherals.

**9.7B3:** Source of title proper.

**9.7B6:** Statement of responsibility.

**9.7B17:** Summary.

**Choice of access points**

**21.4A:** Main entry under personal author responsible for intellectual content of work.

**21.30E:** Added entry for publisher.

**21.30J:** Title added entry.

## 3. INSTRUCTIONAL GAME

Brett, Ruth.
Family finance [computer file] : budget analysis package / by Ruth Brett. -- Rev. 1986 ed. -- Computer program (5 files). -- Austin, Tex. : Falcon Software, c1986.
1 computer disk : col. ; 5¼ in. + 1 manual + 1 pad of budget sheets + 1 packet of play money.

System requirements: Commodore 64; disk drive; color monitor.
Title from title screen.
Edition statement from container label.
Teaches budgeting decisions. For six players. In 8 scenarios, players decide how to allocate family resources.
Contents: Daily expenses -- Monthly expenses -- Savings/ investments -- Income -- Monthly budget status.

I. Falcon Software. II. Title.

```
OCLC MARC Tagging

Type: m    Bib lvl: m   Govt pub:      Lang: N/A  Source: d  Frequn: n
File: b    Enc lvl: I   Machine: a     Ctry: txu  Dat tp: s  Regulr:
Desc: a    Mod rec:     Dates, 1986,

1    040    xxx $c xxx
2    100 1  Brett, Ruth.
3    245 10 Family finance $h computer file : $b budget analysis
package / $c by Ruth Brett.
4    250    Rev. 1986 ed.
5    256    Computer program (5 files).
6    260    Austin, Tex. : $b Falcon Software, $c c1986
7    300    1 computer disk : $b col. ; $c 5 1/4 in. + $e 1 manual +
1 pad of budget sheets + 1 packet of play money.
8    538    System requirements: Commodore 64; disk drive; color
monitor.
9    500    Title from title screen.
10   500    Edition statement from container label.
11   505 0  Daily expenses -- Monthly expenses -- Savings/investments
-- Income -- Monthly budget status.
12   520    Teaches budgeting decisions. For 6 players. In 8
scenarios, players learn how to allocate family resources.
13   710 20 Falcon Software.
14   753    Commodore 64.
```

### *AACR 2* applicable rules

**9.0B1:**   Chief source is title screen.

**Area 1**

**9.1B1:**   Title proper.

**9.1C1:**   GMD.

**9.1E1:**   Other title information as in 1.1E1.

**9.1F1:**   Statement of responsibility as in 1.1F1.

**Area 2**

**9.2B1:**   Edition different from other editions.

**1.2B1:**   Use standard abbreviations from appendix B.

**9.0B2:**   Prescribed sources for edition information include container.

**Area 3**

**9.3B1:**   Type of file.

**9.3B2:**   Number of files.

**Area 4**

**9.4C1, 9.4D1, 9.4F1:**
      Place, name, date.

**9.0B2:**   Prescribed sources for publication area include label.

**Area 5**

**9.5B1:**   Number of units and SMD.

**9.5C1:**   Indicate if color.

**9.5D1:**   Diameter of disk.

**9.5E1:**   Accompanying materials.

**Area 7**

**9.7B1:**   System requirements note: make and model of computer, memory, peripherals.

**9.7B3:**   Source of title proper.

**9.7B7:**   Give source of edition statement if different from that of title proper.

**9.7B17:**   Summary.

**9.7B18:**   Contents. List the parts of a file.

### Choice of access points

**21.4A:**   Enter under heading for personal author responsible for work.

**21.30E:**   Publisher added entry.

**21.30J:**   Title added entry.

## 4. VIDEO GAME WITHOUT COLLECTIVE TITLE

Lord of the lions ; The creatures in the cavern [computer file]. --
Computer program (2 files). -- Elmhurst, IL : Computerscape,
c1984.
1 computer disk : sd., col. ; 3½ in. -- (Vocabulary learning
series)

System requirements: Commodore 128, disk drive, joystick.
Title from disk label.
Program and game concept copyright by William Chapman.
For ages 8-10.
By mastering new words, players find way through the Jungle of
Saturn and get through maze of 28 caverns to final confrontation
with the Cavern Creatures. Helps develop vocabulary and spelling
skills.

I. Computerscape (Firm).   II. Title: Creatures in the cavern.
III. Title: Lord of the lions.   IV. Series.

```
OCLC MARC Tagging

Type: m   Bib lvl: m   Govt pub:     Lang: N/A   Source: d   Frequn: n
File: b   Enc lvl: I   Machine: a    Ctry: ilu   Dat tp: s   Regulr:
Desc: a   Mod rec:     Dates: 1984,

1    040     xxx $c xxx
2    245 00  Lord of the lions ; The creatures in the cavern $h
computer file.
3    256     Computer program (2 files).
4    260     Elmhurst, IL : $b Computerscape, $c c1984.
5    300     1 computer disk : $b sd., col. ; $c 3 1/2 in.
6    440  0  Vocabulary learning series
7    538     System requirements: Commodore 128, disk drive,
joystick.
8    500     Title from disk label.
9    500     Program and game concept copyright by William Chapman.
10   521     For ages 8-10.
11   520     By mastering new words, players find way through the
Jungle of Saturn and get through maze of 28 caverns to final
confrontation with the Cavern Creatures. Helps develop vocabulary
and spelling skills.
12   710 20  Computerscape (Firm).
13   740 41  Creatures in the cavern.
14   730 01  Lord of the lions.
15   753     Commodore 128.
```

### *AACR 2* applicable rules

**9.0B1:** Chief source: if there is no title screen, and information from other internal sources is not available, take information from physical carrier or its labels.

**Area 1**

**9.1G2:** If item lacks a collective title, record titles of individual parts as in 1.1G.

**1.1G3:** Record titles in order in which they appear on chief source. Separate by semicolon if parts are by same person. (While there is no formal statement of responsibility, the copyright statement suggests that one person is responsible for both parts.)

**9.1C1:** GMD.

**1.1C2:** For items without collective title, add GMD immediately following the last title of a group by the same author.

**Area 3**

**9.3B1:** Type of file.

**9.3B2:** Number of files.

**Area 4**

**9.4C1, 9.4D1, 9.4F1:**
Place, name, date. Label is prescribed source.

**1.4F6:** Copyright date.

**Area 5**

**9.5B1:** Number of physical units and SMD.

**9.5C1:** Indicate if sound, color.

**9.5D1:** Diameter of disk.

**Area 6**

**9.6B1:** Record series as in 1.6.

**Area 7**

**9.7B1b:** System requirements note: make and model of computer, memory, peripherals.

**9.7B3:** Source of title proper.

**9.7B6:** Statements of responsibility for persons who prepared or contributed to the production of item. Copyright in this example may imply responsibility.

**9.7B14:** Indicate intended audience, if information is on item or container.

**9.7B17:** Summary.

### Choice of access points

**21.1C:** No personal authorship.

It could also be argued that authorship of the work is suggested by the copyright, and that the main entry should be under the heading for Chapman. This record reflects the more conservative view that main entry should be under title, since authorship has not been definitely established.

**21.30E:** Added entry for publisher.

**21.30J:** Added entry for title significantly different from title proper.

LC will treat headings for computer programs and software as uniform titles. [CSB 38 (Fall 1987): 2-10]. LC omits all initial articles from uniform titles.

**21.30L:** Added entry for series.

### Form of corporate body heading

**24.4B:** Add designation enclosed in parentheses if name does not convey idea of corporate body.

## REFERENCE SOURCES

## Computers and Microcomputer Software Sources

*Bowker's Complete Sourcebook of Personal Computing 1985.* New York: Bowker, 1984.

Contains over 1,000 pages of ready reference information on microcomputers and the microcomputer industry and market. Included are 2,341 citations to reviews of software products found in popular computing magazines.

Provides background in the concepts of computer operations and software program functions. Assists the cataloger and catalog user in identifying the function of software programs, and in determining what equipment is necessary to use them. Also helpful in determining the full name and/or address of software publishers.

Froelich, Robert A. *The IBM PC (and Compatibles) Free Software Catalog and Directory.* Portland, Oreg.: Dilithium Press, 1986.

Introduction explains the difference between public domain software and user-supported software. Directory gives the complete catalogs of the four largest software bulletin boards, cross-referenced by subject and title.

*The Software Encyclopedia 1987-1988.* New York: Bowker, 1988, 2v.

The equivalent of *Books in Print* for software that is commercially produced and marketed. An essential source for cataloging data, since Bowker administers the ISBN system in the United States. Lists over 55,000 packages of over 27,000 programs. Each entry includes author, price, hardware compatibility, description, ISBN, publisher, and operating system requirements. Indexes for applications, title, and expanded applications. Published annually.

## Dictionaries and Glossaries

*American National Dictionary for Information Processing Systems.* Developed by the American National Standards Committee. Homewood, Ill.: Dow Jones-Irwin, 1984.

The official ANSI dictionary of terms used throughout the various fields relating to information processing. Definitions intended to be useful to lay persons.

Christie, Linda G., and John Christie. *The Encyclopedia of Microcomputer Terminology: A Sourcebook for Business and Professional People.* Englewood Cliffs, N.J.: Prentice-Hall, 1984.

More than 4,000 terms focusing on topics of interest to both the layperson and professional microcomputer user.

Gordon, Michael, Alan Singleton, and C. Richards, eds. *Dictionary of New Information Technology Acronyms.* 2d ed. Detroit: Gale Research, 1986.

An international listing of acronyms extending for 232 pages. Technological terms related to the fields of computer science and information technology. Geared toward the library/information science market. Covers a wide range of terms related to microcomputers and software. Each entry is a brief definition, sometimes consisting only of the full spelling of the acronym.

Longley, Dennis, and Michael Shane. *Dictionary of Information Technology.* 2d ed. London: Macmillan, 1985.

A comprehensive dictionary/glossary which includes terms from the fields of printing and publishing, computers and databases, computer networks and communications, photography and cinematography, television and recording, microelectronics and software, and word processing and business systems. Identifies synonymous, broader, and narrower terms for a specific concept. Although most entries are brief definitions, there are extended entries (1-3 pages) for topics such as computer networks, data communications, and microcomputers.

## Microcomputers and Libraries

Costa, Betty, and Marie Costa. *A Micro Handbook for Small Libraries and Media Centers.* Littleton, Colo.: Libraries Unlimited, 1983.

Useful for catalogers in a small library; deals with the types of hardware and software common to those settings. Intended as a general introduction, with a focus on the use of computers and selection of software for library purposes. Could also be referred to for specific information such as the operation of a particular machine, or the uses of types of software.

Rorvig, Mark E. *Microcomputers and Libraries: A Guide to Technology Products and Applications*. White Plains, N.Y.: Knowledge Industry Publications, 1982.

General introduction to and history of the microcomputer and its uses in libraries. Places past, present, and proposed rules into the context of software development in recent years. Also describes programming languages, and defines general types of programs (e.g., database management, word processing). Provides lists of hardware and software producers, publishers of journals and newsletters, and gives a glossary of basic terms.

Woods, Lawrence A., and Nolan F. Pope. *The Librarian's Guide to Microcomputer Technology and Applications*. White Plains, N.Y.: Knowledge Industry Publications, 1983.

Provides a general introduction to the concepts of computer technology. Gives definitions of hardware, storage media, types of software, operating systems, and other topics related to microsoftware programs.

## Cataloging and Classification

In considering the following literature dealing with *AACR 2*'s chapter 9, the reader should keep in mind the 1987 publication date of the draft revision of this chapter. For materials previous to this date, any discussions of *AACR 2*'s chapter 9 will refer to the original chapter 9 rather than the revised chapter.

For an extensive annotated bibliography on the cataloging of computer files, the reader is referred to Nancy B. Olson's *Cataloging Microcomputer Software: A Manual to Accompany AACR 2 Chapter 9, Computer Files* (Littleton, Colo.: Libraries Unlimited, 1988).

### MANUALS AND STANDARDS

American Library Association. Committee on Cataloging: Description and Access. *Guidelines for Using AACR2 Chapter 9 for Cataloging Microcomputer Software*. Chicago: American Library Association, 1984.

These guidelines were published by the ALA in an attempt to address the concerns of librarians trying to catalog microcomputer software using chapter 9 rules which had been designed for program files on mainframe computers. The *1984 Guidelines* were intended as interpretations of, rather than replacements for, the rules in the original chapter 9 of *AACR 2*. Includes glossary with brief definitions for key computer terms needed in the descriptive cataloging process. The guidelines apply only to commercially available software. (See earlier discussion in this chapter.)

Dodd, Sue A. *Cataloging Machine-Readable Data Files: An Interpretative Manual*. Chicago: American Library Association, 1982.

A counterpart to Dodd and Sandberg-Fox's later manual for microcomputer software. Detailed discussion of *AACR 2*'s original chapter 9, with examples. Scope is limited to descriptive cataloging.

Dodd, Sue A., and Ann M. Sandberg-Fox. *Cataloging Microcomputer Files: A Manual of Interpretation for AACR2*. Chicago: American Library Association, 1985.
Covers *AACR 2* and the ALA *1984 Guidelines*. Identifies problems associated with describing microcomputer programs, discusses the hardware and software components of microcomputer systems which must be considered in the cataloging of software.

Discussion focuses primarily on the needs of catalogers in school libraries, public libraries, and college libraries. Since both authors participated in drafting the *1984 Guidelines*, the introductory chapter on the evolution of the rules and guidelines is particularly useful. Contains a fifteen-page glossary which is an extension of that prepared by Sandberg-Fox for the ALA guidelines.

In-depth descriptions of microcomputer systems components are provided, with an emphasis on how those components affect the characteristics of software programs and formats. Unlike more general works on microcomputers, this is written specifically to aid the cataloger, and looks at aspects of computers and software with a view toward the construction of the cataloging record.

The book considers the relative merits of physical and file descriptions. Also discusses classification principles as applied to microcomputer software, concentrating primarily on Dewey Decimal Classification, since many of the largest collections of microcomputer software are in school, public, and college libraries where Dewey is used regularly. Subject cataloging is discussed in terms of both Sears and Library of Congress subject headings. Includes cataloging examples based on the interpretations of *AACR 2* and the ALA guidelines.

Olson, Nancy B. *Cataloging Microcomputer Software: A Manual to Accompany AACR 2 Chapter 9, Computer Files*. Littleton, Colo.: Libraries Unlimited, 1988.
One chapter is devoted to the history of cataloging microcomputer software, and chronicles the evolution of the cataloging rules for this medium. Olson was an active participant in many of these developments. An annotated chronological bibliography gives an extensive listing of the literature on the cataloging of microcomputer software. The author outlines areas of key decisions that must be made before cataloging takes place. Rules from the 1987 Draft Revision of *AACR 2*'s Chapter 9 are listed, with accompanying commentary, LC rule interpretations, and examples.

The central part of the book is a set of 100 bibliographic records illustrating a wide variety of cataloging problems. For each example there is information as presented in the chief source of information, with title screens shown exactly as seen when the computer file is run, and exact reproductions of other information, such as disk and container labels, and manual title pages. Some examples include OCLC MARC coding and tagging.

A glossary, selected from the author's *Audiovisual Materials Glossary* (Dublin, Ohio: OCLC, 1988) gives definitions for computer software terms. Lists of selected subject headings and classification numbers are also included.

Olson, Nancy B., and Jean Aichele. *A Manual of AACR2 Examples for Micro-computer Software*. 2d ed. Lake Crystal, Minn.: Soldier Creek Press, 1985.
Presents a series of examples of interpreting *AACR 2* chapter 9 within the context of the ALA *1984 Guidelines*. The examples illustrate a wide range of materials.

## BOOKS AND ARTICLES

American Library Association. Ad Hoc Subcommittee on Subject Access to Microcomputer Software. *Guidelines on Subject Access to Microcomputer Software*. Chicago: American Library Association, 1986.
A discussion of key issues underlying subject access and classification of software products. Recommendations emphasize that subject access for micro-computer software should follow the same principles as those used for other materials in the collection. Appendixes provide a selective list of subject sources for new subject headings, LC and Dewey classification numbers for computer equipment, and examples of MARC records for software. (See also earlier discussion.)

Coral, Lenore. "Problems in the Cataloging of the Products of Rapidly Chang-ing Technologies: With Special Reference to Machine Readable Files." *International Cataloguing* 13 (April/June 1984): 18-19.
Summarizes the difficulties of applying ISBD standards to machine-readable files. Considers distinction between a work and its physical manifestation. Focuses on the physical/file description area.

Dodd, Sue A. "Changing AACR2 to Accommodate the Cataloging of Micro-computer Software." *Library Resources and Technical Services* 29 (January/March 1985): 52-65.
Discussion of rules for "Extent of File" in *AACR 2*'s chapter 9 and the *1984 Guidelines*. Recommends that the "extent of file" be an optional consideration, and that some of the information currently provided in this field be given in the notes. Does not recommend that a physical description area be added.

Holzberlein, Deanne. "Computer Software Cataloging: Techniques and Exam-ples." *Cataloging & Classification Quarterly* 6:2 (Winter 1986): 1-83. (Also published as separate volume. New York: Haworth, 1986.)
Gives sixteen examples and catalog records, with explanations. Examples are of educational software, educational games, and business software.

Intner, Sheila S. "Problems and Solutions in Descriptive Cataloging of Micro-computer Software." *Cataloging & Classification Quarterly* 5 (Spring 1985): 49-56.
Discusses the inadequacies of *AACR 2*'s original chapter 9 when applied to microcomputer software. Looks in particular at problems relating to terminology, description of the physical manifestation of an item, and notes describing related hardware. Discusses how these problems are addressed by the ALA *1984 Guidelines*, and gives overview of its evolution. Points out difficulties arising from the scope of coverage of the *1984 Guidelines*.

Mitchell, Joan S. "Subject Access to Microcomputer Software." *Library Resources and Technical Services* 29 (January/March 1985): 66-72.

Records the objectives and reports of an ALA subcommittee on subject access to microcomputer software. Specific problems in the subject classification of software are examined. (See also earlier discussion in this chapter.)

Olson, Nancy B. "Cataloging Microcomputer Software: Suggestions for Rule Revision." *Cataloging & Classification Quarterly* 7 (Fall 1986): 3-17.

Recommends a series of rule changes to accommodate specific microcomputer software problems, including using "computer material" as a GMD, and using the screen display as the chief source of information.

_____. "Cataloging Microcomputer Software: Using the Newly Revised AACR2 Chapter 9." In *Policy and Practice in Bibliographic Control of Nonbook Media*, ed. Sheila Intner and Richard Smiraglia. Chicago: American Library Association, 1987.

Lists key rules of revised chapter 9, and gives commentary, brief background, and examples.

Paden, Judith C. "Cataloging Microcomputer Software: A Guide for the Inexperienced Microcomputer User." *Cataloging & Classification Quarterly* 7 (Fall 1986): 19-33.

Intended as a basic introduction for catalogers without computer expertise. Includes descriptions of the parts of a microcomputer system, and the relationship between software programs and the systems for which they were designed. Compares rules from *AACR 2* chapter 9 to the ALA *1984 Guidelines*, with explanations of computer-specific terms. Brief discussion of the issue of file versus physical description. An appendix containing seven examples of catalog records for software is provided, with explanatory comments.

Rohrvig, Mark E. "The 'Bibliographic' Control of Microcomputer Software." *The Electronic Library* 2 (July 1984): 183-95.

Templeton, Ray, and Anita Witten. *Study of Cataloging Computer Software: Applying AACR2 to Microcomputer Programs.* London: The British Library, 1984.

A report of a study in which several British library groups tested the effectiveness of *AACR 2*'s chapter 9 for the cataloging of microcomputer software programs. *AACR 2* rules were applied to a body of software in order to establish principles to be used for cataloging software in general. These principles were then used in cataloging a larger sample of software. From this effort, the researchers developed a set of recommendations to publishers for the inclusion of appropriate information in their programs, and set of recommendations for changes to the rules in *AACR 2* chapter 9. Published in the same year as the ALA *1984 Guidelines*, this study contains similar descriptive information and examples.

# 7

ⵀⵀⵀⵀⵀⵀⵀⵀⵀⵀⵀⵀⵀⵀⵀⵀⵀⵀⵀⵀⵀⵀⵀⵀⵀⵀⵀⵀⵀⵀⵀⵀⵀⵀⵀⵀⵀⵀⵀⵀⵀⵀⵀⵀⵀⵀⵀⵀⵀⵀⵀⵀⵀⵀ

# *Three-Dimensional Artefacts and Realia*

ⵀⵀⵀⵀⵀⵀⵀⵀⵀⵀⵀⵀⵀⵀⵀⵀⵀⵀⵀⵀⵀⵀⵀⵀⵀⵀⵀⵀⵀⵀⵀⵀⵀⵀⵀⵀⵀⵀⵀⵀⵀⵀⵀⵀⵀⵀⵀⵀⵀⵀⵀⵀⵀⵀ

## DECISION AREAS IN DESCRIPTIVE CATALOGING

### Scope

#### DIVERSITY OF THE CATEGORY

"Three-dimensional artefacts and realia" in *AACR 2*'s chapter 10 is a comprehensive category that covers various instructional media (such as braille cassettes, models, dioramas, games), naturally occurring objects (such as microscope specimens, rocks), works of art (such as sculptures, mobiles), and innumerable types of artefacts (such as clothing, furniture, machines) which were not originally intended for communication but can serve as objects of study or appreciation. Materials in this category are "three-dimensional" in the sense that all three dimensions are needed to convey the artistic or intellectual message of the medium.

The range of materials included in the category is as diverse as the uses served and the settings in which they may be found. From toys and games for recreation, to tools for practical application, models and dioramas for instruction, and objects such as realia and art objects for display, three-dimensional objects may be found in school media centers, public libraries, academic institutions, and museums. Some items are from nature and are one-of-a-kind; some man-made items may be unique, while others may be commercially produced. The conditions under which the types of materials may be used are equally varied. Some museumlike objects may be for display only, some may circulate under strictly regulated conditions, while others may be treated as most other library materials.

In her survey of three-dimensional object collections in public libraries, Bierbaum found that the most popular categories were toys, games, and art objects, with a wide variety of "other" three-dimensional items also reported. The "other" category included a range of materials as diverse as puppet theaters, craft equipment, tools and household items, costumes, natural history collections, butterflies, stuffed animals, and live animals. Of the libraries responding to the question 75 percent said that they circulated at least some of these items.[1]

## BIBLIOGRAPHIC CONTROL

Perhaps as a result of special conditions of loan or display, many collections of three-dimensional materials may be less likely to be cataloged in the traditional sense. The lack of uniform standards has also been a factor contributing to gaps in the bibliographic control for these media. Until *AACR 2*, three-dimensional materials were not included in nationally recognized cataloging codes. As with many other materials for which standards were lacking, individual libraries developed their own practices for describing and organizing three-dimensional objects, and these practices and locally developed codes have remained in use well after the emergence of a standard code. In Bierbaum's survey of public libraries, local code or practice was the most frequent basis for cataloging of three-dimensional artefacts, while *AACR 2* was more likely to be accepted for audiovisual materials than for three-dimensional items.[2]

While *AACR 1* excluded three-dimensional materials entirely, in *AACR 2* a method for description is given which is consistent with the description of other library materials. Although three-dimensional objects may have a most "unbooklike" appearance, their description as prescribed by *AACR 2* and ISBD guidelines presents relatively few problems for the cataloger.

# Museum Collections:
## Systems for Description and Organization

Many of the types of media falling into the category of three-dimensional materials are those likely to be collected by museums. A system for description and organization of these materials has already been developed. Museum registration, used for the accessioning and cataloging of museum objects, has been compared with library cataloging and classification procedures. The description of museum materials is far less structured than its analog in libraries, and thus far more likely to vary from institution to institution. No standard format exists for the descriptive record and there are few instances of the development of a consistent and standard terminology, yet certain common features do emerge. For example, as is the case with manuscript, rare book, and special collections cataloging, descriptions of museum objects tend to be more extensive than traditional library cataloging. These descriptions may include the name of the item, its material and size, and an account of its provenance, past history, and condition. In addition one may find documentation associated with the item, such as a codicil to a will, advertisements and clippings, letters, and bills of sale.

The subject organization systems for museum objects have been developed for taxonomic storage, and for the purpose of exhibiting related objects together. Such systems may be hierarchical in nature and according to Bierbaum, "similar to the ordering imposed upon items in a library collection by the classification scheme."[3] The classification is custom tailored to fit the museum's mission; for example, a system designed for a regional history museum might be based on events, persons, and topics of local interest. Such schemes for subject organization are unique to an institution, as opposed to standardized systems which facilitate the sharing of catalog information and resources.

# Sources of Information

## THE WHOLE ITEM AS CHIEF SOURCE

As can be seen from the previous chapters, the consistent pattern in *AACR 2* is to prefer information on the item itself over information on a label or container; if information is lacking on the item, a container permanently associated with it may be used as a chief source instead. A primary exception to this pattern is the case of three-dimensional materials, for which containers and accompanying materials are regularly regarded as chief sources.

Even in the case of three-dimensional materials, however, there is still a distinct order of preference. While the chief source of information is defined collectively as the object, together with its accompanying textual material and container, it is still made clear that information on the item itself is preferred to information found in accompanying textual material or on a container.

Many types of three-dimensional materials, in particular games, are likely to appear as a collection of components issued as a unit. In such instances, logic dictates that the bibliographic description be given for the item as a collective unit. Very often, the data appropriate to the item as a unit are found not on the individual components but on their container. Thus, for three-dimensional objects, the container can be particularly appropriate as a source of information, since frequently there is no label of any kind on the items themselves.

# Title and Statement of Responsibility Area

## SUPPLIED TITLES

Many items falling under the category of "naturally occurring objects" or "artefacts" are likely to contain no labeling or other bibliographic information, and the cataloger will need to supply a title, according to general rule 1.1B7, and indicate the source of the title in a note.

## STATEMENTS OF RESPONSIBILITY
### Nature of Roles

The nature of the intellectual or artistic contribution to be recorded in the statement of responsibility area will vary widely with the type of material. Some types of responsibility will be obvious, such as the artist's role in creating a sculpture, and this can be extended to those responsible for the creation of an artefact. For realia, the roles involved in the display or selection of an item are to be recorded. For instructional materials, such as games, the individuals responsible for the design, development, and other aspects of the intellectual content may be recognized.

## GENERAL MATERIAL DESIGNATION
### Generic versus Specific Terms

Like the category of graphic materials, "three-dimensional artefacts and realia" covers a wide variety of objects and requires a number of GMDs to encompass the scope of media involved. In the original *AACR 2*, there were five terms for GMDs in the North American list (*diorama, game, microscope slide, model,* and *realia*). The revised rules have since added the terms *art original* (formerly used only for graphic materials and now applicable to both two- and three-dimensional objects), *art reproduction* (also to be used for both two- and three-dimensional objects), and *toy.*

The inclusion of the term *toy* will be especially welcome. Formerly, the only term applicable to materials of this kind was *realia,* which was the rubric to be used for a wide variety of objects not covered by the other four, more specific, terms. *Realia* is defined in *AACR 2*'s glossary as "actual objects (artefacts, specimens) as opposed to replicas." As such, the term suggests objects such as a rock or a leaf, and many catalogers found it difficult to apply the GMD *realia* to an item such as a stuffed animal or a puppet.

The British preference is for generic GMDs, and uses the term *object* for all three-dimensional materials.

# Publication Area

## TREATMENT OF UNPUBLISHED AND PUBLISHED OBJECTS

In *AACR 2*, elements of description are sometimes omitted if they are not suitable for a given type of material. Since many three-dimensional objects are not "published" in the usual sense of the word, provision is made to omit the publication place, and name for artefacts not intended primarily for communication, such as a coin. Publication data are omitted entirely for naturally occurring objects, such as a seashell, that have not been packaged for distribution.

Accordingly, rules 10.4C2, 10.4D2, and 10.4F2 and rules 1.4C8, 1.4D8, and 1.4F9 prescribe that "naturally occurring objects" (such as rocks, feathers, and shells) receive no publication data at all, unless they have been mounted for viewing or presentation, or packaged for distribution. For "artefacts not intended primarily for communication," only the date of manufacture is recorded. Thus, *AACR 2* requires the cataloger to make a distinction among the following types of materials:

a. naturally occurring objects that are mounted for viewing or packaged for presentation (e.g., a rock that has been packaged, labeled, and distributed for educational purposes by a commercial producer)

b. naturally occurring objects that are *not* mounted for viewing or packaged for presentation (e.g., the same type of rock, found by a collector in its natural locale, and without packaging)

    c.   artefacts intended primarily for communication

    d.   artefacts *not* intended primarily for communication

Of these categories, "a" and "c" will be treated by *AACR 2* like any other kind of "published" materials, and given the usual place, name, and date of publication. For categories "b" and "d," no place or name of publisher will be given. In addition, no date will be given for naturally occurring objects (category "b"). For artefacts not intended primarily for communication ("d"), the date of manufacture is given.

It is relatively easy to make the distinction between categories "a" and "b," where the difference between the two types of items rests on the physical characteristic of the packaging. To make a decision, however, based on whether an artefact is "primarily intended for communication," seems to require the cataloger to make a philosophical distinction. This writer's experience in teaching *AACR 2* has shown that the phrase "artefact primarily intended for communication" can convey a wide variety of meanings. The rule, however, is not only difficult to apply, but difficult to understand in terms of its basic rationale. It is not clear why a decision on recording publication data should be made on the basis of whether or not an item is primarily intended for communication.

Elsewhere in *AACR 2*, the basic pattern is for such decisions to be made on the basis of whether items are issued in "published" form. *AACR 2* implicitly recognizes certain types of materials as "unpublished," such as realia, art originals, manuscripts, nonprocessed sound recordings, and stock shots, and accordingly provides special treatment for publication data. Since publication data serve as indicators as to how and when an item has been produced or distributed, such data are not appropriate for items that have been issued or that "occur" in unique copies and were never intended for "distribution" in the usual bibliographic sense.

Ben Tucker of the Library of Congress offers a revealing observation:

> The words "not intended for communication" mean nothing more than "not published," or "not issued in an edition," etc., all terms that mean there would be no place of publication, no name of publisher, and no date of publication to record. More direct language was not employed because of the great concern for using book-centric terms that jar audiovisual ears. Another term that might have served is "not commercially available in multiple copies," if it had not been thought that "commercially" and "multiple copies" raise even further questions. In routine situations I should think the difference is obvious between "homemade" and "storebought."[4]

Perhaps another clue as to what is meant by "artefacts primarily intended for communication" can be found in the ISBD (*NBM*), which excludes from its scope all materials that have not been "published" and considers only those materials "having for their primary purpose the transmission of ideas, information or aesthetic content" and that are for the most part published in multiple copies. Excluded from ISBD (*NBM*) are "specimens or found objects, except in so far as such objects are packaged and marketed commercially, as well as original works of art."

# Physical Description Area

## DECISION AREAS FOR THE CATALOGER

Owing to the wide diversity of possible materials that might be cataloged, the cataloger is not restricted to the seven SMDs listed in rule 10.5B1, but can also "give the specific name of the item or the names of the parts of the item as concisely as possible."

Some leeway is also afforded the cataloger in designating the components comprising the item. The components can either be added in parentheses directly following the SMD, or be designated with the term *various pieces* and described later in a note.

Further decision areas arise later in the "other physical details" section of the physical description area. In giving information about the material and the color of the item, a decision is made as to whether such information is "appropriate" and can be stated concisely.

In giving dimensions, the cataloger can indicate which dimension is being given, if necessary.

For three-dimensional objects that are collections of components, such as a game or a jigsaw puzzle, the dimensions of the container may define the size of the unit to be cataloged. In such cases the rules prescribe that the dimensions of the container may be given after the dimensions of the object or as the only dimensions. Even in cases where the item to be cataloged consists of a single unit, the container is named and its dimensions given, following the dimensions of the item itself. This is in contrast to the rules governing media in other chapters in which the statement of dimensions for the container is optional.

In noting "accompanying material," the cataloger should keep in mind that the accompanying material should be clearly secondary to a primary unit, as for example, a teacher's guide accompanying a model. In the case of a game, the various components such as manuals, cards, dice, and playing board all go to make up the basic collective unit of the game, and are not regarded as accompanying material.

# Note Area

Because items in this category will be diverse and often unusual in nature, the cataloger may wish to use the note area to describe in further detail the nature of the item, its physical characteristics, component parts, purpose, and audience.

A note for the source of the title will be mandatory, if the title has been supplied from an outside source or by the cataloger.

# NOTES

[1]Esther Green Bierbaum, "The Third Dimension: Dealing with Objects in Public Library Collections," *Public Library Quarterly* 6 (Fall 1985): 47, 48.

[2]Ibid.

[3]Esther Green Bierbaum, "Records and Access: Museum Registration and Library Cataloging," *Cataloging & Classification Quarterly* (in press).

[4]"Questions and Answers," *OLAC Newsletter* 5 (March 1985): 26.

# DESCRIPTIVE CATALOGING EXAMPLES

## Items to Be Cataloged

1. Marionette

One marionette depicting matador, 40 centimeters long, multi-colored, wooden body, fabric clothes.

No information appears on the item. No information is available concerning title, place and date of "publication," "publisher," etc. The item was mass-produced and was purchased in Mexico in 1972.

2. Game

One Scrabble game: 1 colored cardboard playing board, 35.5 centimeters square, 100 wood tiles, 4 wood racks. In box, 37 x 19 x 4 centimeters.

Front of box:

SCRABBLE
CROSSWORD GAME

Manufactured by Selchow & Righter Co.
Bay Shore, N.Y.                    Made in U.S.A.

Inside of box:

Rules for playing SCRABBLE

Scrabble is a word game for 2, 3, or 4 players. The play consists of forming interlocking words, cross-word fashion, on the SCRABBLE playing board using letter tiles with various score values.

Copyright 1948, 1949, 1953 by Selchow & Righter Co.

3. Map puzzle

Map puzzle consisting of nine six-sided map cubes made of styrofoam and cardboard, green, blue, and black. When assembled, 24 x 24 x 8 centimeters. With instruction guide. In box 25 x 25 x 7 centimeters.

Side of box:

CONTINENT PUZZLE CUBES     6306

Back of box:

Singer Education Division
SVE/Society for Visual Education, Inc.     Chicago, Ill.

Instruction guide:

Cubes combine in six different ways to form complete and accurate maps of the continents of North America, South America, Europe, Africa, Asia, and Australia.

Purposes: to teach and reinforce shapes of the world's major continents, to teach and reinforce place names and locations of bodies of water, countries, and major cities, to provide practice in relative location of map features to excite interest in map study.

Copyright c1976 Society for Visual Education, Inc.

4. Coin

One reproduction of a coin, metal, 3½ centimeters in diameter, with one note. In plastic bag, 9 x 5 centimeters.

From note:

THE CONTINENTAL DOLLAR
c1976

The first silver dollar size coin ever proposed for the United States.

5. Fossil

One fossil, commonly known as a "sand dollar," white, 9.75 centimeters high. The fossil is in the order of Clypeasteroida, in the family of Echinarachniidae.

# *AACR 2* Records and
# OCLC MARC Tagging

## 1. MARIONETTE

[Matador marionette] [toy]. -- [1972?]
1 marionette : wood and fabric, col. ; 40 cm. long.

Title supplied by cataloger.
Purchased in Mexico in 1972.

```
OCLC MARC Tagging

Type: r Bib lvl: m Govt pub: Lang: N/A Source: d  Leng: nnn
       Enc lvl: I  Type mat: w  Ctry: xx    Dat tp: s  MEBE: 0
Tech: n Mod rec:          Accomp mat:
Desc: a Int lvl:    Dates: 1972,

1 040    xxx $c xxx
2 245 00 [Matador marionette] $h toy
3 260    $c [1972?].
4 300    1 marionette : $b wood and fabric, col. ; $c 40 cm. long.
5 500    Title supplied by cataloger.
6 500    Purchased in Mexico in 1972.
```

### *AACR 2* applicable rules

**10.0B1:**   Chief source of information is object itself.

**Area 1**

**10.1B1:**   Title proper as in 1.1B.

**1.1B7:**   Supply title proper for item lacking the prescribed chief source. If no title can be found in any source, devise a brief descriptive title, and enclose in brackets.

**10.1C1:**   GMD added after title proper and enclosed in own set of brackets. GMD is *toy*, a new term added in the revised rules. Formerly, the cataloger was required to use the term *realia* for this type of material, if the GMD were to be applied.

**Area 4**

The assumption is that this is an artefact not intended primarily for communication, and thus no place or name is recorded. An alternative approach would be as follows: If we knew that the item had been commercially produced, and if we used the criterion of "commercially available in multiple copies" in deciding on the appropriateness of including publication data, full publication information would be included. In the latter case, since no·publication information is available, "S.l. : s.n." would be given for the name and place of publication.

**10.4C2, 10.4D2:**
    Omit place of publication and name of publisher for artefacts not intended primarily for communication. In this case, the place of manufacture or publication has not been inferred from the purchase site.

**10.4F2:**    Give date of manufacture for artefacts not intended primarily for communication.

**1.4F7:**    If no date given, supply approximate one. In this case, date of manufacture is inferred from purchase date.

**Area 5**

**10.5B1:**    If none of terms for the SMDs listed in rule is appropriate to use, give the specific name of the item as concisely as possible.

**10.5C1:**    When appropriate, give material(s) of which object is made.

**10.5C2:**    When appropriate, give abbreviation *col.* for multicolored objects. [If two colors or less, the colors can be named.]

**10.5D1:**    Give dimensions of object, when appropriate, in centimeters, to next whole centimeter up. If necessary, add a word to indicate which dimension is being given.

**Area 7**

**10.7B3:**    Give source of title proper if it is not taken from the chief source of information.

**10.7B9:**    Additional publication information.

**Choice of access points**

**21.1C:**    Entry under title for works of unknown authorship.

## 2. GAME

> Scrabble [game] : crossword game. -- Bay Shore, N.Y. :
> Manufactured by Selchow & Righter, c1953.
>
> 1 game (1 board, 4 racks, 100 tiles) : wood and cardboard ; in
> box, 37 x 19 x 4 cm.
>
> Instructions on inside of container.
> For two to four players, with the object of forming interlocking
> words using letter tiles with various score values.
>
> I. Selchow & Righter Co.

```
OCLC MARC Tagging

Type: r Bib lvl: m Govt pub:    Lang: eng Source: d Leng: nnn
          Enc lvl: I Type mat: g Ctry: nyu Dat tp: s MEBE:0
Tech: n Mod rec:            Accomp mat:
Desc: a Int lvl:    Dates: 1953,

1  040     xxx $c xxx
2  245 00  Scrabble $h game : $b crossword game.
3  260     Bay Shore, N.Y. : $b Manufactured by Selchow & Righter,
$c c1953.
4  300     1 game (1 board, 4 racks, 100 tiles) : $b wood and
cardboard ; $c in box, 37 x 19 x 4 cm.
5  500     Instructions on inside of container.
6  520     For two to four players, with the object of forming
interlocking words using letter tiles with various score values.
7  710 21  Selchow & Righter Co.
```

### *AACR 2* applicable rules

**10.0B1:**    Chief source is object itself together with container issued by
publisher.

### Area 1

**10.1B1:**    Title proper as in 1.1B.

**10.1C1:**    GMD *game* from list in rule 1.1C1. Glossary definition: "a set of
materials designed for play according to prescribed rules."

**10.1E1:**    Other title information as in 1.1E1.

### Area 4

The assumption is that this item is an artefact primarily intended
for communication. First, we need to determine whether Selchow &
Righter should be treated as a producer or a manufacturer, since
information about a manufacturer is recorded in a different manner

from that of a publisher. The fact that Selchow & Righter holds the copyright suggests that they are acting as more than just manufacturers. 1.4D7 states that in case of doubt, treat as a publisher.

**10.4C1:** Record place of publication as in 1.4C.

**10.4D1:** Publisher as in 1.4D.

**1.4D2:** Give publisher's name in shortest form ("Co." omitted).

**1.4D3:** Do not omit from the phrase naming a publisher words or phrases indicating functions other than solely publishing.

**10.4F1:** Place as in 1.4F.

**1.4F6:** Give copyright date if this is the only date. (Latest copyright date given.)

**Area 5**

**10.5B1:** SMD *game* is included under terms listed in rule.

**10.5B2:** Add, in parentheses, the number and names of component pieces. If the cataloger decides that the pieces cannot be named concisely, the term *various pieces* can be added instead, and the details of the pieces can be given in a note.

**10.5C1:** Add materials if appropriate. This can be given in a note instead, if the materials cannot be stated concisely.

**10.5D1:** If multiple dimensions are given, record them as height x width x depth.

**10.5D2:** If the object is in a container, the container can be named and given either after the dimensions of the object or as the only dimensions. Since the game does not consist of a single object, it was considered best just to give the dimensions of the box.

**Area 7**

**10.7B10:** Important physical details.

**10.7B17:** Summary.

**Choice of access points**

**21.1B2:** Work emanates from a corporate body but does not fall into one of the categories in 21.1B2.

**21.1C.** Authorship unknown, enter under title.

**21.30E:** Added entry for publisher with responsibility beyond publishing.

## 3. MAP PUZZLE

Continent puzzle cubes [game]. -- Chicago, Ill. : Society for
Visual Education, c1976.
1 puzzle (9 pieces) : styrofoam and cardboard, col. ;
24 x 24 x 8 cm. in box, 25 x 25 x 7 cm. + 1 guide.

Nine six-sided cubes combine in six different ways to form maps
of the continents. Designed to teach names and locations of map
features.
No. 6306.

I. Society for Visual Education.

```
OCLC MARC Tagging

Type: r  Bib lvl: m Govt pub:    Lang: eng  Source: d  Leng: nnn
         Enc lvl: I Type mat: g Ctry: ilu  Dat tp: s  MEBE: 0
Tech: n  Mod rec:            Accomp mat: r
Desc: a  Int lvl: c Dates: 1976,

1   040     xxx $c xxx
2   245 00  Continent puzzle cubes $h game
3   260     Chicago, Ill. : $b Society for Visual Education, $c
c1976.
4   300     1 puzzle (9 pieces) : $b styrofoam and cardboard, col. ;
$c 24 x 24 x 8 cm. in box, 25 x 25 x 7 cm. + $e 1 guide.
5   520     Nine six-sided cubes combine in six different ways to
form maps of the continents. Designed to teach names and locations
of map features.
6   500     No. 6306.
7   710 21  Society for Visual Education.
```

## *AACR 2* applicable rules

### Scope/Choice of chapter

This item could also be cataloged as a map. In this example, the
item is treated as a game. Although the game is cartographic in terms
of its content, and although the chapter on cartographic materials can
include three-dimensional items, the basic purpose of the item is
instructional, and it is designed to be used more as a game than as a
map.

**10.0B1:** Chief source of information is the object itself together with any
accompanying textual material and container.

### Area 1

**10.1B1:** Title proper.

**10.1C1:** GMD.

**Area 4**

The assumption is that this is an artefact intended primarily for communication.

**10.4C1:** Place of publication.

**10.4D1:** Name of publisher.

**10.4F1:** Date of publication.

**Area 5**

**10.5B1:** Record number of physical units. Give specific name of item if appropriate SMD is not listed in rule.

**10.5B2:** Number and name of pieces.

**10.5C1:** Material.

**10.5C2:** Color.

**10.5D1:** Dimensions.

**10.5D2:** Container dimensions. Dimensions are given for both the container and the object since the height of the box is smaller than that of the puzzle cubes.

**10.5E1:** Name of accompanying material.

**Area 7**

**10.7B17:** Summary.

**10.7B19:** Important numbers on the item.

**Choice of access points**

**21.1C:** Entry under title if categories for corporate body main entry in 21.1B2 do not apply and work is not of personal authorship.

**21.30E1:** Added entry for publisher.

**Form of added entry heading**

Name of parent company not needed to identify subsidiary unit.

## 4. COIN

The Continental Dollar [model]. -- c1976.
1 coin : metal ; 4 cm. in bag, 9 x 5 cm. + 1 note.

"The first silver dollar size coin ever proposed for the United States"--Note.

```
OCLC MARC Tagging

Type: r  Bib lvl: m Govt pub:    Lang: eng Source: d  Leng: nnn
         Enc lvl: I Type mat: q Ctry: xx  Dat tp: s  MEBE:0
Tech: n  Mod rec:      :  Accomp mat: r
Desc: a  Int lvl:   Dates: 1976,

1    040    xxx $c xxx
3    245 04 The Continental Dollar $h model
4    260    $c c1976.
5    300    1 coin : $b metal ; $c 4 cm. in bag, 9 x 5 cm. + $e 1
note.
6    500    "The first silver dollar size coin ever proposed for the
United States"--Note.
```

### *AACR 2* applicable rules

**10.0B1:** Chief source is the object itself together with any accompanying textual material.

### Area 1

**10.1B1:** Title proper.

**10.1C1:** GMD *model* from rule 1.1C1. Glossary definition: "a three-dimensional representation of a real thing."

### Area 4

This item is being considered as an artefact not intended primarily for communication. If we based our decision on whether or not the item was issued in multiple copies, full publication information would be given, that is, "[S.l. : s.n.]."

**10.4C2, 10.4D2:** No place of publication or name of publisher.

**10.4F2:** Date of manufacture.

### Area 5

**10.5B1:** Number of units and SMD term.

**10.5C1:** Material.

**10.5D1:** Dimensions. No need to indicate which dimension is given, since the term *coin* implies a round object.

**10.5D2:** Container. If the bag were considered not likely to remain with the item, the container dimensions would not be given.

**10.5E1:** Accompanying material.

**Area 7**

**10.7B17:** Summary.

**Choice of access points**

**21.1C:** Entry under title for works of unknown authorship.


## 5. FOSSIL

[Sand dollar] [realia]
1 fossil : white ; 10 cm. high.

Title supplied by cataloger.
A fossil in the order of Clypeasteroida, in the family of Echinarachniidae.

```
OCLC MARC Tagging

Type: r  Bib lvl: m Govt pub:    Lang: N/A  Source: d  Leng: nnn
         Enc lvl: I Type mat: r Ctry: xx    Dat tp: n  MEBE: O
Tech: n  Mod rec:           Accomp mat:
Desc: a  Int lvl:  Dates:

1    040    xxx $c xxx
2    245 00 [Sand dollar] $h realia
3    300    1 fossil : $b white ; $c 10 cm. high.
4    500    Title supplied by cataloger.
5    500    A fossil in the order of Clypeasteroida, in the family of
Echinarachniidae.
```

Note: Field 754 will contain taxonomic information associated with the organism in hand. Although validated, this field should not be used until a standard list of taxonomic sources and codes has been developed.

### *AACR 2* applicable rules

**Chief source**

No information given on item.

**Area 1**

**10.1B1:** Title proper.

**1.1B7:**     Supplied title. The more technical term would be appropriate for a library with clientele who are specialists in this area.

**1.0C:**      "When adjacent elements are in different areas, enclose each element in a set of square brackets." Thus, separate brackets are given for GMD.

**10.1C1:**    Term *realia* for GMD. Glossary definition: "An artefact or a naturally occurring entity, as opposed to a replica."

**Area 4**

**10.4C2, 10.4D2, 10.4F2:**

Place, name of publisher, and date are not given for naturally occurring objects.

**Area 5**

**10.5B1:**    Number of physical units and SMD.

**10.5C2:**    Color. Specific color can be named, since only one color.

**10.5D1:**    Dimensions.

**Area 7**

**10.7B3:**    Source of title proper if not from chief source.

**10.7B17:**   Summary.

**Choice of access points**

**21.1C:**     Entry under title. (Obviously, there is no possibility of attributing responsibility for a naturally occurring object.)

# REFERENCE SOURCES

Bierbaum, Esther Green. "Realia." In *Non-Print Media: Collection Management and User Services*, edited by John W. Ellison and Patricia Ann Coty, 297-323. Chicago: American Library Association, 1987.

Gives a brief history of realia collections, and describes criteria and tools for selection, commercial sources and suppliers, and the management and maintenance of collections. Also gives a brief overview of considerations affecting organization, storage and retrieval, dissemination, loan, and display.

Bierbaum, Esther Green. "The Third Dimension: Dealing with Objects in Public Library Collections." *Public Library Quarterly* 6 (Fall 1985): 33-49.

Describes the results of a survey that investigated the extent to which public libraries have adopted three-dimensional materials into their collections, the manner in which the materials are circulated, and the cataloging codes used. Found that local code or practice was the most frequent basis for cataloging. Advocates increased use of *AACR 2* to enhance accessibility to collections.

Tessmer, Kathleen M. "Models." In *Non-Print Media: Collection Management and User Services*, edited by John W. Ellison and Patricia Ann Coty, 161-180. Chicago: American Library Association, 1987.

Gives definition of the medium, and of types of models; unique characteristics, criteria for selection, review sources, producers, and suppliers. Section on maintenance and management includes a brief discussion of organization and cataloging. Provides annotated list of additional sources dealing with the medium.

## Museum Cataloging

Abell-Seddon, Brian. *Museum Catalogues: A Foundation for Computer Processing*. London: Clive Bingley, 1988.

Gives critical examination and analysis of existing methods for description, vocabulary control, and classification of museum objects. Proposes a system for museum catalog organization that attempts to reconcile the diverse needs of specialized collections with a uniform basis for description, with a view toward developing a centralized database for improved access to information in museum collections. The proposed model was developed from a study and analysis of the informational content of a wide range of catalogs and museum inventories.

Baker, Sylvia. "Organizing the Collection." In *Museum Librarianship*, edited by John Larsen. Library Professional Publications, 1985.

Bierbaum, Esther Green. "Records and Access: Museum Registration and Library Cataloging." *Cataloging and Classification Quarterly*. In press.

Gives a detailed account of the museum accession, registration, and cataloging processes. Compares and contrasts museum registration and library cataloging procedures. In museum parlance and practice, the description of an object is part of the accession process, while *registration* refers to the creation of a system of records, and *cataloging* refers to the classification of objects. Bierbaum suggests that differences in records management in libraries and museums result from differences in institutional philosophy and mission, and that principles and methods from library and information science may be applied to museum registration.

Chenhall, Robert G. *Museum Cataloging in the Computer Age*. Nashville, Tenn.: American Association for State and Local History, 1975.

Shows how computer systems can be used in the management of museum collections. Gives basic information on how computers work, descriptions and evaluations of computer software packages that can be used in museum documentation, and criteria for selection of an information system. Predates the microcomputer-based systems now prevalent, and includes descriptions of punched card and paper tape systems. Still of value are the sections describing the content of the data categories needed in a museum cataloging record.

_____. *Nomenclature for Museum Cataloging: A System for Classifying Man-Made Objects*. Nashville, Tenn.: American Association for State and Local History, 1978.

Presents a structured system for the naming of man-made objects; designed primarily for museum cataloging purposes. Includes terminology that can be expanded by the user in a controlled manner; gives definitions for major artefact categories, classification terms, and references to publications where users can find definitions of object names. The major artefact categories are structures, building furnishings, personal artefacts, tools and equipment, communication artefacts, transportation artefacts, art objects, recreational artefacts, societal artefacts, and packages and containers. Introductory chapters give detailed information on the system's purpose, structure, and use. Listings are alphabetical and by class.

*Museum Documentation Systems: Developments and Applications.* Edited by Richard B. Light, D. Andrew Roberts, and Jennifer D. Stewart. London: Butterworths, 1986.

Collection of essays ranging "from statements of principle to practical description of working systems" by museum practitioners from a wide spectrum of countries. Gives review of current application of information technology to museum documentation: "the procedures used by museums to manage information concerning their collections or of relevance to their curatorial functions." Selected to "provide a representative cross-section of some of the major documentation and developments now taking place." Developments referred to are during 1982 and 1983.

Reibel, Daniel B. *Registration Methods for the Small Museum: A Guide for Historical Collections.* Nashville, Tenn.: American Association for State and Local History, 1978.

# 8

BBBBBBBBBBBBBBBBBBBBBBBBBBBBBBBBBBBBBBBBBBBBBBBBBBBBBBBBBBBBBBBBBBBBBBBBBBBBBBBBBBBBBB

# *Microforms*

BBBBBBBBBBBBBBBBBBBBBBBBBBBBBBBBBBBBBBBBBBBBBBBBBBBBBBBBBBBBBBBBBBBBBBBBBBBBBBBBBBBBBB

## TRENDS AND ISSUES IN THE DEVELOPMENT OF BIBLIOGRAPHIC STANDARDS

Since rules for microforms have been the subject of considerable controversy, this chapter will begin with an overview of issues underlying major decisions in the implementation of cataloging rules for these materials.

With microforms, as with many other nonbook media, the cataloger is likely to encounter reproductions which retain the intellectual content of the original but appear in a markedly different physical format and with different publication characteristics. The controversy over the treatment of microform reproductions in *AACR 2* has brought into prominence two opposing viewpoints, one emphasizing the original, and the other the reproduction.

In *AACR 1*, microform reproductions were described in terms of the original text, and data pertaining to the microform were given in a note. Many have voiced the opinion that microform reproductions should be similarly treated in *AACR 2*. Instead, *AACR 2* proposed a radical change when it prescribed that the starting point for the description be the microform reproduction rather than the original.

## Response of the Library Community to *AACR 2*'s Approach

Widespread dissatisfaction with *AACR 2*'s treatment of microform reproductions became apparent from the outset of the publication of the rules. Those objecting to this approach argued that, to the user, the information pertaining to the original was of greater importance. Also frequently stressed were economic implications of preparing new records for "copies" issued in microform. There was far less agreement, however, on an alternative solution. As a result, LC announced the adoption of a policy in which works issued in microform reproductions would be described in terms of the original, with details of the microform given in a note. This "policy" was issued as a rule interpretation.[1] As such it has been adopted as a standard by major U.S. libraries and bibliographic utilities. Since this policy has not been submitted as a rule revision to the Joint Steering Committee for Revision of AACR for a vote, libraries in other countries, for example, the National Library of Canada, are applying the chapter on microforms as it was issued in *AACR 2*.

# The "Facsimile" Theory
## Emphasis on the Original

In *AACR 1,* microform reproductions of a printed work were treated as "facsimiles" of the original. Emphasis was given to the intellectual content of the work, and thus to the description of the original publication from which the microform was made. Information concerning the microform reproduction was added, in a note, to the bibliographic description for the original work.

One practical advantage to pursuing the *AACR 1* approach is that the library is able to deal more quickly and inexpensively with a microform reproduction. Existing cataloging copy for the original can be modified by including a note describing the microreproduction. In addition, it can be argued that if important information about the original work is relegated to the notes portion of a catalog entry, problems arise when catalog records are abbreviated by omitting the notes area.[2] This is a consideration worth noting if brief records without notes are to be stored in the library's own catalog, and if the corresponding full records are to be available only from a centrally shared mainframe, as is the case with some distributed processing configurations.

# The "Edition" Theory
## Emphasis on the Reproduction

The "edition" approach is reflected in *AACR 2*, and gives precedence to describing the work as a physical object and to treating the microform in hand as a separate edition of the original rather than as a photographic reproduction.

Description of the item in hand is viewed as a "cardinal principle" in *AACR 2*. Principles of description are applied consistently to all materials as far as possible. Since the microform reproduction is the item in hand and is markedly different from the original in its physical appearance and publication data, a separate bibliographic record is made for the reproduction.

# DECISION AREAS IN
# DESCRIPTIVE CATALOGING
## AACR 2 and LC POLICY

# Scope
## A Category Defined by Format

*AACR 2*

Chapter 11 covers the description of "all kinds of material in microform." Physical formats include microfilms, microfiches, microopaques, and aperture cards (11.0A). The content represented in these formats may be textual or nonverbal (e.g., pictorial, cartographic, or music), published or manuscript, serial or monographic.

The resulting combinations of content, form, and publication pattern will require that rules from other media chapters be combined with the rules for microforms. For example, in cataloging a microform reproduction of a serial map, the chapter for maps would be used along with the chapters for microforms and serials.

*AACR 2* requires the cataloger to keep in mind rule 0.24's "cardinal principle" when using the rules for description in Part 1:

> The description of a physical item should be based in the first instance on the chapter dealing with the class of materials to which that item belongs. For example, describe a printed monograph in microform as a microform (using the rules in chapter 11).

The rule goes on to point out that

> there will be need in many instances to consult the chapter dealing with the original form of the item, especially when constructing notes. So, using the same example, consult the chapter dealing with printed books (chapter 2) to supplement chapter 11. In short, the starting point for description is the physical form of the item in hand, not the original or any previous form in which the work has been published.

Accordingly, *AACR 2* regards any item appearing in microform as a microform first and a book, music score, picture, map, and so on second. This important principle has far-reaching implications for the cataloging of the item.

## LIBRARY OF CONGRESS POLICY

As stated earlier, LC decided to adopt its own policy for the cataloging of works issued in microform reproductions. This policy runs counter to *AACR 2*'s chapter 11 and as such is not so much a "rule interpretation" as a divergent practice. Since the policy applies only to microreproductions, LC will apply *AACR 2* in the cataloging of publications issued originally as microforms. Relevant portions of the LC policy will be included in the discussion of corresponding sections of *AACR 2*'s chapter 11. The following excerpt deals with the scope of coverage.

> [The Library of Congress policy for the cataloging of microforms] applies to reproductions in micro- and macroform of previously existing materials. Specifically the policy applies to micro- and macroreproductions of
>
>> books, pamphlets and printed sheets
>> cartographic materials
>> manuscripts
>> music
>> graphic materials in macroform
>> serials

It applies to reproductions of dissertations issued by University Microfilms International and "on demand" reproductions of books by the same company.

Rule 1.11 and chapter 11 of AACR 2 will not be applied to these materials except to provide directions for the formulation of the note describing the microform or macroform characteristics of the reproduction.

Items that are microreproductions of material prepared or assembled specifically for bringing out an original edition in microform will be cataloged as instructed in chapter 11 of AACR 2.

The practical effect of the LC policy is to apply the chapter appropriate for the original work (e.g., chapter 2 for books, chapter 5 for music), as the basis of the description and to use the microforms chapter as a guideline for composing a note containing the microform description.

Regardless of whether the microform reproduction is described in terms of the original or in terms of the reproduction, the cataloger will need to be familiar with the chapter on microforms as well as the chapter pertaining to the original form of the work. In either case, both the original and the reproduction aspects will be described in the catalog record, the major difference being which aspect of the work appears in the body of the record and which is described in a note.

# Sources of Information

## *AACR 2*

The preferred source of information is the item itself. Analogous with books and printed materials, information on a microform is sequentially presented, and key bibliographic data usually appear at the beginning of the item. The title-page comparison is even more noticeable in the reproduction of a book, since the title page of the original will also be present on the microform. Thus, for microfilms, the chief source is the title frame, defined as "a frame, usually at the beginning of the item, bearing the full title and, normally, publication details of the item." For microfiches and microopaques, the chief source is also the title frame. Criteria for determination of the chief source are based on both location (the preferred location occurring at the beginning of the sequence), and completeness, with eye-readable data at the top of the fiche or opaque used as chief sources if the title frame information is insufficient.

## LC POLICY

The chief source of information would be appropriate to the original form of the work being reproduced.

# General Material Designation

The LC policy adds the GMD "microform" according to *AACR 2*'s rule 1.1C2.

# Publication Area

## *AACR 2*

While a microform reproduction and its original counterpart are likely to be identical in terms of title, statement of responsibility, and edition, the two formats will inevitably differ in their publication data.

*AACR 2*'s "cardinal principle" outlined in rule 0.24 must be kept in mind in recording the publication data, since there is no explicit mention of this principle in the chapter on microforms. Since the starting point for description is the item in hand, the information recorded in the publication area relates to the "publisher," that is, reproducer, of the copy rather than the publisher of the original.

Analogous considerations arise in videorecording copies of motion pictures, and tape recording copies of sound discs. Those who maintain that catalog descriptions of microform reproductions should give primacy to the original work argue that, since the intellectual content is the focus of attention, the place, producer, and date of the reproduction are of marginal interest to the catalog user. A second major argument maintains that such information is not only of marginal interest but is also quite likely to change, since the "producer" can vary with each reproduction activity. The implications of this situation for multilibrary databases are especially noteworthy.

### UNPUBLISHED MICROFORMS

Revised rules now provide for unpublished microforms. The date of an unpublished microform is not recorded if this information is not readily available (11.4F2).

### LC POLICY

LC's policy requires the cataloger to "transcribe the bibliographic data appropriate to the work being reproduced" in the publication area. Thus, this area would include the place, publisher, and date of the original publication, rather than information pertaining to the microform.

For original microform publications, *AACR 2*'s chapter 11 will apply, and publication data appropriate to the microform will be given.

# Physical Description Area

*AACR 2*

The physical description area describes the microform. In the "other physical details" section, some of the information given may pertain to the original as well as the microform, such as color and the presence of illustrations, while other details may be unique to the microform, for example, whether or not the microform is negative.

In revised rules, standard dimensions have been recognized for microfiche: The dimensions for this format are not given if the item is the standard 10.5 x 14.8 centimeters (11.5D3). In contrast, the original *AACR 2* required dimensions for all microfiche. Another revised rule (11.5D4) requires that only the width be given for microfilms (similar to the treatment for motion picture films). In a previous rule, the diameter of the microfilm reel was given if it were other than the standard three inches.

## LC POLICY

In the case of microform reproductions, the physical description given is that appropriate for the original. If access is not available to either the original or to cataloging copy for the original, some of the data needed for description of the original will not be included.

For original microform publications, the physical description of the microform will be given according to the rules in *AACR 2* chapter 11.

## OCLC MARC BOOKS FORMAT

Since OCLC follows LC policy, microforms are covered in the OCLC Books Format, which provides physical description information for microforms in the physical description fixed field (007). Subfields allow coding for data elements prescribed in *AACR 2*'s physical description area, and also go beyond this to code for additional aspects such as the microform's reduction ratio, emulsion on film, generation, and base of film (i.e., whether or not the film is a safety base).[3]

# Series Area

*AACR 2*

A distinction must be made between a series relating to the microform reproduction and a series relating to the original. The series statement is given in the series area only if it relates to the microform. If the original was published in a series, this is recorded in the note area (11.6B1).

## LC POLICY

The series statement that relates to the original is recorded in the series area.

For original microform publications, the series statement appropriate to the microform will be given in the series area.

# Note Area

*AACR 2*

The note area in *AACR 2* is used to describe the original item that has been reproduced in microform. Other essential notes give details about physical characteristics affecting the use of the microform, such as reduction ratio, and requisite equipment.

## LC POLICY

In the note area, the cataloger records "all details relating to the reproduction and its publication/availability." The note should be introduced with "the word that is the specific material designation appropriate to the item."

The note area should contain

bibliographic details relating to the reproduction required by 11.4 [publication, distribution, etc., area] in the order and form provided by this rule, followed by the details required by 11.5-7 [physical description area, series area, and note area]. If a note of the 11.7B10 type [physical description] is necessary, transcribe it before any series statement required by rule 11.6 [series area].

# ACCESS ISSUES AND DEVELOPMENTS

## Bibliographic Control

In the past few decades, microform materials have come to comprise a substantial percentage of libraries' collections. Figures from studies made in 1978-79 show that two out of five items held by larger academic libraries were microforms. For smaller academic libraries, the percentage is even higher.[4]

Microforms are recognized as a preservation tool and as a means of providing copies of scarce materials. Perhaps foremost among the advantages of this medium are storage economies resulting from shelf space saved in libraries, and economies resulting from purchase prices that are generally less than those of original printed counterparts.

For many decades, the savings realized by purchasing microforms were rendered far less effective because these materials were largely underutilized. In part this underutilization can be attributed to resistance to inconveniences attendant upon the use of microform copies. A more crucial barrier to use, however, has been the lack of adequate bibliographic control, particularly in regard to monographs in microform. Microforms have been largely neglected by traditional means of access on both the national level – in indexes, bibliographies, catalogs, databases, and so on, and at the local level – in individual libraries' catalogs.

Lack of coverage on the national level was evident in a number of ways. Microforms were not included comprehensively in the standard national bibliographies for printed materials, and they were often omitted as well from union catalogs since these items were not being cataloged by most libraries submitting cataloging copy (LC included). The bibliographic tools that were specifically devoted to microform, such as the *Union List of Microforms* and *Newspapers on Microfilm*, were limited in their scope of coverage and had failed to gain the necessary support from participating libraries and publishers.

One of the most formidable challenges to bibliographic control on both the national and the local levels has been the preponderance of large microform collections which are comprised of thousands of titles, and which lack adequate bibliographic access. For both trade and union catalogs, the failure to list individual titles in sets constituted a major gap in bibliographic coverage of microforms. On the local level, libraries often found it prohibitively expensive to provide analytics for such collections. Series entries provided access to the titles of the sets, while printed indexes and guides were relied on for access to the individual works. The lack of adequate bibliographic control for microform materials on the national level was particularly crucial in view of the corresponding lack of coverage in local library catalogs.

Since microforms, like many other types of nonprint materials, were not among the types of materials acquired and cataloged by LC in significant numbers, LC was not in a position to assume a leadership role as a source of cataloging copy and standards for these materials.

## RECENT ADVANCES

Recent developments point to encouraging advances in bibliographic control of microforms on a number of fronts: (1) the emergence of bibliographic reference tools such as *Microforms in Print* and *Micropublishers' Trade List Annual*, (2) increasing uniformity in the provision of bibliographic information on the microforms themselves, and (3) cooperative cataloging efforts among libraries.

In the 1980s, significant strides have been taken to improve bibliographic access. "Microforms have come out of the closet in the 1980s," Joachim proclaims in his description of completed and ongoing efforts to bring previously inaccessible microform sets under bibliographic control. He credits the progress made in this area to the efforts of major organizations such as OCLC, The Association of Research Libraries (ARL), and The Research Libraries Group (RLG) in initiating projects and activities instrumental in achieving bibliographic control.

The ARL Microform Project was established in 1981 "to assist libraries, microform publishers and the bibliographic utilities in their efforts to achieve bibliographic access to titles in microform sets." Toward this end a clearinghouse was established for the bibliographic control of microforms. Libraries can use the clearinghouse to acquire records on the bibliographic utilities, or to acquire tapes of machine-readable cataloging from other libraries. The ARL Microform Project has been working with the bibliographic utilities to enable member libraries to receive cataloging on a set-by-set rather than title-by-title basis. As a result, libraries wanting to use the records generated by specific projects will not have to call up each title individually.

The clearinghouse also provides information on individual library holdings of specific sets. Details on the bibliographic control of the individual sets document such information as the existence of local finding tools, the proportion of the contents of sets that have been cataloged, cataloging codes observed, source and level of cataloging, proportion of cataloging in machine-readable form, and the name of the database into which machine-readable records have been entered.

Over 47,000 titles which have been filmed as part of cooperative preservation projects funded by the National Endowment for the Humanities and undertaken through RLG have also been cataloged and added to the RLIN database. Another major source of grant funding for projects involving the cataloging of microform sets has come through HEA Title IIC of the U.S. Department of Education.[5]

## Alternative and Supplemental Methods for Access

### CONTROL OF INDIVIDUAL COLLECTIONS
**Finding Aids**

The lack of adequate cataloging for microforms has forced many libraries to employ a variety of alternate methods in providing access to specific contents in their collections.

For titles published in sets, often the only source of external control may be the paper copy finding aids which have been prepared specifically to accompany the collections they document. Such aids include reel guides, calendars, bibliographies, catalogs, indexes, and abstracts.

Many libraries have used printed finding aids as a less expensive option to creating separate catalog entries when it comes to organizing and providing access to individual titles in large microform sets. Some argue that, for microform sets based on established bibliographies such as Pollard and Redgrave's *Short Title Catalogue*, there is already sufficient access to individual titles. In some cases, information in established bibliographies is supplemented by special bibliographic tools, prepared by the micropublisher, which can provide additional description or improved access to individual titles.

However, since not all libraries include finding aids in their catalogs, these tools may be as hard to locate as the collections themselves. As bibliographic adjuncts, separate from the library catalog, they fall outside the author, subject, and title groupings which make up the catalog's access points. It is thus important that library users be alerted to the availability of these tools. Information pointing to finding aids can be provided in catalog records for each microform set, in orientation booklets, or in guides to local microform holdings.[6]

## IN-HOUSE GUIDES

Locally developed guides to the microform collection of an individual library sometimes serve as an alternative or as a complement to full cataloging. Many are designed as reference tools for the use of both staff and patrons and include items insufficiently represented in the library's catalog. By themselves, catalog records for materials such as manuscript collections and personal papers may not adequately reflect the collections' relevance for a wide variety of research topics.

In-house guides will vary from library to library as to their purpose, scope, style, format and overall quality. Useful features can include descriptive annotations, citations for accompanying finding aids, call numbers for both collections and finding aids, and a detailed index including authors, titles and their variants, and subject terms.

Since in-house guides are limited to materials of a given format and are separate from traditional author, title, and subject approaches in the catalog, they may often be overlooked by patrons and librarians who are seeking documents or information in its original printed form, and are unaware of the existence of a microform reproduction. Therefore, it can be argued that collection guides should be used to supplement but not supplant full cataloging, if users are to be provided adequate access to microforms.

# Systems for Organization of Materials

As with many other types of nonbook materials, convincing arguments can be presented in favor of separate storage of microforms. Such arguments are based on the need for special shelving configurations, as well as the need for controlled temperature, humidity, and acidity. While most libraries keep their microforms separate from other materials, libraries differ as to whether materials should be available on an open or closed stack basis, and also as to whether materials should be classified by subject. Some libraries arrange microforms primarily by type of physical format (e.g., fiche, film, print), and others according to the content of the original (e.g., serials, dissertations, documents), with subarrangement by accession number or alphabetically. For smaller libraries, whose microform collections consist mostly of serials, microforms are sometimes intershelved with hard-copy serial backfiles.

Subject classification for microforms is appropriate, of course, only for open-stack arrangements. For microforms, classification has its limitations since the items cannot be browsed, and any information gleaned by the user is limited to what the labeling on the container can provide. Moreover, subject classification is of relatively little value for items that have been grouped under broad subject categories, as is the case with general serials and large collections of titles in sets. While broad classification has its disadvantages, it is sometimes necessary, since splitting up a set would render the corresponding finding aids useless and thus negate the effectiveness of another kind of search.

An ARL survey by Reichmann and Tharpe revealed that microforms are classified by less than 30 percent of responding libraries. For the libraries that do classify, the classification is often broad, indicating only the first few characters of Library of Congress Classification or Dewey Decimal Classification notation. The approach most frequently used consists of an abbreviated class mark, an indicator of microform type, and an accession number or shelf designator.[7]

# Alternatives to Full Cataloging

## PUBLISHERS' CARD SETS

Since some publishers supply card sets with their microform collections, purchased cards have been used as an alternative to the full cataloging of large microform sets. This option has not been without its drawbacks, however: Initially the quality of purchased cataloging was poor, and although standards are now reported to be much higher, the cards may still not be a cost-effective option because they necessitate extensive authority work and other revisions to meet local requirements. In addition, only a small number of publishers sell cataloging.

Included among the publishers that sell cataloging is University Microfilms International (UMI), which supplies catalog cards for its Early English Books series.[8] Micropublishers such as UMI and Research Publications have also contributed to the bibliographic control of microforms through funding for cataloging of some of their products.[9]

## ANALYTICS

Analytics may provide an alternative to the full cataloging of the individual works within a large microform set. Two approaches are possible. The most complete (and costly) method is to provide full cataloging for each bibliographic unit in the set, applying all author, title, and subject tracings appropriate to each individual item. Some may feel that full cataloging for each separate title is not a viable option in view of the massive number of titles, sometimes in the tens of thousands, which make up some large microform sets. Costs become even higher if original cataloging must be provided for rare or esoteric materials.[10]

Alternatively, libraries may provide author/title analytics for items in sets, adding authors and/or titles of the individual works to unit cards representing the set as a whole. This latter approach lacks a subject approach as well as descriptions for individual items in a collection, but is an improvement over the type of access provided only under the title of the collection.

# Bibliographic Utilities and Microforms

## MICROFORMS IN MARC

A significant step toward bibliographic control of microforms was made possible through the inclusion of microforms in the online databases of the major bibliographic utilities. This in turn was made possible through the accommodation of microforms within the existing MARC structures for books, serials, and other types of materials.

## COOPERATIVE CATALOGING THROUGH
## BIBLIOGRAPHIC UTILITIES

Since the creation of OCLC and other utilities, libraries and publishers have been inputting microforms on a moderate scale. While libraries report finding some copy for about 50 percent of the microform titles they search in bibliographic utilities, about two-thirds of the copy found is for the hard copy publication, but not necessarily for the same edition.[11] Aside from the quantitative problem of overall hit rate, one drawback cited in cataloging microforms on OCLC had been that titles in sets must be searched and processed individually. Fortunately, this problem has been addressed by recent developments on the part of OCLC and ARL to enable access on a set-by-set rather than a title-by-title basis. Another encouraging development in regard to bibliographic utilities has been the agreement reached by OCLC and RLG to exchange tape records for microform sets cataloged with the use of federal grant funds. One publisher, UMI, has begun to enter on OCLC all the cataloging it prepares for its new publications.[12]

# NOTES

[1]*Cataloging Service Bulletin* 14 (Fall 1981): 56-58.

[2]William Saffady, *Micrographics*, 2d ed. (Littleton, Colo.: Libraries Unlimited, 1985), 189.

[3]OCLC, *Books Format*, 3d ed. (Dublin, Ohio: OCLC, 1986).

[4]Information Systems Consultants, Inc., "Bibliographic Control of Microforms: A Planning Study for the Association of Research Libraries" (final report, October 1, 1980), 1.

[5]Martin D. Joachim, "Recent Developments in the Bibliographic Control of Microforms," *Microform Review* 15 (Spring 1986): 74-86.

[6]Saffady, *Micrographics*, 192.

[7]Ibid., 194.

[8]Ibid., 192.

[9]Joachim, "Recent Developments in the Bibliographic Control of Microforms," 81.

[10]Saffady, *Micrographics*, 191-92.

[11]"Bibliographic Control of Microforms," 55.

[12]Joachim, "Recent Developments," 84.

# DESCRIPTIVE CATALOGING EXAMPLES

## Items to Be Cataloged

1. Reproduction of dissertation on microfilm

One microfilm reel, black and white, 176 frames, 3 inches in diameter; 35 mm. gauge.

The original text consists of a cover page, an abstract page, and leaves numbered 1-174. There is a bibliography on pages 172-74. Height 28 cm.

First frame of film:
> AUTHOR: James William Frost, Ph.D.
> New York University

> TITLE:   Photon Correlation Studies of Motile Microorganisms
> University Microfilms International, Ann Arbor
> Michigan, 1978.

Second frame:

> Photon Correlation Studies of
> Motile Microorganisms
> by
> James W. Frost

> A dissertation in the Department of Physics submitted to the faculty of the Graduate School of Arts and Sciences in partial fulfillment of the requirements for the degree of Doctor of Philosophy at New York University.

> October, 1977

> Approved by: Herman Z. Cumins
> Research Advisor

> Henry Stroke
> Thesis Advisor

2. Reproduction of novel on microfiche

One microfiche, black and white, negative, 36 frames, in envelope. Microfiche is 10.4 x 14.8 centimeters (height x width).

Envelope:
> NCR Micrographic Systems, Inc.
> 5011 Herzel Place

Beltsville, Md.

Top of fiche:

THE ALBANY DEPOT by William Dean Howells
HARPER'S BLACK AND WHITE SERIES. Harper and Brothers 1893.
Reproduced with permission of Harper & Row, Publishers Inc.
1979

Right side of fiche:

NCR Micrographic Systems
Producers of quality microforms

First title frame: [cover of the original book]
THE
ALBANY DEPOT
by
W.D. Howells
Harper's Black & White Series

Second frame: [title page of original book]
THE ALBANY DEPOT
by
W.D. Howells
New York
Harper and Brothers
1893

The last numbered page of the original text is page 68. Each frame contains two pages of the original text. There are seven pages of illustrations.

3. Reproduction of research report on microfiche

One microfiche, black and white, negative, 48 frames, in envelope. Microfiche is 10.4 x 14.8 centimeters (height x width). Original item is an unpublished typescript; last numbered page is 43; 28 centimeters.

Envelope:

ERIC Clearinghouse on
Information Resources
Syracuse University
School of Education
Syracuse, N.Y. 13210

[There is no date on the envelope, which is postmarked June 1986.]

Top of fiche (eye-readable):

ED 264 872 STUDENT AND FACULTY SUBJECT SEARCHING IN A
UNIVERSITY ONLINE PUBLIC CATALOG
1 of 1       MCKINNEY, EMMA T.
AUG 85 48P.

First frame of microfiche:

ED 264 872

AUTHOR     McKinney, Emma T.

TITLE        Student and Faculty Subject Searching in a
University Online Public Catalog
SPONS AGENCY Council on Library Resources, Inc.
Washington, D.C.
PUB DATE     Aug 85
NOTE        48p. ....

Second frame:

STUDENT AND FACULTY SUBJECT SEARCHING
IN A UNIVERSITY ONLINE PUBLIC CATALOG

A Report to the Council on Library Resources

Emma T. McKinney

August 1985

## *AACR 2* Records and OCLC MARC Tagging

### 1. REPRODUCTION OF DISSERTATION ON MICROFILM

#### *AACR 2* record

Frost, James W. (James William)
  Photon correlation studies of motile microorganisms [microform] / by James W. Frost. -- Ann Arbor, Mich. : University Microfilms International, 1978.
    1 microfilm reel ; 35 mm.

  Bibliography: leaves 172-174.
  Microreproduction of: 1977. 174 leaves. Typescript. Thesis (Ph.D.)--New York University, 1977.

  I. Title.

## LC version

> Frost, James W. (James William)
>    Photon correlation studies of motile microorganisms
> [microform] / by James W. Frost. -- 1977.
>    174 leaves ; 28 cm.

>    Typescript.
>    Thesis (Ph.D.)--New York University, 1977.
>    Bibliography: leaves 172-174.
>    Microfilm. Ann Arbor, Mich. : University Microfilms
> International, 1978. 1 microfilm reel ; 35 mm.

>    I. Title.

```
OCLC MARC Tagging (Follows LC policy)

Type: a  Bib lvl: m  Govt pub:     Lang: eng  Source: d  Illus:
Repr: a  Enc lvl: I  Conf pub: 0  Ctry: miu  Dat tp: r  M/F/B: 10
Indx: 0  Mod rec:    Festschr: 0  Cont: b
Desc: a  Int lvl:    Dates: 1978,1977

1  040     xxx $c xxx
2  007     h $b d $c $d a $e f $f u---- $g b $h a $i c $j a
3  100 10  Frost, James W. $q (James William)
4  245 10  Photon correlation studies of motile microorganisms
$h microform / $c by James W. Frost.
5  260 1   $c 1977.
6  300     174 leaves ; $c 28 cm.
7  500     Typescript.
8  502     Thesis (Ph.D.)--New York University, 1977.
9  504     Bibliography: leaves 172-174.
10 533     Microfilm. $b Ann Arbor, Mich. : $c University
Microfilms International, $d 1978. $e 1 microfilm reel ; 35 mm.
```

### *AACR 2* applicable rules

#### Scope

**0.24:**      Cardinal principle: describe item in hand.

**4.0A:**      (Manuscript chapter): "For reproductions of manuscript texts published in multiple copies, see chapter 2 or chapter 11, as appropriate."

#### Chief source of information

**11.0B:**     Chief source for microfilms is title frame.

#### Area 1

**11.1B1:**    Record title proper as in 1.1B.

**11.1C1:**    GMD as in 1.1C1, *microform*, following title proper, in brackets.

**Area 4**

**1.11C:** Describe reproduction.

**11.4C1:** Place of publication (of microform) as in 1.4C.

**11.4D1:** Name of (microform) publisher as in 1.4D.

**11.4F1:** Microform publication date as in 1.4F.

**Area 5**

**1.11D:** Describe reproduction.

**11.5B1:** Number of physical units; SMD is *microfilm*. Add term *reel*.

**11.5D4:** Give width of microfilm in millimeters.

**Area 7**

**11.7B22:** [new] Give information relating to original. (Chapter on manuscripts must be consulted to describe original document):

**4.4B1:** Give date of manuscript.

**4.5B1:** Record sequences of leaves.

**4.7B13:** If manuscript is a dissertation, describe as in 2.7B13. (Chapter on books, pamphlets, and printed sheets.)

**2.7B13:** For dissertations, give designation of the thesis followed by statement of degree for which author was candidate, name of institution, and year degree was granted.

**Choice of access points**

**21.4A:** Work of single personal authorship.

**Form of heading**

**22.1A:** Choose name by which person is commonly known.

**22.1B:** Determine name by which commonly known from chief source of information.

**22.18A:** If part of name is represented by initials and full form is known, add spelled out form in parentheses. Optional if not necessary to distinguish between identical names; LC is applying the optional provision [CSB 11 (Winter 1981): 26].

## 2. REPRODUCTION OF NOVEL ON MICROFICHE

### AACR 2 record

> Howells, W. D. (William Dean), 1837-1920.
> The Albany depot [microform] / by W.D. Howells. -- Beltsville,
> Md. : NCR Micrographic Systems, 1979.
> 1 microfiche (36 fr.) : negative, ill.
>
> Microreproduction of: New York : Harper and Bros., 1893.
> 68p. (Harper's Black and white series)
>
> I. Title.

### LC version

> Howells, W. D. (William Dean), 1837-1920.
> The Albany depot [microform] / by W.D. Howells. -- New
> York : Harper and Bros., 1893.
> 68 p. : ill. -- (Harper's Black and white series)
>
> Microfiche. Beltsville, Md. : NCR Micrographic Systems, 1979.
> 1 microfiche (36 fr.) : negative.
>
> I. Title.

```
OCLC MARC Tagging (Follows LC policy)

Type: a  Bib lvl: m  Govt pub:      Lang: eng  Source: d  Illus: a
Repr: b  Enc lvl: I  Conf pub: 0   Ctry: nyu  Dat tp: r  M/F/B: 11
Indx: 0  Mod rec:    Festschr: 0   Cont:
Desc: a  Int lvl:    Dates: 1979,1893.

1 040    xxx $c xxx
2 007    h $b e $c $d b $e m $f u--- $g b $h a $i c $j a
3 100 10 Howells, W. D. $q (William Dean), 1837-1920.
4 245 14 The Albany depot $h microform / $c by W.D. Howells
5 260 0  New York : $b Harper and Bros. ; $c 1893.
6 300    68 p. : $b ill.
7 490 0  Harper's Black and white series
8 533    Microfiche. $b Beltsville, Md. : $c NCR Micrographic
Systems, $d 1979. $e 1 microfiche (36 fr.) : negative.
```

### *AACR 2* applicable rules

**0.24:** Cardinal principle.

**Chief source of information**

**11.0B1:** Chief source for microfiche is title frame.

**Area 1**

**11.1B1:** Title proper.

**11.1C1:** GMD.

**11.1F1:** Statement of responsibility. Reflects form of name taken from chief source.

**Area 4**

**Publication area appropriate to reproduction.**

**11.4C1; 11.4D1; 11.4F1:**
Place, name, date.

**Area 5**

**Physical description area appropriate to reproduction.**

**1.11D:** Describe reproduction.

**11.5B1:** Number of physical units; SMD is *microfiche.*

**11.5B2:** Add number of frames of microfiche.

**11.5C1:** Indicate if negative.

**11.5D3:** Omit dimensions for microfiche if 10.5 x 14.8 cm.

**Area 7**

**11.7B22:** Information relating to original. Size of original not known, hence dimensions left blank.

**Choice of access points**

**21.4A:** Single personal authorship.

**Form of heading**

**22.1A:** Name by which person is commonly known.

**22.1B:** Determine name from chief source of information.

**22.18A:** Add spelled out form of name in parentheses. Optional.

## 3. REPRODUCTION OF RESEARCH REPORT ON MICROFICHE

### *AACR 2* record

McKinney, Emma T.
Student and faculty subject searching in a university online public catalog [microform] : a report to the Council on Library Resources / Emma T. McKinney. -- Syracuse, N.Y. : ERIC, [1986?]
1 microfiche (48 fr.) : negative.

ED 264 872.
Microreproduction of: 1985. 43 leaves. Typescript.

I. Title.

### LC version

McKinney, Emma T.
Student and faculty subject searching in a university online public catalog [microform] : a report to the Council on Library Resources / Emma T. McKinney. -- 1985.
43 leaves ; 28 cm.

Typescript.
Microfiche. Syracuse, N.Y. : ERIC, [1986?] 1 microfiche (48 fr.) : negative. ED 264 872.

I. Title.

```
OCLC MARC Tagging   (Follows LC policy)

Type: a  Bib lvl: m  Govt pub:     Lang: eng  Source: d  Illus:
Repr: b  Enc lvl: I  Conf pub: 0   Ctry: nyu  Dat tp: r  M/F/B: 10
Indx: 0  Mod rec:    Festschr: 0   Cont:
Desc: a  Int lvl:    Dates: 1986,1985

1 040     xxx $c xxx
2 007     h $b e $c $d b $e m $f u---- $g b $h a $i c $j a
3 100 10  McKinney, Emma T.
4 245 10  Student and faculty subject searching in a university
online public catalog $h microform : $b a report to the Council on
Library Resources / $c Emma T. McKinney.
5 260 1   $c 1985.
6 300     43 leaves ; $c 28 cm.
7 500     Typescript.
8 533     Microfiche. $b Syracuse, N.Y. : $c ERIC, $d [1986?]
$e 1 microfiche (48 fr.) : negative. ED 264 872.
```

### *AACR 2 applicable rules*

**Scope**

**0.24:**     Cardinal principle.

**Chief source**

**11.0B1:**     Chief source is title frame.

**Area 1**

**11.1B1:**     Title proper.

**11.1C1:**     GMD.

**11.1F1:**     Statement of responsibility.

**11.1E1:**     Record other title information.

**Area 4**

**Publication area appropriate to reproduction.**

**11.4C1; 11.4D1; 11.4F1:**
         Place, name, date.

**Area 5**

**1.11D:**     Describe reproduction.

**11.5B1:**     Number of physical units and SMD; number of frames.

**11.5C1:**     Indicate if negative.

**11.5D3:**     Omit dimensions for microfiche if 10.5 x 14.8 cm.

**Area 7**

**1.7A4:**     [revised] Give notes relating to reproduction (i.e., ERIC number) and then notes relating to original.

**11.7B22:**     Give information relating to original.

**4.4B1:**     Date of manuscript.

**4.5B1:**     Record sequences of leaves.

**Choice of access points**

**21.4A:**     Single personal authorship.

# REFERENCE SOURCES

## Microform Librarianship

Dodson, Suzanne Cates. "Microfilm Types: There Really Is a Choice." *Library Resources and Technology Services* 30 (January/March 1986): 84-90.
An overview of the advantages and disadvantages of the basic microfilm types currently available for library usage.

Folcarelli, Ralph J., Arthur C. Tannenbaum, and Ralph C. Ferragamo. *The Microform Connection: A Basic Guide for Libraries.* New York: Bowker, 1982.
Primary focus is the small to medium-sized library with little or no current micrographic services, but most of the information is pertinent to any size library. Basic information on the software and hardware of microformats. Bibliography includes selected lists of micrographic reference books. Includes lists of micropublishers, micrographic associations and organizations, and a glossary.

*Microforms in Libraries: A Manual for Evaluation and Management.* Edited by Francis F. Spreitzer. Chicago: American Library Association, 1985.
Basic information about the various formats of microforms. Discussion topics include areas such as film polarity, the advantages and disadvantages of film and fiche, as well as collection management and microform evaluation. Also included is a glossary of terms, a selected list of standards, specifications, recommended practices, and a bibliography. Chapter on public service includes consideration of the user in relation to cataloging and maintaining a microform collection.

Saffady, William. *Micrographics.* 2d ed. Littleton, Colo.: Libraries Unlimited, 1985.
Broad coverage of various aspects of micrographics, such as types of microforms, micropublishing, equipment, and recent technologies. The chapter on bibliographic control of microforms covers national bibliographic control (union lists and trade bibliographies), local bibliographic control (catalog entries and printed guides), and internal bibliographic controls (bibliographic targets and microfiche heading areas). Discusses approaches to cataloging and classification, and alternatives to cataloging. Aimed at practicing librarians and library school students.

## Directories

*Microforms Annual.* 7th ed. Elmsford, N.Y.: Pergamon Press, 1986.
International directory and bibliographic information on the literature and services in the field of microforms. Arrangement is by subject coverage of collections or by publisher of journals. A separate section contains information on equipment and services of the industry.

Wasserman, Ellen S., ed. *Microform Market Place: An International Directory of Micropublishing 1986-87.* Westport, Conn.: Meckler Publishing, 1986.

Provides comprehensive information about micropublishers. All entries are compiled from information submitted by micropublishers listed. Includes a directory of micropublishers, a subject index, geographic index, organizations listing, mergers/acquisitions/name changes listing, and a bibliography of primary sources. Name and telephone numbers of the publishers listed are given in addition to microformats and micropublications programs offered. Published every two years.

Waugh, Barbara, ed. *1984-85 International Micrographics Source Book.* New Rochelle, N.Y.: Microfilm Publishing, 1984.

A biennial publication listing micrographic dealers, consultants, service bureaus, storage centers, associations, products, and sources. Arrangement is alphabetical, by state in the United States, and then by country and title of organization. Entries provide primarily address information, with subject coverage of micropublishers also included.

## Sources of Materials Available

### UNION CATALOGS

Library of Congress Catalogs. *National Register of Microform Masters.* Washington, D.C.: Library of Congress, 1965- . Annual.

Provides a listing of library materials that have been filmed and for which master negatives exist (for copying only), and identifies those designated as "master preservation negatives" (for archival storage only, not for copying). Reports master microforms of foreign and domestic books, pamphlets, serials and foreign doctoral dissertations but excludes technical reports, typescript translations, foreign or domestic archival manuscript collections, and U.S. doctoral dissertations and master's theses.

Arrangement is alphabetical, by main entry. Cross-references are included. Entries include main and condensed titles, and publication and physical description statements.

*Newspapers in Microform.* Washington, D.C.: Library of Congress, 1973- . Annual.

A bibliographic source listing newspapers published in microform. Serves as a supplement to *Newspapers in Microform: Foreign Countries, 1948-1972* and *Newspapers in Microform: United States, 1948-1972.* Foreign and domestic newspapers are covered in separate sections. Includes index.

### COVERAGE IN LC UNION CATALOGS

For the most part, the Library of Congress issued independent union catalogs specifically devoted to microforms, instead of integrating these materials in LC's national bibliographies and catalogs for other materials. The two earliest catalogs, *Union List of Microforms* and *Newspapers on Microfilm*, attempted to locate master negatives of micropublications. These tools suffered from a lack of inclusion of all microformats, and from a lack of complete and accurate information submitted by libraries and publishers.

In 1965 LC established a new union catalog to replace the *Union List*. The *National Register of Microform Masters* was intended to provide a complete listing of all master negatives. The *Register* does not attempt to report all service copies for each title included, thus limiting its usefulness for interlibrary loan.

Even in terms of its stated scope, there were other initial problems with the *Register*: Its arrangement by LC number and overly technical reporting forms resulted in poor acceptance by libraries and micropublishers. Even after arrangement had been improved and the laborious forms eliminated, lack of support continued to cripple the *Register* as a key tool in a national bibliography of microforms. Ongoing problems included voluntary nature of participation, the effect of changing personnel situations on the consistency of reporting by participating libraries, and incomplete and inaccurate information submitted by commercial publishers unaware of bibliographic needs.

Companions to the *Register* and successors to *Newspapers on Microfilm, Newspapers in Microform: United States*, and *Newspapers in Microform: Foreign Countries* list master and service microform holdings submitted since 1948. Both suffer to some degree from the same problems that afflict the *Register*. But because their scope is limited to one original format and because newspaper holdings are relatively easy to report, these tools are better supported than the *Register*.

Two other union catalogs provide information on microforms: *The National Union Catalog of Manuscript Collections* indicates master and service copies of archives and manuscripts that have been filmed. *The National Union Catalog: Pre 1956 Imprints*, the first of the national union catalog sets to attempt systematic listing of all reported service copies, gives microform holdings for works previously submitted to the *National Union Catalog*. However, there are still gaps and overlapping coverage in these bibliographies. As a result of incomplete reporting and overlapping coverage, reliable and easily obtained information about existing micropublications is not always available.


## TRADE AND OTHER EXTERNAL BIBLIOGRAPHIES

*Guide to Microforms in Print*. Edited by John J. Walsh, Jr. Westport, Conn.: Microform Review, 1976- . Annual.

Provides information much the same as the traditional *Books in Print*, for domestic and international micropublishers. Publishers are indexed alphabetically and by code. There is a subject classification listing, a general index, and the entries themselves of those microforms currently published by micropublishing organizations. Microform titles are entered if they are offered for sale on a regular basis, except for dissertations and theses. Includes books, journals, newspapers, government publications, archival material, collections, and other projects. Listings include author, title, volume, date, price, publisher, and type of microfilm. An international source of information on microforms that are currently in print. A companion publication, *Subject Guide to Microforms in Print*, has been published annually since 1962.

*An Index to Microform Collections.* Edited by Ann Niles. Westport, Conn.: Meckler Publishing, 1984.

A guide to what is available on selected microform sets with broad series titles. Includes a list of the contents for each of the collections and a comprehensive author and title index. Part 1 gives a contents listing for each of the twenty-six collections included in the index. Parts 2 and 3 are author and title indexes respectively. Arrangement is by subject content of the collections; international in scope.

*Micropublishers Trade List Annual.* Westport, Conn.: Meckler Publishing, 1975- . Annual.

A compilation of the catalogs of micropublishers. The scope is worldwide and arrangement is alphabetical by publisher's title. Published on microfiche. Hard copy indexes list fiche number for each catalog.

*Serials in Microform.* Ann Arbor, Mich.: University Microfilms International, 1972- . Annual.

A listing of serials published in microform by subject, title, and journal identification. Also included are common abbreviations in the field, a section of the quarterly microfiche titles, and a section of *New Serials Titles* entered since the last publication.

### COVERAGE IN TRADE BIBLIOGRAPHIES

"In-print" trade bibliographies for microforms are more comprehensive than the union catalogs. Because they parallel the familiar sources for hard-copy books, they are also easier to use. All are now produced by Microform Review, Inc., major publisher of secondary literature relating to microforms.

Because microforms tend not to go out of print, the trade bibliographies for this medium can serve as useful, though not authoritative, retrospective sources. They are not, however, without certain limitations. *Microforms in Print* is limited in that individual titles in sets are not always listed. The *Subject Guide* is a classified listing based on general categories; no index is provided. Locating microforms on a desired topic usually requires tedious scanning of pages of alphabetical entries under broad headings. These sources are also limited in their currency. *Microforms in Print* appears biennially with one separate interim supplement, while the *Subject Guide* is revised only biennially.

# Glossaries

Avedon, Don M. *NMA Standard Glossary of Micrographics.* 5th ed. Silver Spring, Md.: National Microform Association, 1971.

Terminology and concise definitions of important micrographic terms. Arrangement is alphabetical. Trademarks and tradenames are also included.

# Periodicals

*Journal of Micrographics.* Silver Spring, Md.: National Micrographics Association, 1967- . (Formerly the *NMA Journal.*)
Monthly journal covering topics relating to micrographics and other information management technologies.

*Microform Review.* Westport, Conn.: Meckler Publishing, 1972- . Quarterly.
Provides a wide variety of current information on microforms and microform equipment. It also contains reviews of books that deal with microforms, and evaluations of microforms.

# Cataloging and Bibliographic Control

Boss, Richard W. *Cataloging Titles in Microform Sets: Report of a Study Conducted in 1980 for the Association of Research Libraries by Information Systems Consultants, Inc.* Washington, D.C.: Association of Research Libraries, 1983.
Overview of problems and controversies relating to bibliographic control of microforms. Discusses microform sets and problems relating to their access. Concludes with a summary of research and recommendations. Describes proposals that have been set forth to resolve the *AACR 2* chapter 11 controversy and to bring better access to microform collections.

Dodson, Suzanne Cates. "Bibliographical Control of Microforms: Where Are We Today?" *Microform Review* 12 (1983): 12-18.
Outlines the controversy between cataloging microforms by chapter 11 of *AACR 2* or by the LC Rule Interpretations, and stresses the need for consensus as a prerequisite to cooperative cataloging.

Graham, Crystal. "Rethinking National Policy for Cataloging Microform Reproductions." *Cataloging & Classification Quarterly* 6 (Summer 1986): 69-83.
Discusses the current practice of creating unique cataloging records for an original publication and each of its microfilm reproductions. Advocates the adoption of a single record approach consisting of several tiers, with the third and final tier containing local holdings information.

Heynen, Jeffrey. "Microform Project for the Bibliographic Control of Microforms: Report on a Survey of Microform Sets on U.S. and Canadian Libraries." *Cataloging & Classification Quarterly* 4 (1983/1984): 31-41.
Describes the project established to assist libraries, microform publishers, and the bibliographic utilities in achieving bibliographic access to titles in microform sets. Detailed account of the Microform Project's survey of cataloging practices of various research libraries for their microform sets.

Hill, Janet Swan. "Descriptions of Reproductions of Previously Existing Works: Another View." *Microform Review* 11 (Winter 1982): 14-21.
Describes some of the controversy which surrounds the treatment of microforms in *AACR 2*. Gives reasons why describing the item in terms of the original

may not be the solution, asks if there is a rationale for treating some types of reproductions differently from others, and states points often overlooked by those who object to *AACR 2*'s approach to microforms.

Joachim, Martin D. "Recent Developments in the Bibliographic Control of Microforms." *Microform Review* 15 (Spring 1986): 74-86.
Survey of trends recognizing importance of bibliographic control, and major microform projects undertaken by the Association of Research Libraries, OCLC, and the Research Libraries Group. Also discusses projects involving centralized authority work for cataloging projects, cataloging of sets with grant funds, and machine-readable cataloging provided by micropublishers.

Niles, Ann. "Bibliographic Access for Microform Collections." *College and Research Libraries* 42 (November 1981): 576-80.
Discusses problems of providing bibliographic access to individual titles in microform collections. Suggests that libraries abandon full cataloging in favor of indexing, using the information provided by micropublishers.

Swanson, Edward. *A Manual of AACR2, Examples for Microforms*. Crystal Lake, Minn.: Soldier Creek Press, 1982.
Part 1 includes a number of examples of original microform publications, and individual items in a collection. Chapter 11 of *AACR 2* is used as originally written. Part 2 of the manual uses *AACR 2* and the LC rule interpretations. Gives examples of microform reproductions of previously existing works, including monographs, manuscripts, and serials. Explanations are given.

Willard, Louis Charles. "Microforms and *AACR2*, Chapter 11: Is the Cardinal Principle a Peter Principle?" *Microform Review* 10 (Spring 1981): 75-78.
Addresses problems associated with implementation of *AACR 2*'s chapter 11 for both the user and the cataloger. Provides a historical context for later developments.

# Index

Videodisc
 Use in retrieval of graphic images,
  154-55
Videorecordings, *see* Motion pictures
  and videorecordings
Videotapes, *See* Motion pictures and
  videorecordings


WLN, 19, 20